Advance Praise for Ashley Davis Prend's
Claim Your Inner Grown-up:

"What an insightful, hopeful, and practical guide to emotional, psychological, and spiritual maturity! Ashley Davis Prend's *Claim Your Inner Grown-up* is a must-read for anyone interested in personal development. Her tough love with a soft touch approach will lead readers to the deep soul satisfaction that comes from choosing transcendence over indulgence."

—Dave Pelzer, author of *A Man Named Dave*

"Mix a pinch of Dr. Laura's ethic of responsibility with a teaspoon of M. Scott Peck's compassion and an ounce of Gibran's spirituality, heat and serve Ashley Davis Prend's *Claim Your Inner Grown-up*. Your body, mind, and spirit will jump with joy (er . . . responsible joy)."

—Warren Farrell, Ph.D.,
author of *Why Men Are the Way They Are*

"Ashley Davis Prend's *Claim Your Inner Grown-up* is an indispensable guide to eliminating the shortage of real maturity among adults. Like any good teacher, she asks us to set our sights high, then provides us with the tools and instruction we need to achieve those goals. Ashley Davis Prend offers guidance and encouragement, but not doctrine or dogma. The practical, powerful exercises are especially helpful. I can't think of anyone who wouldn't benefit from this wise and warmhearted book."

—Harold Bloomfield, M.D.,
author of *Making Peace with Your Past*

"In this thought-provoking and inspirational book, the self-help movement itself finally comes of age. Both your life and the world we share will be the better for it."

—Forrest Church, author of *Lifecraft*

"What a wise book! It will bring blessings to many who read it."
—Rabbi Harold Kushner,
author of *When Bad Things Happen to Good People*

ASHLEY DAVIS PREND, A.C.S.W., is a psychotherapist and grief counselor, and the author of *Transcending Loss: Understanding the Lifelong Impact of Grief and How to Make it Meaningful*. She lives in New Hampshire with her husband and their three children.

Claim Your Inner Grown-up

4

Essential Steps to
Authentic Adulthood

Ashley Davis Prend,
A.C.S.W.

A PLUME BOOK

PLUME
Published by the Penguin Group
Penguin Putnam Inc., 375 Hudson Street, New York, New York 10014, U.S.A.
Penguin Books Ltd, 27 Wrights Lane, London W8 5TZ, England
Penguin Books Australia Ltd, Ringwood, Victoria, Australia
Penguin Books Canada Ltd, 10 Alcorn Avenue, Toronto, Ontario, Canada M4V 3B2
Penguin Books (N.Z.) Ltd, 182–190 Wairau Road, Auckland 10, New Zealand

Penguin Books Ltd, Registered Offices: Harmondsworth, Middlesex, England

First published by Plume, a member of Penguin Putnam Inc.

First Printing, June 2001
10 9 8 7 6 5 4 3 2 1

Quotations from *The Prophet* by Kahlil Gibran, Copyright 1923 by Kahlil Gibran
and renewed 1951 by Administrators C T A of Kahlil Gibran Estate and Mary G.
Gibran. Used by permission of Alfred A. Knopf, a division of Random House, Inc.

Ⓟ REGISTERED TRADEMARK—MARCA REGISTRADA

LIBRARY OF CONGRESS CATALOGING-IN-PUBLICATION DATA
Prend, Ashley Davis.
    Claim your inner grown-up : four essential steps to authentic adulthood /
Ashley Davis Prend.
        p.   cm.
    Includes bibliographical references and index.
    ISBN 0-452-28250-0
    1. Emotional maturity.   2. Inner child.   I. Title.

BF710.P74 2001
155.6—dc21

                                                            00-066562

Printed in the United States of America
Set in Garamond Light
Designed by Eve L. Kirch

To my beloved husband, David,
whose inner grown-up is an inspiration

CONTENTS

Part III: The Best of Both

ACKNOWLEDGMENTS

I'm aware that the "Acknowledgments" section in any book runs the risk of sounding like an endless acceptance speech at the Oscars, and the temptation is to bring out the hook and haul the speaker (or the writer, as the case may be) offstage. I'll try not to be *too* laborious.

I want to first thank my co-agents from the Sanford J. Greenburger Associates Literary Agency: Faith Hamlin and Nancy Stender. Faith, your support and consistent dedication are deeply appreciated. And Nancy, your enduring passion for this project sustained me throughout the entire process of publication. Thanks to you both!

I am grateful to my editor, Gary Brozek, who graciously shepherded this book into its final form. I was impressed with his thoughtful attention and his helpful suggestions. I also thank all the talented folks at Plume and Penguin Putnam who helped in the process of bringing this book to life. And a special thanks to Jennifer Dickerson Kasius, who played a vital role in bringing me to Plume in the first place.

I am especially grateful to dear family members who have graced me with their love and unwavering support, especially my mother, Peyton Lewis, my father, William Davis, and my sister, Rebecca Davis.

My husband, to whom the book is dedicated, was my first reader, my cheerleader, and my friend during every step of this journey. I thank him with enduring love. I wish also to make a special note of love and adoration to my three precious children, who bring out the best in my inner grown-up.

A special gratitude goes to my religious community at South Church, who supported me and unwittingly nurtured this project along from its inception.

I also thank my friends and my various fellow group members who listened patiently to all the monthly progress reports. And a special thanks to Martha Nossiff, who was an outstanding supporter through this work—the mala beads were an inspiration!

I also want to express my deepest gratitude to my clients, those from the past and those from the present, seen individually and in support groups, who have taught me so much about life. It has been an incredible honor for me to accompany them on part of their life's journey. And I also thank those individuals, clients and otherwise, who volunteered to talk with me about the topic of the inner grown-up, generously sharing their thoughts and personal experiences with me.

In closing, last but in no way least, I humbly acknowledge my Muse, that divine Spirit of the universe, who sustains, guides, inspires, and grounds me. Without such holy influence, this book would not have been possible.

Introduction

*The real voyage of discovery consists not in seeking
new landscapes, but in having new eyes.*

—Marcel Proust

She looked up at me with the simple innocence that seemingly only a few fortunate six-year-olds are still privy to. "Mom, how can you tell the difference between a kid and a grown-up?" Of course I couldn't help but smile. This was precisely the question I had been trying to answer for the past several years in my work with the adult clients of all ages that I counsel. I have a private practice working with individuals, couples, and groups.

"Why do you ask?" I countered.

"Well, you have pierced ears and Kara in my class has pierced ears, too. So how can you really tell the difference between a kid and a grown-up?"

My first thought was that considering the piercing craze, having your ears pierced wasn't a clear indicator of much. But, considering that it was late and we were trying to finish our bedtime routine, not to mention that she just wanted a simple answer to her question, I responded concisely, "It's the size. Grown-ups are bigger than kids." She seemed satisfied, at least enough not to press further for the moment. I was also relieved that she didn't see through the holes in my logic, since one of our young teenage baby-sitters is actually taller than I am. So much for my size explanation.

What I didn't tell my daughter is that often adults act like kids and many kids act like adults. Nor did I mention the complexities in our society that force some children to grow up too quickly and allow some adults to apparently never grow up at all.

Discovering the Inner Grown-up

The truth is that it often seems difficult to tell the difference between kids and grown-ups these days. This idea was brought home to me in stark reality one day when I was driving around running errands and doing all the things that "grown-ups" do and I was listening to the nationally syndicated talk radio program hosted by Dr. Laura Schlessinger.

Now there is no question that Dr. Laura is a controversial figure. She is known for having extremely conservative views. And, yes, she has a no-nonsense, sometimes abrasive style with her callers. I don't always agree with her content or style, but I have to admit that I think she often offers excellent advice. She pushes her callers on to find answers of high moral integrity. She challenges in a way that causes people—both the actual callers and the listening audience—to evaluate their options in life and to make better choices.

So as I was driving around on this errand day, somewhere between the bank and the dry cleaners, I heard a caller on Dr. Laura's program whining on and on about this and that and the other thing. I honestly can't even remember exactly what her plight was, but I do remember thinking to myself, "Oh, come off of it . . . you sound like such a baby, so full of self-pity." And then I thought the words that would change the entire direction of my practice as a psychotherapist. I thought, "Your inner child has run amok; you should try developing your inner *grown-up*."

Your inner grown-up. I remember chuckling to myself at

first. "That's pretty funny," I thought. In recent years we have become obsessed with nurturing our inner children—looking back at past wounds, honoring that pain, coddling the child inside who was hurt—but we've forgotten about looking forward and claiming our inner grown-ups.

Well, I didn't think much else about it at first. If anything, I thought it was just an amusing play on words. But then situations kept coming up that would make me think, "Oh, they need to develop their inner grown-up." It reminded me of a great line in the movie *Babe*, which is about a farmer who decides to enter his unusual pig in a sheepdog competition. Although it seemed ridiculous on the surface to enter a pig in a competition for dogs, "Farmer Hoggett knew that little ideas that tickled and nagged and refused to go away should never be ignored, for in them lie the seeds of destiny."

Okay, perhaps "seeds of destiny" is a bit dramatic; nevertheless, I was haunted, if you will, by the idea of the inner grown-up. So I mentioned the notion to a few people, and I was often met with the same initial response that I had experienced: people laughed. It was a funny twist on a commonplace concept. You may have even laughed yourself when you read the title of this book. Or thought to yourself, "I know someone who needs *that*." Ha-ha.

But then I started to think about the term "inner grown-up" more seriously. What does that mean? Clearly, we have a youth-obsessed culture that often scoffs at the idea of growing up. Think of Peter Pan, who sings to Wendy about his refusal to grow up. To Peter, growing up is a fate worse than death.

How many of us secretly feel that way, too? Most elements in our society and our media urge us consciously and unconsciously to seek the proverbial fountain of youth. Consider popular television series, such as *Seinfeld* or *Friends*, that exalt the lives of adolescentlike adults who bounce through life in a humorous, juvenile manner. Don't get me wrong—I enjoy watching these shows, too, but think about what role models those characters actually are for us aging adults, let alone the messages they send to teens.

Why We Need This Book

Many people consider being regarded as a grown-up an insult. I just read a print advertisement for an automobile that read "Giggle. No, laugh. No, howl as if you've never grown up." Grown-ups, after all, are boring, stodgy, dull, and hopelessly burdened by the heaviness of life—aren't they? Even when many youngish grown-ups enter the "real world" of work and responsibilities, they do so with childlike attitudes. If we're to believe the popular conception, our culture is dominated by a generation of computer wizards who go to work in jeans, ride skateboards, and get paid to play video games or surf the Internet.

And look at how our advertising not only encourages us to stay youthful—any cream or powder or lotion to hide the wrinkles and stave off that dreaded process of aging—but how it also encourages childlike self-absorption. A popular potato chip's recent tag line was "Grab Your Own Bag." Heaven forbid you should act like a grown-up and actually share!

Which reminds me of the newest craze in the self-improvement world, a trend toward utter self-involvement called "personal coaching." These coaches are professionals from a variety of backgrounds who have a range of credentials and are hired to cheer you on to create a better life for yourself. How do they do this, you ask? They give you permission to indulge in excessive self-care. Thus, they advise things like "pamper yourself," "take a nap," "have a massage," "do what you want, not what you should," "have fun," "put yourself and your own needs first."

Now, I'm all for having fun and taking care of your needs, *but* the coaching philosophy sounds suspiciously self-indulgent and shallow. It appears to be encouraging your inner child to take control in his or her most demanding, spoiled, and self-centered way.

Where has all of this obsession with the self and youth brought us? Largely to a place in Western cultural development where we are a self-serving, shortsighted group of grown-up children. Even the *New York Times Magazine* proclaimed on its November 1, 1998, cover that a new version of the American Constitution might be:

> We, the relatively unbothered and well off, hold these truths to be self-evident: that Big Government, Big Deficits and Big Tobacco are bad, but that big bathrooms and 4-by-4's are not; that American overseas involvement should be restricted to trade agreements, mutual funds and the visiting of certain beachfront resorts; that markets can take care of themselves as long as they take care of us; that an individual's sex life is nobody's business, though highly entertaining; and that the only rights that really matter are those which indulge the Self.

A narcissistic nation. Is that how we really want to live? Has narcissism brought any of us true, lasting satisfaction? Has our attitude of "entitlement" or our culture of immediate gratification or our tacit approval of eternal adolescence done anything to fill the existential void? Is it possible that living as a true grown-up is actually a positive experience and not one of Dante's hellish circles? Maybe.

So, I reflected on what exactly the inner grown-up ought to be, or has the potential to be—the inner self that is wise, brave, strong, mature, selfless, loving, spiritual, committed, responsible, meaningful. It could be your best self, really, your highest self—the inner self that is rooted in the present and conscious of the future though not beleaguered by baggage from the past.

Grieving and Growing Up

Eventually I realized that this higher self, this most authentically adult self, is the self that often evolves after a period of *bereavement*. My first book, *Transcending Loss: Understanding the Lifelong Impact of Grief and How to Make It Meaningful*, is precisely about the kind of transformation that is possible over time after a major loss. I describe "transcenders" as people who are changed irrevocably by their losses but are changed in ways that are ultimately meaningful and redemptive.

In that book, I identified four pathways to transcendence, four key avenues in which people make their losses meaningful. They are framed by the acronym SOAR: Spirituality, Outreach, Attitude, and Reinvestment. *Spirituality* refers to the intense change in one's faith that can occur after a loss, a faith that becomes perhaps more complex and less innocent, but ultimately stronger, richer, and deeper. *Outreach* refers to the change that can occur whereby a griever becomes more giving, choosing to reach out to others, recognizing that we are all connected. It is a perspective that lifts one out of oneself. *Attitude* is the change in one's stand toward life, death, suffering, the world, the self. The transcendent griever looks at life through a different lens, seeing what's important in life and what is merely trivial. And finally, *Reinvestment* refers to the avenues in which transcendent grievers choose to channel their pain and reconnect to life, whether it is reinvesting in a cause or mission, a new career, a new creative project, or love and life itself.

Any of these four pathways is ultimately a choice. Grievers transcend because they are determined, insistent, and exert their will to get them where they want to be. And in the final analysis, the pathways of SOAR are roads that *any* evolved grown-up should travel, whether he or she has had a major loss or not. Spirituality, service-oriented outreach, a positive and wise attitude, investment in important and meaningful activities—these very qualities lead to a more fulfilled and enriched life, a more grown-up existence. Why wait for a major loss to become your wake-up call to life?

The Buddhists say that death is the greatest teacher, but one does not need to experience death intimately to glean its lessons. It is enough that death is the constant backdrop of our lives, a persistent reminder that our time here is limited. Daily we press against the veil of death—just read a newspaper or watch the evening news. There is no more time to waste. The opportunity for knocking on the door, the occasion to plunge deeply into a richly satisfying grown-up life, is *now*.

Choosing to Grow

How do we work toward this worthy goal? Unlike physical maturity, we have control over when, how, and to what extent we will develop emotionally, psychologically, and spiritually. Claiming your inner grown-up, just like transcending a loss, is ultimately a *choice*. It is a conscious decision to work toward the goal of discovering your best self—a conscious decision that anyone can make at any time on his or her personal pilgrimage.

But it does help to have some guidance along the way so you know that you're taking the best route. I developed the Four-Pillar Program for claiming your inner grown-up as a kind of map, one that I hope will act as a guide for you on your journey. The four pillars (Responsibility, Maturity, Love, and Spirituality) are largely inspired by the four pathways to transcendence for grievers. Both of these frameworks are based on the possibilities of change and transformation. And just as it is never too late to do grief work, no matter how many years have gone by, it is never too late to claim your inner grown-up, no matter what age you are.

RESPONSIBILITY   MATURITY   LOVE   SPIRITUALITY

The Four Pillars of Your Inner Grown-up

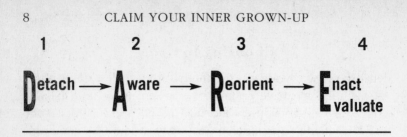

The Four Steps to Access Your Inner Grown-up

The key technique that actually stimulates the change, that literally connects you with your inner grown-up, is the DARE technique. DARE stands for Detach, Aware, Reorient, and Enact/Evaluate. These are the four essential steps that will ultimately harness the power of your inner grown-up. The four steps of DARE can be used anytime, anywhere. They will be specifically applied throughout the book to the four pillars (the critical aspects of your inner grown-up). Think of this approach as a 4-by-4 "vehicle" to help you overcome any obstacle to getting you where you want to be!

By the end of this book, you will become quite familiar with how the four steps of DARE can diffuse problematic attitudes and behaviors and can tap into the wisdom and strength of all parts of your inner grown-up. This process will help you "dare" to reach your potential as an authentic adult. And as the child in me might taunt, I dare you to try it.

How to Use This Book

The first section of this book provides a look at your inner child. Since the 1980s people have embraced the inner child concept that celebrates and honors the childlike spirit within each of us. Because it was also a movement to help heal childhood wounds, the addiction and recovery communities (twelve-step programs and substance abuse treatment centers) embraced it. Whether you actually participated in any aspect of the inner child movement is not especially relevant. Some of you will have found those concepts life changing, whereas others of you will have thought of your inner child as nothing more than a joke. Regardless of your views on the inner child movement, you can still claim your inner grown-up. But it is useful to understand the movement that made such an impact on our societal psyche. Consequently, in chapter 1 I review the many positive aspects of this cultural phenomenon.

Unfortunately, even as many positive directions emerged from this trend, there also emerged a certain "victim" mentality. Focusing on and healing wounds from one's childhood is, in and of itself, a very therapeutic endeavor. But one problem that arose is that many people got stuck in the pain from their pasts. They found that holding on to their wounds provided them with an identity of sorts. Perhaps unwittingly they adopted a victim mentality. Others seem trapped by inner child "problem" qualities, such as immaturity, dependence, and fear. Chapter 2, then, looks at how our inner children can develop into problem children.

When we pay too much attention to the dysfunctions of the past and use them as an excuse to explain all manner of dysfunctions in the present, then we know it's time to grow up. Growing up does not mean eliminating the past, of course. It is fantasy to think we can all move forward with a clean slate. Claiming your inner grown-up does mean honestly appraising the past, having respect and compassion for the self that suffered childhood wounds, and then using that understanding as a springboard to personal responsibility and free will.

A therapist friend of mine once told me that the problem with most therapy (including inner child work) is that if you picture therapy as a horizontal number line, we've done a great job of moving people from negative numbers to zero. We've looked back, dealt with the past, and brought them to the present. But then we tend to stop there. How do you move into the positive numbers? How do you move forward? What's the next step? Claiming your inner grown-up is that next step.

Section 2 of the book looks at your inner grown-up. It examines the road to authentic adulthood, explains the Four-Pillar Program, and then offers a chapter on each pillar. Much of the material in this book corresponds to a six-week workshop that I designed to help people grow and develop on all levels. Each week has a reading, a visualization, journal questions, and exercises to help facilitate change. These tools will be offered in each chapter.

Each reading (a poem or excerpt) is a preparation before the visualization to help induce a reflective state. The visualizations in each chapter are powerful agents of change. I would strongly recommend speaking each reading and visualization into a tape recorder in a slow, relaxed voice. Later, you can listen to the words as they direct you instead of having to read them. Doing this frees you to enter a trancelike, meditative state. In this state, as you listen to the recorded words, you absorb the material into your unconscious, on a deeply healing level, which can profoundly assist you in your goal of personal growth.

I also would urge you to be open to responding to the journal questions. Many people tell me that they're not writers and that keeping a journal just doesn't work for them. I understand that people do resonate better with one type of activity over another, but I must confess a strong bias in favor of writing as a therapeutic aid. I truly believe that it makes an emotional difference to actually write about one's reactions, to reflect thoughts in the written word. Don't concern yourself with grammar or sentence construction—this isn't about getting a good grade. No one needs to see your writing, either; the journal is for you and only for you. Writing from the heart pulls an emotional experience into the body and through the fingertips. It allows for a more thorough healing. Please be open to trying anything. What do you have to lose?

In fact, I recommend that you keep two journals: a smaller one for note-taking as you process this material and log entries that you can carry with you in a purse or a pocket; and a larger one for some of the letters, drawings, and other responses. At first you may feel some discomfort with the journal process, but ultimately you will find it an invaluable aid.

The Four-Pillar Program and the four essential steps of DARE, in the end, are more than mere exercises, tools, or psychological devices—they are in essence a new framework for viewing yourself and the way in which you interact with your world. This paradigm becomes a personal philosophy, one that shapes the way in which you think about life. It offers a new perspective for analyzing situations, helps you develop a heightened awareness of what is and what can be, and encourages a mindfulness that leads to empowerment.

The third section of the book is about the necessity for integrating one's inner child with one's inner adult. I certainly wouldn't recommend throwing out the baby—or in this case the inner child—with the bathwater. Both inner selves are vital components to being whole. One without the other leads to a skewed identity. I will offer an integration plan for blending the best parts of each self.

Throughout the book you will find stories, anecdotes, and clinical vignettes to illustrate points and highlight how this program can work for you. All names and identifying characteristics have been changed to protect privacy, but I think you will find that their experiences are universally applicable.

The Premise and the Promise

For me, working with this material professionally has been very exciting and gratifying. Whenever someone can release the bondage from the past and move forward to a happier, more peaceful place in his or her life, or whenever someone simply decides that it's time to move on emotionally and then succeeds, something sacred takes place. It is a privilege to be a companion to people on this intimate and worthwhile journey.

What I didn't expect, but have been pleased to note, is that ever since the inner grown-up concept entered my life, I have been changed personally as well. I have a much broader and more complex understanding of my own emotional and spiritual development.

Like a lot of you, as a child I just couldn't wait to become an adult. When someone thought I was younger than I really was, it was an insult, not a compliment. I remember aching to be sixteen to get my driver's license. Then I wished to be eighteen so that I could move away to college. Then I dreamed of being twenty-one so I could graduate from college and have my own apartment in the "real world." Finally I graduated and moved to New York City, where I got a full-time job, paid all of my bills, and was responsible for cooking all of my meals (or ordering takeout, which was more likely!). Finally I was all grown up . . . at last.

Of course, then, with the ironic messages of our society, I discovered all manners of products and articles and ideas to help me achieve the illusion of eternal youth, with the implicit message of "Why did you want to grow up anyway?"

Actually I was always pretty comfortable with my roles in life as a grown-up, but I never thought much about it. Being conscious of the inner grown-up concept has opened my eyes and raised my awareness on a daily basis about how to connect with this inner self that is calm and rational and strong. I feel like I have discovered a new resource, a wealth of internal treasure that was there all along but was obscured by my lack of attention.

Thus, when I find myself short-tempered and yelling at the kids to hurry up, I'm more apt to stop now and take a deep breath and notice how my inner child is acting in a rather immature manner. Then I call upon my inner grown-up to take charge in a less reactive way, which she is happy to do. Or when I find myself anxious over little things, such as a doctor's appointment (I've never liked doctor's examinations, neither as a child nor as a grown-up), rather than cower internally with my inner child fear, I just call upon the reservoir of strength that my inner grown-up presides over, and I'm instantly more relaxed.

Claiming your inner grown-up is very much a process, just as growing physically is very much a process. I don't always succeed in being my best self, but I'm committed each day to giving it another try. This journey is about hope and possibility and being open to a new mind-set.

I believe that true happiness and fulfillment lie in claiming your inner grown-up, the inner self that is wise, transcendent, and honorable. And the best part is that you already have this inner grown-up inside of you. You just have to learn how to access this valuable resource. While you may have searched for answers and solutions outside of yourself, the truth is that the answers are and have been within you all along. Just as Dorothy in *The Wizard of Oz* possessed the power to return home at any time because of her ruby slippers (only she didn't know it), you possess the power to find inner peace and a deeper sense of meaning in your life. Understanding the keys and unlocking the doors to your inner grown-up are what will take you there.

As a final introductory note, you may have noticed my propensity for quoting children's materials (*Peter Pan, Babe, The Wizard of Oz* . . . with many more references to children's movies and books to come). This may seem odd in a book about becoming an authentic *adult*. One reason I use these examples is that as a mother of young children, that's the primary entertainment that I am exposed to these days! More significantly, classic children's media endures the test of time because it speaks to us on many levels. These stories may be entertaining, but, like parables, they contain deeper meanings and subtle lessons that speak to our adult selves. These stories provide, if you will, a bridge from the world of the child to the adult. Let them connect to your inner worlds, spanning from your inner child to your inner grown-up.

So I invite you to take the next step in *your* personal growth— to work on fulfilling your potential. If you feel that something is missing in your life or that it's just time to grow, if you worry that the past is affecting your present in negative ways, if you feel like you're faking it as an adult, well, then, the time is now for taking this journey.

PART

I

Your Inner Child

CHAPTER ONE

The Beauty of Your Inner Child

I am still every age that I have been. Because I was
once a child, I am always a child.

—Madeleine L'Engle, *A Circle of Quiet*

She sat in front of me with her eyes closed. I had my eyes closed as well. We had reached a point in our therapeutic work together when I felt she needed to meet, comfort, and nurture her inner child. We did a visualization exercise where I asked Brenda to go back in time, to picture the little girl that she was, and to talk with her.

Not only did my client Brenda end up "talking" with little Brenda, but she held her in her lap and stroked her hair and hugged her. Brenda sat in my office and tears streamed down her face as she engaged in this visualization and made an emotional connection with her inner child. She realized that this sweet child was all innocence and goodness. She was not bad or flawed or responsible for what was later to happen . . .

Brenda was a forty-year-old woman who was quite capable and accomplished and personable. She had a booming laugh and a beaming smile, and I found myself looking forward to my sessions with her. But as put together as Brenda appeared, deep down she felt inadequate. More than just underlying insecurity or low self-esteem were responsible for her unhappiness. Brenda felt that she was inherently flawed, "damaged goods," she said.

After some months of therapy, it became clear that this negative self-perspective stemmed from a childhood experience with her father when he sexually molested her. "Little Brenda must have caused that; little Brenda must be bad; it was her fault," Brenda told herself. The burden of this secret weighed on her soul for many, many years.

But when Brenda had the occasion to meet with little Brenda and to hold her and hug her and braid her hair, Brenda realized on some deeply rooted level that this child was pure and good and was in no way responsible for what had happened with her father. This realization, at such a profound level, changed things for Brenda. She forgave herself and learned to love herself in a way that made her feel whole. Seeing herself as a child changed the way she saw herself as an adult. Knowing that that child was still a part of her helped her feel more at peace with herself.

The Inner Child Phenomenon

In the 1980s the inner child concept burst onto our cultural scene. The idea itself was not especially new. Carl Jung, for example, at the beginning of the twentieth century spoke of an inner child as a "wonder child." Object relations theorists later in the century spoke of a "true" inner self. In 1985 Dr. W. Hugh Missildine was one of the first mental health professionals who addressed the issue of working therapeutically with one's inner child in his book *Your Inner Child of the Past*. Later therapists Claudia Black and Sharon Wegsheider-Cruse introduced the idea of the dysfunctional family to the field of substance abuse and chemical dependency.

But John Bradshaw can be credited with linking together the ideas of the inner child, the dysfunctional family, and addiction. With his PBS television series and his many books, including *Homecoming: Reclaiming and Championing Your Inner Child* (1990), he launched a self-help explosion that lasted well into the late 1990s. In fact, the repercussions are still being felt to this day.

Suddenly, a profusion of books were published to address the inner child. Therapeutic workshops and weekends and lectures and seminars and classes and vacation packages all devoted to nurturing the inner child were held throughout the country. Other spin-offs followed: music for your inner child, herbs for your inner child, food for your inner child, affirmations for your inner child, toys for your inner child . . . the list goes on and on.

Some people took this movement very seriously and found the work life transforming, helping them to change their self-perceptions and/or their behaviors. Others saw the trend as merely humorous. The idea was easily mocked by late-night talk show hosts and comedians. It may have even caused you to chuckle on more than one occasion.

But whether you actually participated in and benefited from the therapeutic movement is not especially relevant to claiming your inner grown-up. Looking at the child within is merely a starting point. This chapter will describe some of the healthy and positive insights that have evolved from the inner child movement. For some of you, this discussion will be a review, whereas for others of you this discussion will be an introduction to what all the hype was about.

The Magic of Your Inner Child

On one level, the concept of the inner child highlights aspects of childhood that are inherently wonderful: creativity, imagination, magic, spontaneity, joy, freedom, wonder, innocence, vulnerability, sensitivity, lack of inhibitions, artistic expression, humor, enthusiasm, playfulness, and so on. Children have all of these qualities, making them seem enchanted in many ways.

Have you ever watched children playing at the park or sifting through sand on the beach? They possess an appealing leisure, an in-the-moment carefree ease. Or have you seen their faces light up when they go to an amusement park or unwrap a birthday present? Childhood has a true magic that we all yearn to return to. Kids typically aren't burdened by grown-up worries, such as rent, mortgage, bills; they don't worry whether the stock market is up or down. The only up and down they are concerned with is a seesaw.

This aspect of the inner child is known as the wonder child—the childhood captured in Disney World or Kodak commercials. Many people feel that this aspect of the inner child is your true self, the essential you. It's the you before you add layer upon layer of defenses, the protective cushion that adults learn to insulate themselves with. In the best sense of the word, it's the naive you before you're taught to be fearful and prejudiced and cynical and jaded. Remember the words from the classic movie *South Pacific*: "You've got to be taught to hate and fear. You've got to be taught from year to year." The wonder child is the core happy you before you were wounded by life.

A friend of mine described his wonder child as the "original voice." He told me, "I think we all come into the world from pure love. And then stuff happens—family things happen—and the kernel keeps getting covered with other stuff. But the original beauty is still there and my job now is to uncover that lost beauty, that love essence, whatever you want to call it. That's the voice I'm looking for."

So, of course, the idea of connecting with the essential self, a romanticized version of the inner child, became extremely appealing. It sounded fun, indulgent, almost like a great vacation. I believe part of the reason that the movement became so popular was that it drew upon our unconscious desire to get that pure, unsullied core back into our lives again—even if it was never there to begin with.

The Wounds of Your Inner Child

The truth is that few childhoods were pure amusement. As we grew from infant to toddler to child, we were exposed more and more to various levels of pain, abandonment, fear, confusion, and powerlessness. So on a deeper level, the inner child movement became very much about uncovering and healing those wounds from the past. This step is critical, because healing the wounded child gives you access to the wonder child.

Every child, inner and otherwise, has been wounded. Perhaps you weren't beaten or tortured or abused, but every child has felt lost, afraid, and unloved, even if only for a moment. Maybe you got lost in the grocery store. Or you were afraid to be left with unknown baby-sitters. Or maybe something terrible and life shattering happened such as your parents getting divorced or your mother dying. We've all been wounded one way or another, and we carry the fragments of these shatterings with us.

With the inner child movement, long-closeted skeletons were released from their dark chambers to be examined. Issues were brought into the light, including abuse (emotional, physical, and sexual), neglect, growing up in an alcoholic home, growing up with a dysfunctional family, divorce, losses, and so on. These issues had always been around, but the inner child movement gave people permission to look honestly at their painful pasts and acknowledge their needs for restoration.

Bradshaw's Inner Children

John Bradshaw, a recovering alcoholic and ACOA (adult child of an alcoholic) himself, realized that his wounded inner child was contaminating his life. He experienced "spontaneous age regressions" when he was consumed by rage and then withdrew, much in the same way his eleven-year-old self had been consumed by rage and then withdrawn. He began doing inner child work to reclaim and champion that inner child and found it completely life transforming. Then he began sharing the work with others through his workshops, books, and television programs.

Bradshaw offers a developmental framework that subdivides the inner child into the infant self, the toddler self, the preschool self, the school-age self, and the adolescent self. So not only do you have an inner child, but also many inner children! All of these inner children, he claims, are inside of you, and any single one may be dominating at any given point in time. One minute your demanding toddler self could be in control, whereas at another time your sad school-age self, the you who felt awkward and shy, seems to have taken over. Bradshaw's approach is to take each inner self on a journey of embracing and reclaiming.

So what exactly does the "work" involve? To begin with, it means going backward in time and connecting to the past. Usually this brings up some uncomfortable feelings that require doing "original pain work" or *feeling* the painful feelings rather than avoiding them or being numb to them. The therapeutic principle is that you must feel in order to heal. The "work" also means, perhaps most important, developing a relationship with your inner child, nurturing and loving and meeting his or her previously unmet needs. Many people were transformed by this connection.

Techniques to facilitate this process include things like going on guided visualizations to connect with your wounded inner child, writing letters to your wounded inner child, having meditations to console your inner child, stating affirmations to comfort your inner child, and engaging in corrective exercises (like play therapy) to meet your inner children's desires. This process helps you reclaim your inner infant, and then you can repeat the process for your inner toddler, your inner preschool self, and so on.

Bradshaw realized that by engaging in this work, he was able to stay clean and sober. Healing the wounds from the past, he felt, was key to his recovery from addiction. Others in the field of addiction and recovery felt the same way. Soon, many inpatient and outpatient treatment centers for substance abuse began employing inner child work to help secure long-term recovery. It was believed that if painful issues from the past weren't eventually dealt with, many addicts would ultimately relapse.

Inner Children of Dysfunction

But, of course, the inner child movement goes beyond the field of addiction. Its therapeutic power can be applied to any type of dysfunction.

Sara was a young woman who was devastated by the breakup of her relationship with the man she thought would become her husband. After years of his inability to commit on that level, they finally agreed to call it quits. Simultaneously, Sara decided to leave a job that was unfulfilling and chronically stressful. Unfortunately, these two major losses, even if they might ultimately be for the best, plunged Sara into a serious depression.

Sara had trouble concentrating and sleeping. She found herself crying constantly, and, worst of all, she virtually stopped eating. Thin to begin with, she became positively gaunt over the course of a few weeks. She knew that she was on a slippery slope of self-destruction and decided to enter therapy.

Sara's therapist asked her if she would be willing to do some inner child work. Her therapist realized that Sara was reacting to more than just these recent losses in her life. She was unconsciously recreating a similar time in her life, a time when she also felt lost and alone and afraid, another time when she stopped eating and felt uncared for . . . when she was nine years old. Not coincidentally, Sara's parents had divorced when she was that age. And Sara's mother had been so overwrought with her own issues of loss and survival, that she had not been able to parent Sara in the way that Sara needed. At that time Sara plunged into a similar depression, feeling utterly bereft.

Sara said, "When I visualized little Sara with her pigtails not knowing how to take care of herself and feeling like she had done something terribly wrong, well, my heart just ached for her. I could see that she was taking me over in a weird sort of way and taking control of my life now. So I learned to comfort her and tell her that she didn't do anything wrong."

Sara started taking care of her inner child, which ultimately translated to taking care of her adult self. She told me that it felt sort of crazy at times, like she was some sort of split personality. But she admitted that working with the inner child healed her. "Little Sara doesn't get out of control anymore. I did a lot of work to comfort her. I self-parented her."

For whatever reasons, our parents weren't always able to parent us in the way that we needed. In fact, they were wounded children themselves and didn't get everything they needed in their own childhoods. Mostly they just did the best they could with the internal resources that they had. But we were left feeling needy and began searching for that parenting, perhaps in unlikely places. Ultimately we must reparent ourselves, at least partially, to begin healing the inner child. You can't go back and change what your parents did or didn't do, so you have to deal with who you are now and where you are now. The solutions won't spontaneously emerge from your spouse, your own children, or anyone else. The solution, that is, self-parenting, must come from within.

The Reparenting Process

When I was in graduate school in social work in New York City, one of our required courses was in group therapy. Not only did we have the usual academic approach to the subject— that is, lectures, papers, and readings—but we also participated in our own group therapy experience with our fellow classmates. I was in a group with seven others, and we engaged together in this type of live laboratory experiment.

Being in the group provided support, and we also got to see group dynamics emerge in a fresh, vibrant way. I remember one of my fellow group members talking about his fear of going on a job interview (this was the end of graduate school and we were all stressed about finding jobs). The woman sitting next to me said, "Well, don't you just automatically comfort yourself with your inner parent?" We all looked at her quizzically. She continued, "Whenever I'm feeling scared or sad or whatever, I just listen to my inner parent. That's the voice inside me that says, 'Oh, it's okay. Everything is going to be fine, honey. Here's a hug . . . you'll be all right. Don't worry; I'm here with you.' "

The way she talked was mesmerizing—she clearly felt so comforted by this inner voice that it was able to carry her through most any frightening or sad situation in her life. It stands out vividly in my mind that she had claimed an important inner voice, ultimately an inner grown-up voice.

Disciplining Our Inner Children

In general, the inner child movement encouraged a protective reparenting process that emphasized a nurturing, gentle approach to the inner children. This is also one of the movement's limitations, however, since sometimes firm discipline is necessary for teaching an inner child how to behave himself. A friend of mine, Thom, a thirty-seven-year-old gay man, told me that inner child work was extremely valuable for him, but that his inner child needed not to be coddled, but to be reined in and disciplined.

Thom got into therapy after a brief love affair ended, leaving him devastated and depressed and acting out with self-destructive behaviors like drinking, taking drugs, and having promiscuous sex. What Thom discovered was that he had a lot of unfinished business from the past to deal with. Feelings toward his grandfather (who had sexually abused him); toward his mother, who he felt didn't protect him; feelings toward his father, who was homophobic—all these issues and more needed to be addressed therapeutically.

Thom's therapist recommended inner child work. He suggested that Thom begin by carrying a stone with him in his pocket to represent his inner child. Thom thought this sounded silly at first, but he agreed to try it. He found that it helped to keep his inner child more consciously in his awareness. Then if he found himself in a questionable situation, he would stop and ask, "Would I be behaving this way if my 'child' was with me? How would I behave differently?"

He found it useful to picture his "child" with him and developed a protective attitude toward this inner child. This child doesn't belong in bars or drug dens. He shouldn't put this child in dangerous situations. Thom was able to act in a more loving and respectful way toward himself because he was being more loving and respectful toward his inner child.

Then Thom began to do grief work in his therapy. He mourned the rejections and misunderstandings of the past. He grieved over the ways in which he'd been wronged. And he came to understand much about his inner child's motivations. But simply realizing what's going on is not necessarily enough to change behavior. That's when Thom realized it was time to re-parent his inner child.

In conversations with others, Thom heard how his friends self-parented by coddling and hugging and holding their inner children. Thom realized that his inner child was out of control and had been running the show for quite a long time. The fears and pain of his inner child had been driving much of his self-destructive and potentially dangerous patterns of behavior.

So Thom engaged in an art therapy exercise of his own design and created a three-panel painting. In the first panel he drew an outline of an adult, filled with pulleys and levers, and inside a child manipulated the adult-size puppet. That is exactly how he felt—he was a mere puppet to the demanding and out-of-control needs of his wounded inner child. Then he asked himself, "What are the steps that I'm going to take to change this?" So in the next panel he drew himself lecturing to this inner toddler and disciplining him. He told the child, "I'm the adult here and I'm in charge." In the final panel Thom drew himself embracing the inner child. "But for me," he said, "the real healing came not in the third panel but in the second panel when I told the child that he wasn't in control anymore." Of course, eventually Thom had to develop an action plan to change his behaviors and to insure that his inner grown-up stayed in charge.

The Inner Grown-up

The inner grown-up concept is not entirely new. Within the inner child movement, many of the leaders and authors did, in fact, make reference to an inner adult or an adult within. They employed this vital aspect of the self to help heal the wounded inner child. Cathryn Taylor in *The Inner Child Workbook* describes a ceremonial bathing ritual for cleansing your body of the childish ways that interfere with being the adult you want to be. And she also recommends a "Crossing the Bridge" ceremony to symbolically leave the past behind and connect with your adult self. She acknowledges that it's your inner adult who is responsible for orchestrating all of these rites of healing.

And yet, somehow, in the end, the inner grown-up didn't receive top billing. The inner child was so vocal and so pained that its cries were often heard above the voice of the inner grown-up. As the movement unfolded, what became most powerful for people was the going back and acknowledging the secrets from the past, embracing the wounded inner child, and grieving for his or her pains and losses. We existed in a culture of repression and denial for such a long time that the inner child movement lifted the lid off Pandora's box. A lot of stuff had to come out before we could put the lid back on.

Claiming your inner grown-up is about putting the lid back on Pandora's box. Now is the time. But before you can put the lid back on, you have to make sure that everything that needs to come out has had an opportunity to do so.

Beginning with the Inner Child

Before I begin inner grown-up work with a client, either individually or in a group, I usually start with the inner child. Each person is coming from a different place in terms of his or her inner child work. Some people have focused for years on the many ways that they were wounded as children. Others haven't thought much about their pasts. Some are veterans of therapy, whereas for others this is their first experience with a mental health professional. Some people have had sad and tragic histories to contend with, whereas others had generally happy and uneventful childhoods.

So in order for everyone to have at least a minimal common frame of reference, in the first week of the Claim Your Inner Grown-up support group, I ask group members to bring in an object that represents/expresses/symbolizes their inner child. I ask them to tell us about the object, share any memory associated with it, and reflect on what it says about them as children.

People bring in a wide variety of things. Dana, for example, brought her childhood wallet, a prized possession, one which she remembered purchasing with her own hard-earned dollars. The leather was worn and crumpled, darkened by years of handling. Inside, the wallet was brimming with school photographs of long-ago friends. One of these friends, in fact, had just recently died—Dana had lost touch with her years ago but read about her death in the obituaries. The wallet also held schoolgirl notes secretly traded with friends, full of gossip and wide-eyed innocence and fun. As Dana shared the wallet and its contents with us, her eyes twinkled.

Joshua brought the blocks that he used to play with as a child. Sandra said she couldn't bring the item that most represented her inner child because it was the piano that she grew up playing. "That piano is where I spent hours of my childhood, just happy as could be," she recalled.

Some of the items people bring recall the wonder aspects of their inner child, whereas other items reflect a more painful past.

Yvonne brought her childhood teddy bear, one of the few items that brought her comfort in a childhood filled mostly with pain and abandonment. Her father died when she was a preteen and her mother, suffering from schizophrenia, had been unfit to raise her own children for some time. Yvonne had floated from foster home to foster home until finally her maternal grandmother took in Yvonne and her two siblings. If her grandmother had been a nurturing woman, perhaps Yvonne might have healed from her already traumatic childhood. However, this woman was cruel and abusive. Yvonne said, "I never smiled when I was young. There was nothing to smile about."

But when Yvonne held her teddy bear in our group session, she became misty eyed. This teddy bear had brought her solace when her family members could not. This worn-out, moth-eaten brown bear—as real and beloved to her as the Velveteen Rabbit becomes real in Margery Williams's classic children's book—kept her going. Seeing how tenderly she held it spoke volumes about its importance to her.

A necessary part of understanding your inner child is understanding how vulnerable our inner children were and are. It's just as important to review the memories of pain, disappointment, and abandonment as it is to recall the memories of fun and magic. Confronting all that the past was, for better or for worse, is the only way to reach any deep level of healing. The inner child movement helped many people do just this. And it prepared the way for them to move on and claim their inner grown-ups.

Try This . . .
Select an object that represents your own inner child. Look at it. Hold it. What does it mean to you? What does it tell you about you? In your journal write about a particular moment in your life or experience you had that is related to this object.

The Inner Child in Review

The inner child movement brought to our awareness two key concepts: first, *the wounded inner child,* including past hurts and how our history can continue to have an impact on us. There's no doubt that healing the wounded inner child was a goal of the inner child movement, as well. And many people did, in fact, find healing in the nurturing and connecting and reclaiming of their past inner selves. For this we owe a great psychological debt.

And secondly, the movement also brought us the *wonder child*, helping us to reconnect with our own personal lost city of Atlantis. *Gourmet* magazine proudly displayed cotton candy on the cover of its February 2000 issue. The inside story tells how the Four Seasons restaurant in New York City now offers a mountain of white cotton candy as one of its delicacies. Julian Niccolini, the managing partner of the restaurant, explains that the reason cotton candy is so popular (selling around two dozen servings per night) is that "it gives [adults] their childhood back, and everybody wants to be a child again. Our guests have everything—this is the only thing they don't have." The inner child movement gave us back our childhoods to a certain extent as well.

A Reminder: At the end of each chapter, you will have a reading and a visualization for your consideration. They will be more effective as processing tools if you first read them aloud into a tape recorder in a very slow, relaxed tone of voice. Be sure to pause between sentences. Then, later, when you have time, listen to your recording. This will produce a deeper, more hypnotic effect. Also, if a gender is mentioned that doesn't match your own, substitute the correct pronoun.

READING
From *Where the Wild Things Are*
by Maurice Sendak

"Now stop!" Max said and sent the wild things off to bed without their supper.

And Max the king of all wild things was lonely and wanted to be where someone loved him best of all.

Then all around from far away across the world he smelled good things to eat so he gave up being king of where the wild things are.

But the wild things cried, "Oh please don't go—we'll eat you up—we love you so!"

And Max said, "No!"

The wild things roared their terrible roars and gnashed their terrible teeth and rolled their terrible eyes and showed their terrible claws but Max stepped into his private boat and waved

*good-bye and sailed back over a year and in and out of weeks
and through a day and into the night of his very own room
where he found his supper waiting for him and it was still hot.*

VISUALIZATION

Note: The beginning and end of each visualization in virtually all of the chapters will follow the same process. The
middle section of each guided imagery will be specific to the
topic of that particular chapter. You should plan on spending
at least ten minutes on each visualization. While many people
use quiet music when they meditate, I would not recommend
it for this type of visualization. While when accompanied by
music the experience does become meditative, it is different
from an actual meditation. The purpose of a visualization is to go
somewhere—be led somewhere—and consequently to *feel*
something. Music can be a distraction from the focus of this task.

Begin by getting your body into a comfortable position. You
may prefer to sit in a chair or to lie on the ground. Whichever you
choose, have your palms open, facing upward. Before you settle
into a relaxed position, stretch your arms high over your head.
Then stretch them to your sides, reaching out. Drop your arms,
and gently roll your head from side to side. Close your eyes.

Think about the words that you just heard from the reading.
What do they make you think of? Did the reading evoke a feeling? Did the reading remind you of any experience from your
own life? Take whatever message it is that you need from the
reading.

Now bring your attention to your body and where you
are in the room. Notice your breath, breathing in and breathing out. Notice the air around you and how it feels on your
skin. Listen for any noises that may be near you. Notice any
smells in the air. Become *mindful* of your environment and
your place in it. Feel the weight of your clothes on your body.
Feel the weight of your body on the floor or in your chair. Take
three slow, deep breaths. Your consciousness is going on a
journey.

Imagine yourself going down a flight of stairs. Down you go, and when you get to the bottom, there is a door. The door opens, and as you go through it, you realize that you've gone back in time. Picture yourself when you were a child, of any age that feels right for you. I want you to remember a time, an event, a situation that brought you great joy. Take your time as you sift through memories to decide on a time that was truly delightful, a time when you were filled with happiness. Perhaps it was a birthday or a special holiday. Maybe it was a vacation, or a visit to the zoo, or a picnic in the park. Or maybe it was just playing with a favorite toy in your room or skipping outside on a summer afternoon.

Take this memory and try to envision it clearly in your mind's eye. Where exactly were you? What were you wearing? What were you doing? Who else was there? Try to remember exactly what it felt like to be in that moment. Were you smiling . . . laughing? Was it sunny—warm or cold? Were you breathless with excitement? Rest in this moment, basking in its pleasure. How does it make you feel now, remembering and imagining it? The feelings of this moment are always accessible to you. Sit for a few moments in the silence.

Now, when you are ready, your consciousness returns to your body on a wave of light. Start to sense your body in the room. Feel your mind and body getting grounded and integrated. Wiggle your fingers and toes. Take a deep breath. Start to move your arms and legs gently from side to side. Take another deep breath. Allow yourself to feel a vibrant energy coursing through your body, revitalizing you. I'm going to count from one to five, and when you are ready, after the count of five, you may open your eyes. One . . . two . . . three . . . four . . . five. You may open your eyes.

JOURNAL QUESTIONS

What was a magical moment in your childhood? Write about a time when you felt filled with joy.

What was a painful time in your childhood? Write about an experience that was terribly hurtful to you as a child.

Is there a special skill or hobby that you enjoyed as a child? Is that a part of your life now? Why or why not?

How do you treat your inner child now? What kind of relationship do you have with him or her?

EXERCISES

A note on the exercises: All of the exercises in this book are designed to help you claim your inner grown-up. You will benefit most from them if you set aside both a quiet time and a place to do them. This is your opportunity to spend time with yourself in solitude, without the interruption of phones, children, spouse or the other distractions that often occur. Keep the products of the exercises in a place where you are likely to come across them and/or have easy access to them if you want to work on them again.

Picture: Draw a picture of your favorite room as a child.

List: Make a list of values and lessons that you were taught as a child by your parents, either by their words or by their examples. Which of these values do you embrace now? Which of these values do you choose to discard now?

Letter: Write a letter to your inner child asking him what he needs from you, what he has to tell you, and how he wants to be integrated into your life. Then, write a reply letter back from your inner child to your present self, responding to your thoughts and questions.

Reflection: Consider the following list of positive inner child qualities:

Creativity	Vulnerability
Living in the moment	Fun
Joy	Lack of inhibitions
Spontaneity	Artistry

Imagination	Humor
Magic	Enthusiasm
Freedom	Playfulness
Wonder	Exhilaration

How many of these qualities are active in your life now? How can you incorporate more of them into your life? Choose an activity this week that will exhibit one or more of these positive inner child qualities. Do it! Afterward, write about how it felt. How can you plan to do this more regularly?

CHAPTER TWO

When Your Inner Child Becomes a Problem Child

*Life can only be understood backwards; but it must
be lived forwards.*

—Søren Kierkegaard

It was almost Mother's Day when Elizabeth received a call from her daughter. "Hi, Mom," Irene said. "You know, since Robert just had his sinus surgery, I really need to stay with him . . . things are hectic here. I was thinking that I'd like to take you out to brunch *next* week."

Silence. "You mean we can't get together this Sunday on Mother's Day?" asked Elizabeth incredulously.

"Well, it would just be more convenient, Mom," answered Irene.

Elizabeth countered, "I really want to see you, honey, on that day. It's special to me. How about if I just come by for half an hour. We don't even have to eat. I'll just come by briefly."

"I would *prefer* to take you out to brunch *next week*, Mom," said Irene with conviction.

Silence. Then finally, with a wavering voice, Elizabeth said, "That's really upsetting to me." And she slammed down the phone.

Many mothers might have said, "Sure, no problem, whatever works best for you, honey." But for Elizabeth, her daughter's response struck a nerve. What she heard was, "You're not important. You don't matter. You're not lovable. You mean nothing to me." Those were the subtle messages that Elizabeth grew up hearing from her narcissistic and clinically depressed mother. And her inner child remembers those feelings . . . vividly.

The fact that Elizabeth was wounded as a child is not, in itself, extraordinary. We were all wounded to one degree or another, as we discussed in the last chapter. And the fact that her emotional button was pushed is also not unusual. We all get our buttons pushed by certain triggers. Elizabeth was momentarily controlled by an example of what I call the retriggered wounded child. She acted out by slamming down the phone.

What becomes of vital importance, however, is *what happens next?* Will the retriggered wounded child now seize control? Will Elizabeth continue to pout and hold a grudge? Will she pull the silent treatment for days, weeks, or even months? Will this evolve into a family feud? Or will Elizabeth follow the four DARE steps: *detach* and observe the situation from afar, become *aware* of what was really happening with her inner child, *reorient* to and use her inner grown-up, and *enact* a new course of action by reaching out to her daughter with an apology?

The Ongoing Nature of Pain from the Past

No matter how much you've nurtured, embraced, and reparented that inner child, it is bound to cause occasional problems. In other words, while much *healing* can take place, the wounded inner child is never completely *healed*. This is a normal and natural and perfectly acceptable phenomenon. As time goes by, circumstances will retrigger the pain, when the vulnerabilities are momentarily exposed, when the anguished inner child awakens from its slumber because of key events, smells, sounds, dynamics, people, reactions, or memories. The question is, will those fleeting brushes with the past *dominate* you or will you be able to move past them?

As one of my workshop participants confirmed, "I still get the negative voices, my old inner child wounding stuff that says, 'You can't do that; you're rotten; you're going to screw this up.' It's heavy stuff but now I just say, 'You've got to get on with it. You have to do this or that.' So, for me, the negative voices don't necessarily go away, but I've learned not to let them control me."

Our society loves to believe in emotional "closure"—you hear and see it touted in the media all the time. So, many of us assumed that if we did proper inner child work and healed the demons from our past, we would achieve "closure," never to be adversely affected by our histories again. Well, I have some news for you: *Closure does not actually exist.* Closure applies to real estate transactions and business deals but not to the human heart.

This truth can be illustrated effectively by the reality of bereavement. When I began doing research for my book *Transcending Loss*, I realized that many of our traditional grief models emphasized an ending phase of grief, a resolution, a sense of "closure" that could allegedly be acquired with the proper amount of grief work. The implicit goal was that after you grieved sufficiently for the lost loved one (which should only take a few months or maybe a year), then you would "move on" and feel no more pain.

What I found in my own research was quite the opposite. I concluded that, yes, grievers could and did heal, that they could and did move on, but not in the ways that we customarily had been led to believe. I developed a new model of grief to account for this, which includes a lifelong stage of grieving called synthesis. Synthesis is the interweaving of loss into life, the ongoing phase of internalizing and integrating all that this loss means throughout the years. Synthesis means that even after dozens and dozens of years go by, grievers are still impacted by their losses and occasionally continue to feel searing pain. The relationship with the loss continues, just as the relationship with the loved one continues as well. Grief is not something you "get over," like the flu; it's something you learn to live with.

John came to my office just to make sure that he wasn't "crazy." You see, his eleven-year-old son died suddenly from a rare blood disease, and that was *twenty-seven* years ago. But still John cries when he tells the story. Still he has a hole in his heart that cannot be filled. And he still misses his little boy and is pained that his son's life was cut short.

And yet John is a vibrant man who enjoys life. He leads an active lifestyle and is involved in many fulfilling activities. He has made his peace with God. He has satisfying and loving relationships with his wife of forty-two years, his daughter, and his grandchildren. He manages a scholarship fund in his son's name. John is not bitter or stuck or depressed. He is simply a man who had a terrible tragedy happen in his life and is still affected by it. He still has moments of retriggered pain, but this is not a sign of pathology. This is just the nature of life and love and loss.

So, just as a griever has moments of retriggering pain, even after many years, an authentic adult will also have moments when his retriggered wounded child is activated. The trick is to be aware of what's happening and not let the inner child seize control. This is a time for the inner grown-up to observe what's happening and to step in with authority. As Elizabeth later told me, "Part of the woundedness will always be there—you can't rewrite your past; I can never have a mother who wasn't limited by her own emotional illness. But I've learned to live with it and how to move on in spite of it and because of it." Thus you will find that you don't just reparent your wounded inner child once and then are done with the process; you reparent again and again as triggers come up. That is not a sign of a problem.

The problem occurs when the wounded inner child is noncompliant and won't respond to the reparenting, that is, when she refuses to be silenced, when he's holding you back, when she succeeds in becoming your victimized identity, or when the wounded inner child consistently dictates behavior that is either irresponsible, immature, unloving, or evil. Then you've got a problem child on your hands.

In order to do your inner grown-up work like the logging exercise that follows, you will need a small pad of paper or a notebook that you can carry with you. As these incidents occur, write them down as soon as possible to avoid forgetting about them. Later, you can review them and assess your responses and what you might change. If you find the logging process helpful, continue to use it to keep track of any changes you'd like to make or behaviors that are important to you to take note of.

Try This . . .

For one week, keep track of when you experience instances of the retriggered wounded child (RWC). How did you react? How could you have reacted differently? Keep the information recorded in a chart like this:

	RWC	How I Reacted	How I Could Have Reacted Differently
Sunday			
Monday			
Tuesday			
Wednesday			
Thursday			
Friday			
Saturday			

Stuck in the Past

In the 1958 Lerner and Loewe musical *Gigi*, based on the novel by Colette, Gigi lives with her grandmother and is ultimately courted by the handsome bachelor Gaston. In the film version, there is a scene in which the grandmother serves chamomile tea to Gaston. He inquires, "How is your sister? I haven't seen her for quite a while." She responds, "I don't wonder . . . she never sets foot out of her apartment or her past."

What a line. That's exactly the problem for many of us. We may never set foot outside our pasts. In her case it was a lovely past—being romanced by kings and dukes and sultans. It doesn't really matter whether the past was terrific or terrible, today if your primary emotional and mental residence is in the twentieth century, you're probably stuck.

The more common situation, of course, is remaining transfixed and entangled by wounds from the past. Sometimes the wounds create a sort of badge, a sense of self, and there ensues almost a pride in the victimization. This victim mentality creates a new language of intimacy, which Caroline Myss in *Anatomy of the Spirit* calls woundology, defined as "the revelation and exchange of our wounds as the substance of conversation." This is a quicksand pit into which we are all tempted to fall. She describes how we've built a culture of wound support that implicitly encourages our identification with our painful pasts. She says, "Because our culture for so long did not allow time for healing the heart nor even recognize the need for it, we have overcompensated for this earlier failing by now failing to place any time boundaries around that healing."

She tells an amazing story to illustrate her point. Myss was in a restaurant having coffee with two friends while she was waiting for another friend to meet her there. She writes:

When Mary arrived, I introduced her to Ian and Tom, and simultaneously another man approached us to ask Mary if she was free on June 8. . . . Note that the question put to Mary was "Are you free June eighth?"—a question requiring a yes or no reply.

Instead, Mary responded: "June eighth? Did you say June eighth? Absolutely not. Any other day, but not June eighth. June eighth is my incest survivors workshop, and we never let each other down. We are committed to supporting each other, and no matter what, we are there for each other. Absolutely not that day. You'll have to find some other person. I simply will not break my commitment to this group. We all have a history of broken commitments, and we are dedicated to not treating each other with the same disregard."

Mary didn't even know these men and yet she felt instantly compelled to reveal that she was an incest survivor. She wore her emotional history, her childhood wounds, like a red badge of courage. Isn't it possible that she's become a victim of her wounded inner child?

In our society we have people processing every type of emotional trauma from incest to grief to domestic violence, sharing it openly, and then remaining there in a supportive, cushioned attachment to this identity. Sometimes therapy even encourages a wallowing in the pain. Now I don't deny that these experiences were traumatic. And of course it is important and healing to work through them. But for some of us, we forgot about the business of healing and *moving on*—moving on even with the pain.

The paradox is that you learn to move on in spite of the fact that there is no clear closure. Think of it this way: The inner grown-up carries the baggage, but he also puts wings on it so that it is no longer heavy and no longer weighs him down.

Mark Epstein, M.D., offers us another way to think about this paradox. He does a wonderful job of explaining Buddhism and applying it to Western psychotherapy in his book *Thoughts without a Thinker*. He describes the Wheel of Life concept—six realms of existence through which we cycle and recycle on our round of rebirths. Epstein suggests that we may find release, ironically, not in the traditional notion of nirvana, but in actually changing our perception of the nature of each realm. Thus the causes of our suffering are also the means by which we are released from our suffering.

The reason I mention this at all is that my interest was piqued by his concept of the Realm of the Hungry Ghosts, which struck me as a poetic description of the wounded inner child. Epstein writes:

> The Hungry Ghosts are probably the most vividly drawn metaphors in the Wheel of Life. Phantomlike creatures with withered limbs, grossly bloated bellies, and long, thin necks, the Hungry Ghosts in many ways represent a fusion of rage and desire. Tormented by unfulfilled cravings and insatiably demanding of impossible satisfactions, the Hungry Ghosts are searching for gratification for old unfulfilled needs whose time has passed. They are beings who have uncovered a terrible emptiness within themselves, who cannot see the impossibility of correcting something that has already happened. Their ghostlike state represents their attachment to the past.

Sound familiar? The ghosts remain "obsessed with the fantasy of achieving complete release from the pain of their past and are stubbornly unaware that their desire is fantasy. . . . The Hungry Ghosts must come in contact with the ghostlike nature of their own longings." In other words, the wounded child who might be ruling your life must confront its own ghostlike nature in order to be freed from its own tyranny.

Darkness and Shadows

A problem child, however, is even more than a wounded self in control. Stop and consider the darker sides of childhood, the truly unpleasant aspects. Children can be cruel, mean, insecure, impulsive, fearful, and emotionally volatile (and that's without any trauma or dysfunction). They are naturally immature, jealous, self-indulgent, dependent, and prone to tantrums. For children this behavior is developmentally appropriate. For adults it is not.

And yet we are human beings with a human nature. An area of interest to many mental health professionals is called shadow psychology. Essentially it looks at the darker sides of our nature, aspects of the problem inner child that invariably rise to the surface. The basic premise of shadow psychology is that we may disavow these unpleasant aspects of ourselves. However, denying that these aspects exist is dangerous to our mental health. We need to learn how to integrate and work with these tendencies rather than trying to repress or deny them. If we don't, they will express themselves eventually in ways that can cause harm to ourselves and often to others.

I use the words "dark side" to refer to those unattractive childish traits within us that were developmentally appropriate yet unpleasant aspects of ourselves even when we were young, and are even more unpleasant when we are grown up (in particular, narcissism, blame, jealousy, rage, envy, fear, and dependency). These feelings are responsible for a great deal of adult pain and misunderstanding. And I use the words "shadow side" to refer to those traits that are seemingly positive inner child qualities (such as fun, freedom, carefreeness, and play) that when taken to the extreme can lead to problems. In the sections that follow, I'll illustrate these two important concepts.

The Dark Side

"I Have a Secret to Tell You"—that was the topic of a mid-morning talk show. I was taking a break from my writing, waiting for water to boil for tea, when I stumbled upon this juicy subject. I knew it was bound to be embarrassing for guests and audience alike—as so many of these talk shows are—but rather than turn the TV off, I kept it on, drawn into the voyeuristic web just like the rest of America.

The television screen was split for simultaneous viewing: on the right-hand side of the screen was a young attractive blond woman (dressed in symbolic black no less) who would soon be revealing her secret, and on the left-hand side of the screen was her unsuspecting twin sister (dressed in white—did they rig this?) as seen from the backstage waiting room. The talk show host noted, "And your twin sister who is backstage has no idea why she is here today, right? She has no idea what you've come to say to her?"

"Right," the already tearful twin admitted.

"What secret did you come here to tell her today?" goaded the host.

"I have to tell her that I've been sleeping with her husband," she responded. The audience gasped, groaned; some people booed.

"What?" I asked out loud, incredulously. "Is this for real? Wasn't this the plot in a recent Hollywood movie? I shouldn't be watching this; it's shameful. It's disgusting." But I kept watching. Truth is sometimes stranger and more compelling than fiction.

Out came the innocent twin. She smiled shyly, unsure of why she was there. I winced when the twin prefaced her remarks to her sister by saying, "You know that I would never do anything to hurt you." ("Except betray you by sleeping with your husband and then announce this to you in front of millions of people," I thought to myself.) The cameras zoomed into the unsuspecting twin's face when the bomb was dropped, recording every tear of trauma. The adulterer continued, "It was just sex; it didn't mean anything; you know he loves you."

That's enough. The kettle on my stove whistled. The twin walked offstage, sobbing. She wasn't going to play this exhibitionist game. I turned off the television in disgust. What has our society come to?

Watching this talk show reminded me of just a few of the major ways that the dark side of one's inner child can run amok. The adulterer twin demonstrated an inner child that was selfish, immature, and downright cruel. She betrayed not only her sister, but her own self. The fact that Americans, including myself, hung on to watch this immature display reflects our overall childish cultural obsession with voyeuristic, egocentric, naughty behaviors. We all have dark sides.

It is important to understand these dark qualities since they are a natural part of the self. And yet the inner grown-up learns how to temper these tendencies. She recognizes them for what they are, understands their childish origins, and learns to master their unruly powers by finding more appropriate and safe outlets for them.

You, Wonderful You

When you are a child, the whole world revolves around you. You think only of your own needs, how to get them met and fulfilled all the time—and fast. You are the center of the universe. When I was a child, my sister used to taunt me, calling me in a disparaging, accusatory voice, "You think you're Queen of the World." Yep, I was Queen of the World—like many children—mostly egocentric.

Typically we think of narcissism as vanity or excessive self-love. But actually, from a clinical perspective, the disorder of narcissism is more about self-absorption, self-centeredness, and a lack of empathy for others. There is an ancient legend that warns of the dangers of narcissism. Once upon a time, a dog wandered into a house of mirrors. Wherever he looked, he saw himself—a dog. So many images of dogs irritated him and frightened him. He bared his teeth. He barked. Suddenly all the other dogs bared their teeth and barked. He did not notice that the barking, resounding from all sides, was his own. He saw only bristling hair, vicious teeth. He heard menacing growls. So he started to run—and around him, the other dogs ran, too. He ran faster and faster in circles trying to keep the dogs off his heels. But he couldn't escape from them. Finally, whipping himself into a frenzy, he collapsed dead, persecuted by no one other than himself.

It can be dangerous to become so insular, lured into the house of mirrors of oneself. Focusing on oneself is paradoxically likely to leave you feeling empty as well. And when you're feeling empty, you strive to fill the void. It's a vicious circle.

This is a loop that we, in our pursuit of happiness, know only too well. You might say that our culture, to some degree, encourages the dark side of our inner children. We look out for number one, thinking more of our own concerns than that of our neighbors. Forget about the golden rule.

We focus on our power, our success, our acquisitions. Like little children leaning out of the shopping cart and pointing to each new sugary product, we proclaim, "I want this" and "I want that." And accordingly we spend way beyond our means, maxing out our credit cards.

And like little children banging our forks on the table, we want what we want when we want it . . . and that's *now*. And accordingly we have fast food, prepackaged salads, one-hour photo development, instant message e-mail. We don't want to wait!

The narcissism in our nation prods us to think only of ourselves, striving to fulfill our every need immediately. Unfortunately, this impulsive, egocentric dark side of the inner child leaves us feeling profoundly empty.

The inner grown-up response to narcissism is selflessness.

Entitlement

Because the dark side of our inner children urges us to be self-centered and materialistic, we begin to feel in our narcissism that we are *owed* things; we feel entitled. Rather than seeing life and its blessings as a gift, we conclude that good things are owed to us. And if we don't receive them, then someone else is to blame.

This leads to a victim mentality that contributes to the litigious nature of our society. If something goes wrong, someone else is at fault, and we're going to find them and hold them accountable (as if suing could make it all better). To frustrated children, vengeance seems to be the only way. Rather than seeing others as fellow sojourners in life—as our friends—viewed through a prism of entitlement and blame, we see others as our enemies.

A recent mini-trend in book publishing has lovelorn women lashing out at their lovers in caustic tell-all memoirs. Imagine a book entitled *How to Heal the Hurt by Hating* by Anita Liberty. Okay, the title is meant to be amusing and humorous. But I have always felt that every little joke has a kernel of truth. Even in jest, this is a terribly unhealthy attitude, in my opinion. These books spew venom, vengeance, and utter superiority since, of course, they, the writers, played no part in the breakdown of the relationship.

Remember energy attracts like energy—that's a karmic law. Therefore, blaming others, holding on to grudges, has the effect of drawing that kind of negative energy right into your life. Likewise, spreading positive, loving energy draws the same into your life.

The inner grown-up response to entitlement and blame is forgiveness and love.

Envy

Envy is an insidious emotion based on the ill will felt at another's prosperity, or the underlying hostility felt while admiring someone else's traits, possessions, accomplishments. It means comparing that person to ourself and wishing to have/own/be whatever the other person has/owns/is.

Envy is an inner darkness that underlies the lose-lose mentality that runs rampant in our society. Women's magazines are famous for encouraging this ridiculous "catfight" mentality among women. Magazine covers proclaim, "She's gorgeous. She's smart. We hate her!" This attitude is based on a scarcity myth that there is only so much to go around in life, and so one person's success takes away from mine, thus equaling my failure. Of course, this scarcity of abundance is only a myth.

Maybe it's a genetic predisposition to see another person's blessings as our own curse, some hardwired survival of the fittest strategy, but the inner grown-up response is a win-win philosophy. Think, "You have good fortune and I bless you. I am enriched, as are you." Stephen Covey gives a marvelous explanation of win-win solutions in his *The Seven Habits of Highly Effective People*. As Covey states, "Win/Win is based on the paradigm that there is plenty for everybody, that one person's success is not achieved at the expense or exclusion of the success of others."

The dark side of the inner child has a hard time believing this can be true. The inner child is naturally insecure and often threatened because he or she is so frightened of potential loss.

*The inner grown-up response to
envy is maturity and love.*

Try This . . .
Our problem children love to compare themselves to each other in an insecure and often mean-spirited way. Think of the evil queen in *Snow White* who asks, "Mirror, mirror on the wall, Who's the fairest of them all?" When she hears that Snow White is the fairest, she begins to plot her murder. But envy, wishing others ill, and outright hatred are actually toxic emotions that poison our own systems. A friend of mine had a tarot card reading after breaking up with a boyfriend. The so-called psychic gushed, "I can advise you on some powerful revenge strategies." My friend, knowing that energy attracts like energy, declined her advice. In other words, putting out negative and hateful energy only draws that back into your life. Spreading loving and positive energy comes back to bless you tenfold. So let the jealousy and the envy go.

Fill in the following chart: Just as you did with the Retriggered Wounded Child Log, keep track of your responses for a week. Note the times when a flash of envy occurs. Also, at the end of the week, list those peoples you are envious of. Examine your list to look for trends.

Who You Are Envious Of	Why You Are Envious	What You Could Do to Have That in Your Life and/or What Other Things You Have That Are Valuable That You Can Focus On

How can you be supportive and enthusiastic for that person's success/good fortune?

Jealousy

That old green-eyed monster. Jealousy is the more volatile cousin of envy. It is based on relationships and perceived loss or threat of loss. Children are naturally emotionally jealous of each other and prone to subsequent temper tantrums.

What child hasn't at some point felt threatened by his brothers or sisters and what they have, what they get to do, and how much more they're loved by mommy? It's just the way kids are. If I spend time alone with my daughter, my son naturally wants time alone with me as well. He might throw himself on the floor screaming until I promise him an equal outing.

Unfortunately, adult jealousy may not be benign. It may even turn deadly. A client of mine was the best friend and roommate of a victim of inner child distortion. My client Brenda and her friend Trish, both attractive women in their early thirties, had been best friends since high school. Both were outgoing, smart, and popular. Then Trish began dating a man that no one else seemed to like much. She moved in with him and proclaimed to all how happy they were. Because Brenda didn't like Trish's new boyfriend, the friendship naturally drifted.

Eric, it turns out, was not only immature but irresponsible. He had financial troubles. He couldn't keep a job (more inner child problems). Because of his jealousy and possessiveness, he prevented Trish from socializing with her old friends. It turns out that he abused her and manipulated her into believing she was dependent upon him.

Over time Trish realized the net of deceit and danger in which she was caught and broke up with Eric and moved out. She renewed her friendship with Brenda and moved in with her. But Eric would not be dropped lightly. He harassed her. He stalked her. Trish, in turn, took out a restraining order against him.

Then one night Brenda and Trish came home from going out to dinner. They were planning on watching television and turning in early. Trish went upstairs to change clothes. She screamed. A shot rang out. Brenda ran for help. When she returned with the police, Eric had taken not only his own life, but Trish's as well.

Many extreme examples like homicides and domestic abuse can, in the end, be traced to childish emotions turned dangerous. Impatience. Jealousy. These are the dark sides, the deepest chasms of one's inner child.

The inner grown-up response to jealousy is love.

Rage

You see it on the highway; you see it waiting in long lines; you see it in Hollywood movies; you see it on airplanes; you see it in violence on school playgrounds: free-floating rage. People are angry, frustrated; they have tantrums; they become violent. And if they have guns, their rage can be lethal. When children have temper tantrums, they are out of control. Adult rage may also be as reactive, spontaneous, and uncontrolled as a child's anger. Or adult rage may be more channeled, more calculated. It can serve as an internal fire, smoldering within, providing fuel for a life filled with hatred.

On August 19, 1997, the idyllic North Country of New Hampshire was stunned by an act of unspeakable violence. A disgruntled loner vented his rage by shooting and killing four prominent community members in Colebrook. It turns out that he had grievances, harbored grudges. He collected firearms, nursing his private rage, stoking the fires of his dark side. And then he put his plan into action, systematically killing anyone in his path of revenge. He murdered two state troopers, a local judge, and the editor of the local newspaper. Colebrook was shocked by the horror.

America was also shocked, just as they were shocked by the bombing in Oklahoma City, the shootings at Columbine High School, and other national disasters born of rage. Unbridled rage may be understandable in children, but rage both controlled and uncontrolled in adulthood is nothing but a destructive force.

*The inner grown-up response to rage (and its underlying
existential angst) is spirituality and love.*

Fear

Sometimes rage is a defensive reaction against fear. It is common for children to be afraid—afraid of the dark, afraid of swimming, afraid of bugs, afraid of monsters. But what happens to adults who carry inner fears? Perhaps we no longer are afraid of monsters per se, but instead we are afraid of public speaking, flying in airplanes, driving on highways, sitting in dentist chairs, having commitments, losing the people we love, dying. Instead of managing our fears, we can sometimes become phobic, obsessive, even paralyzed by our fears.

I once had a client terrified of riding in elevators. When in an elevator, she felt claustrophobic, had trouble breathing, and broke into a full-blown panic attack. She avoided elevators because of this fear, at times climbing dozens of flights of stairs.

We worked on calming techniques and mental imagery to help her combat this phobia. We discussed the physiological nature of fear and panic, and discussed techniques for managing excess adrenaline in order to relax. She eventually found it tolerable to go into an elevator if a friend was with her holding her hand. But even so, she mostly confined herself to stairs.

Anytime we let fear win, when we avoid the activities that we so dread, then the monster has won and the grown-up has lost.

*The inner grown-up response to fear
is maturity and courage.*

Dependency

Fear is a part of the childish disposition because so much of the world is large, unknown, and unmanageable. The adult self, by contrast, comes to know about his environment, comes to understand his own powers, abilities, and limitations. The inner grown-up discovers both his independence and interdependence.

The child self, however, is utterly dependent on his or her guardians. Unlike some infants in the animal kingdom who can walk or fly within a few days or weeks of birth and are generally self-sufficient within a few months, the human infant is totally at the mercy of its caregivers for its survival. Through the years, the goal of growing up is to become increasingly more independent. Eventually, after one's acquired independence (usually sometime in adolescence), the goal then becomes to be interdependent in a healthy marriage, or other partnership, for example. But the journey to get there is complex and awesome, indeed.

Children are in many ways dependent, with relatively few choices in their lives. It can be a time of incredible frustration at one's limitations. I remember moments of pure agony when I couldn't control my food choices—my mother forcing me to eat yellow squash. She would set a timer, and if I didn't finish the squash by the time the bell rang, I would be sent to my room for the remainder of the evening. To this day I cannot eat yellow squash! I remember the sheer sense of powerlessness being at the mercy of those tall grown-ups all around me. I remember the blow of not being able to control my world around me, like when my parents divorced when I was twelve—terrible, life-changing things happening without my consent.

It is no doubt a struggle to acquire a solid sense of self, and the journey toward autonomy is fraught with detours and boulders in the road. But some grown-ups never seem to take the trip. They remain dependent on their loved ones; they assign absolute authority to those around them; they even give others the key to their emotions.

The *Diagnostic and Statistics Manual* of the American Psy-

chiatric Association (known as the DSM-IV) gives criteria for di-
agnosing mental disorders. It defines a dependent personality
disorder (DPD) as "a pervasive and excessive need to be taken
care of that leads to submissive and clinging behavior and fears
of separation, beginning by early adulthood and present in a
variety of contexts." Then it lists eight conditions, five or more
of which must be present to classify someone as having DPD,
including things like "needs others to assume responsibility for
most major areas of his or her life" and "has difficulty making
everyday decisions without an excessive amount of advice and
reassurance from others." Sounds like a child, doesn't it? For a
child, being dependent but moving toward separation is developmentally natural. For a grown-up, giving away your power is
a problem.

*The inner grown-up response to dependency is
responsibility.*

Unseen Powers

The dark sides of our inner children may wield undue influence even without our conscious awareness. Jennifer, a woman
in her late forties, was advised by a counselor through her employee assistance program that she should consider antidepres-
sant medication. Jennifer had been through a Claim Your Inner
Grown-up support group and came to me for a second opinion.

For the past few months, she had been experiencing extreme stress at work, feeling overwhelmed and depressed, to
the point that she was thinking about leaving her job (a position that she had held for six years). Her depression did not
seem to extend beyond the boundaries of work, however. She
was generally happy with the state of her life and her marriage.
Already I was drawing the conclusion that medication wasn't
the solution in this situation.

I asked, "Has anything changed at work in the past few
months to make your job more stressful?"

Jennifer answered, "Well, yes, we're changing computer systems and it involves lots of training. Also, we're changing a filing system and a billing system because of the computer change, which involves me single-handedly reviewing the files and learning a new procedure."

As Jennifer kept emphasizing the new systems and the training and the learning, it dawned on me that she sounded like a frightened student. I asked her to tell me about her experiences in school when she was a child. That opened a floodgate of memories about her scary experiences in Catholic school.

"I used to have terrible stomachaches before I went to school. The nuns just scared me to death. They told me I was stupid and used to slap my hands with rulers. I was a totally mediocre student, mostly because my fear was so overwhelming and I just got blocked in my ability to learn. I spent most of those years in total fear. I was just terrified of going to work—I mean school."

"Wait a minute," I interrupted. "Did you hear what you just said? You said you were terrified of going to *work*."

"I meant school," she repeated.

"Isn't it possible," I persisted, "that your slip of the tongue means something? Maybe all this new training at work is retriggering your fears of being a student. It's bringing back all that childhood fear of inadequacy and causing you to be overly stressed at work, which in turn is causing your depression. Your fearful inner child is getting in your way."

Ding. Ding. Her jaw nearly dropped to the floor. She really had no idea that unconsciously she was, in fact, terrified of work just as she had been terrified of school as a child. In this instance I have to side with Dr. Freud: her slip of the tongue was a meaningful insight into her unconscious. Once this realization was brought to her conscious awareness, she knew she needed to claim her inner grown-up.

Jennifer had already completed the Four-Pillar Program, so we talked about how she could apply some of those techniques to this situation. And once she realized that the problem inner child had been in control, she could choose to take away its power. Letting go of those past limitations, she was free to move into a new relationship with her present.

Universality

No matter how much we grow and develop, we will *always* have certain dark sides of our inner children to contend with . . . seen and unseen, known and unknown. Dark sides are, in fact, part of human nature. In my inner grown-up support groups, I ask people to write on an index card three problem inner child qualities that hold them back in life, that interfere with their functioning. Then we pass around the index cards to each other in a circle of silence. This exercise, called the silent witness, highlights that we all wrestle with the same demons. Fear, insecurity, and anger seem to top most people's lists. Claiming your inner grown-up is not about eradicating these dark aspects; it is simply about not letting them *rule*.

It's also about changing our relationship to them, so that they are not feared parts of ourselves but merely pieces of our personality. So after we pass around the index cards, we participate in a ritual of transformation. On the back of each index card is a part of a picture. Turning over and joining the index cards, we are able to piece together a picture of a flower in bloom. Visually, the cards of dark-side qualities, when turned over, create a beautiful image. In this ritual we light a candle as well and symbolically recall our spirits from the past, honoring the possibility of transformation, and releasing the negative energy from our wounds.

Try This . . .

On an index card, write down three problem inner child qualities that hold you back in life. In what ways do they affect your behaviors? Keep these cards in a place where you can see them this week, like on your refrigerator door. How do you feel about their power over your life?

Shadows

We have been looking at the dark side of one's inner child—the characteristics that were unpleasant then and are equally if not more so unpleasant now. We looked at narcissism, entitlement, envy, jealousy, rage, fear, and dependency. But there's another class of problems that appears at first positive, only later to show its true nature as a negative characteristic. I call these qualities shadows. In moderation, these positive inner child attributes are wonderful. But taken to an extreme, these characteristics show their shadowy sides, a gray manifestation that can lead to trouble. For example, it's the inner child characteristics of being pampered and enthusiastic that have as their flip side excess and self-indulgence. It's the inner child characteristic of free-spiritedness that can flip to irresponsibility and recklessness.

In fact, the same is true in basic marriage counseling theory. That which most attracted you initially is often what later drives you crazy. His "wildness" is now "immaturity." Her "passion" is now "emotional volatility." What once seemed attractive has retreated into the shadows and no longer seems appealing.

Freedom

Although children are becoming more responsible all the time, the essence of true childhood is still to be relatively free from adult cares and concerns. Kids lose things. Kids forget things. They don't keep the appointment books and pay the critical bills or take care of household management. They don't grocery shop or worry about mortgages or rent. They're not supposed to, remember? They're kids.

Ironically, children tend to imagine that grown-ups are free. After all, grown-ups can stay out late, go to bed when they want, eat what they want, choose how to structure their time, and so on. Grown-ups do have a lot of freedoms, of course, but these must be tempered with responsibility and maturity.

Take the grown-up who wants to remain eternally "free," who thinks he "can't get caught," who has difficulty with the responsible duties in life—suddenly this doesn't seem so cute or developmentally appropriate. Freedom always comes with the price of responsibility, just as "carefreedom" comes with limitations.

Dr. Viktor Frankl, a Viennese psychiatrist and author of *Man's Search for Meaning*, was fond of saying that the Statue of Liberty on the East Coast should be supplemented by a Statue of Responsibility on the West Coast. I couldn't agree more.

The inner grown-up response to the urge
for freedom is responsibility.

Fun

Many grown-ups remember childhood as being a time of lots of fun—afternoons on the swing set, lazy summer days, hours of unstructured play. Grown-ups don't want to lose that sense of fun. Nor should they as long as it is balanced with inner grown-up sensibilities. It is a problem when one's inner child sense of fun is excessive, when it develops into a shadow.

I have a girlfriend in her late thirties who has never married, largely because she keeps choosing men whose inner child shadows prevail. Whenever she meets a responsible, orderly, settled grown-up man, she runs for the hills thinking he is stodgy and boring. Instead, she selects men who are wild and crazy. These men are in touch with their inner children all right. They are free and fun. They are thrill seekers. But do they settle down? Do they earn a steady living? Do they have security or stability? Do they commit? No, their shadows prevail, leaving them, at least emotionally, forever young. Fun to such an extreme is no longer fun.

The inner grown-up balance to fun is maturity.

Forever Young

The idealized version of childhood is that it was all sand cas-tles, ice cream, and hopscotch. The reality is that it also in-cluded the many dark sides and shadow sides of vulnerability that we have discussed. You would think we would be de-lighted to grow up, delighted to leave those miserable phases behind! However, such is often not the case. We cling to the il-lusion that youth is to be treasured. M. Scott Peck writes elo-quently in his book *Further Along the Road Less Traveled: The Unending Journey Toward Spiritual Growth*:

Those who stop learning and growing early in their lives and stop changing and become fixed often lapse into what is sometimes called their "second childhood." They become whiny and demanding and self-centered. But this isn't because they have entered their second childhood. They have never left their first, and the veneer of adulthood is worn thin, revealing the emotional child that lurks underneath.

We psychotherapists know that most people who look like adults are actually emotional children walking around in adult's clothing. And we know this *not* because the people that come to us are more immature than most. On the contrary, those who come to psychotherapy with genuine intent to grow are those relative few who are called out of immaturity, who are no longer willing to tolerate their own childishness, although they may not yet see the way out. The rest of the population never manages to fully grow up, and perhaps it is for this reason that they hate so to talk about growing old.

Why are we so afraid to grow up, to take responsibility, to settle down, as it were?

Fountains of Youth

Our youth-crazed culture fixates on staying young, on staving off the dreaded aging process as long as possible. The cosmetics and plastic surgery industries depend on our fear of aging. A Russian fairy tale tells of an old man who is convinced that he will have eternal youth if he jumps into a vat of boiling water. He willingly jumps into the vat—anything, he reasons, if it will bring eternal youth. In reality he was being tricked. Many of us would likewise jump into a vat of boiling water if it promised eternal youth. Maybe we unconsciously associate growing up with growing old.

In a remarkable book by Mitch Albom called *Tuesdays with Morrie*, the author records life's lessons as taught by his elderly dying professor. Morrie had particularly strong feelings about society's fear of aging:

> "All this emphasis on youth—I don't buy it," he said. "Listen, I know what a misery being young can be, so don't tell me it's so great. All these kids who came to me with their struggles, their strife, their feelings of inadequacy, their sense that life was miserable, so bad they wanted to kill themselves. . . .
>
> "And, in addition to all the miseries, the young are not wise. They have very little understanding about life. Who wants to live every day when you don't know what's going on? When people are manipulating you, telling you to buy this perfume and you'll be beautiful, or this pair of jeans and you'll be sexy—and you believe them! It's such nonsense."
>
> Weren't you *ever* afraid to grow old, I asked?
>
> "Mitch, I *embrace* aging."
>
> Embrace it?
>
> "It's very simple. As you grow, you learn more. If you stayed at twenty-two, you'd always be as ignorant as you were at twenty-two. Aging is not just decay, you know. It's growth. It's more than the negative that you're going to die, it's also the positive that you *understand* you're going to die, and that you live a better life because of it."
>
> Yes, I said, but if aging were so valuable, why do people always say, "Oh, if I were young again." You never hear people say, "I wish I were sixty-five."
>
> He smiled. "You know what that reflects? Unsatisfied lives. Unfulfilled lives. Lives that haven't found meaning. Because if you've found meaning in your life, you don't want to go back.

You want to go forward. You want to see more, do more. You can't wait until sixty-five."

And the truth is, why fight the process? We're all going to age no matter what we do. We will all grow up, at least physically, whether we like it or not. Why not view all growth—emotional and spiritual—as opportunities for making more meaning?

The inner grown-up response to aging is maturity.

Making Choices

I had a friend who told me he had peaked at the age of twenty-five. That was when he was at the crest of his powers, or so he thought. His life was a line that went up, peaked early, and then descended in a steady decline—sort of like the proverbial high school football star who spends the rest of his adult life reliving that past peak glory. I prefer to think of life as a line that starts low and continually moves in an ascending climb, continually going up and up. The future always holds opportunities for more growth, more development, more maturation.

I also like to think of life like a fine red wine. In the grape nectar's infancy, it is astringent. It is only through aging slowly and patiently that it acquires its richness, its unique complexity. Wine doesn't have much choice in its maturation process—humans do.

Some of us may choose to let our inner children rule forever, because in many ways the inner child is all of what Freud called the id—instincts, base drives, pleasure-oriented behaviors. Choosing the inner grown-up is more a combination of what Freud called ego and superego—that which is based on logic and morality. It is this self that transcends our core instincts; it is this self that makes civilization possible. And it is this self that ultimately seeks and finds meaning in life.

While we may have physical limitations that accrue over time, emotionally and spiritually there are no limits. We can choose to reach to the sky, limitless. And from above, the view is quite beautiful. We will continue, as grown-ups, to wrestle with our human dark and shadowy sides. But each day we can make a choice to transcend these characteristics, choose to allow the inner grown-up to tame the problem inner child.

Incidentally, the Mother's Day story from the beginning of the chapter did resolve itself. Elizabeth worked the Four-Pillar Program and was eventually able to draw upon her inner grown-up resources. In particular, she took the four DARE steps to *detach* herself; to become *aware* of how she was responding from a wounded child position; to *reorient* to her inner grown-up, reminding herself that she was lovable; and to *enact* differently: first she sent her daughter a note to tell her that she loved her; later she called her daughter to apologize, and they made plans for a belated Mother's Day brunch.

She didn't automatically respond from this inner grown-up perspective, but again, this takes time to truly internalize. She was able to analyze the situation from an inner grown-up viewpoint a few days later, after the heat of the moment. And that's when she chose to confirm that her daughter did care about her, and that she was validated both as a mother and as a person.

Growth is always a process, one that requires work, patience, and persistence. Remember, it's never too late to claim your inner grown-up.

The Problem Child in Review

The wounds from the past will always continue to affect you on some level. There is no true "closure." But you need not remain haunted, ruled, or even controlled by the past. The present and the future are up to you now. They are your responsibility.

Dark aspects, childish aspects, of our nature—narcissism, impatience, entitlement, envy, jealousy, rage, fear, and dependency—

will inevitably show themselves. But the inner grown-up can soften these traits, helping to balance and ultimately quiet them.

The problem inner child also may make an appearance in the shadows, disguised as forms of fun, freedom, youthfulness, and impulsivity. These initially pleasing experiences may become insidiously excessive to the point where problems arise. The inner grown-up knows how to keep these traits in check, retaining only the positive essence of each.

The inner grown-up rejoices in the aging process knowing that the adventure of life gets richer as it evolves. It is possible as the years fly by to not only be getting older, but to be getting better.

READING
From *The Book of Qualities*
by J. Ruth Gendler

"Fear"

Fear has a large shadow, but he himself is quite small. He has a vivid imagination. He composes horror music in the middle of the night. He is not very social, and he keeps to himself at political meetings. His past is a mystery. He warned us not to talk to each other about him, adding that there is nowhere any of us could go where he wouldn't hear us. We were quiet. When we began to talk to each other, he changed. His manners started to seem pompous, and his snarling voice sounded rehearsed.

Two dragons guard Fear's mansion. One is ceramic and Chinese. The other is real. If you make it past the dragons and speak to him close up, it is amazing to see how fragile he is. He will try to tell you stories. Be aware. He is a master of disguises and illusions. Fear almost convinced me that he was a puppet-maker and I was a marionette.

Speak out boldly, look him in the eye, startle him. Don't give up. Win his respect, and he will never bother you with small matters.

VISUALIZATION

Begin by getting your body prepared to relax. Stretch your arms high over your head. Then stretch them to your sides, reaching out. Drop your arms, and gently roll your head from side to side. Settle your body into a comfortable position and close your eyes.

Think about the words that you just heard from the reading. What do they make you think of? Did the reading evoke a feeling? Did the reading remind you of any experience from your own life? Take whatever message it is that you need from the reading.

Now bring your attention to your body and where you are in the room. Notice your breath, breathing in and breathing out. Notice the air around you and how it feels on your skin. Listen for any noises that may be near you. Notice any smells in the air. Become *mindful* of your environment and your place in it. Feel the weight of your clothes on your body. Feel the weight of your body on the floor or in your chair. Take three slow, deep breaths. Your consciousness is going on a journey.

Imagine yourself going down a flight of stairs. Down you go, and when you get to the bottom, there is a door. The door opens, and as you go through it, you realize that you've gone back in time. Picture yourself when you were a child, of any age that feels right for you. I want you to remember a time, an event, a situation that was difficult for you, that brought you great pain. Take your time as you sift through memories to decide on a time that was truly wounding for you as a child. Know that you are safe and that no one can harm you right now. Were you being hurt by someone? Were you neglected by someone you loved? Did you just find out that your parents were getting divorced? Was someone being cruel to you?

Take this memory and try to envision it clearly in your mind's eye. Where exactly were you? What were you wearing? What were you doing? Who else was there? Take your time and try to remember exactly what it felt like to be in that moment. Were you crying? Sit with this moment, and know that you are safe. How does it make you feel now, remembering and imagining it? The feelings of this moment do not have to control you or contaminate your life.

Now imagine your current adult self entering the scene where your wounded inner child is. Your adult self sees how distraught your inner child is. Imagine your adult self walking over to your child self and reaching out to touch her. If it feels comfortable, let your adult self embrace your wounded inner child. Let her stroke her hair, wipe her tears, and envelop her in a big bear hug. Let your wounded inner child accept the comfort. Let her feel loved and cared for. Let your wounded inner child know that your adult self is there for her, now and always. Sit for a few moments in the silence.

Now, when you are ready, your consciousness returns to your body on a wave of light. Start to sense your body in the room. Feel your body getting grounded and integrated. Wiggle your fingers and toes. Take a deep breath. Start to move your arms and legs gently from side to side. Take another deep breath. Allow yourself to feel a vibrant energy coursing through your body, revitalizing you. I'm going to count from one to five, and when you are ready, after the count of five, you may open your eyes. One . . . two . . . three . . . four . . . five. You may open your eyes.

JOURNAL QUESTIONS

How do you self-parent your inner child?

Consider the following list of problem inner child qualities:

Fear	Immediate gratification
Anger/temper tantrums	Irresponsibility
Jealousy	Foolishness
Paranoia	Self-indulgence
Panic	Selfishness
Self-centeredness	Recklessness
Woundedness	Impatience
Childishness	Insecurity
Irrationality	Dependence

How many of these qualities are active in your life; in other words, how is your problem child interfering with your grown-up life?

If your problem child qualities weren't affecting you negatively, how would your life be different?

If you gave up feelings of identification with your past, what would you be losing? What would you be gaining?

How do you feel about aging? Do you ever lie about your age? What do you think is the "perfect" age?

EXERCISES

Pictures: Draw a picture of yourself with your problem child inside of you. (You don't need to be a great artist to do this. The point is not to create a gallery-quality image. The point is to visually see your problem child's influence in your life.) How large is your problem child in relation to yourself? Draw several scenes in which your problem child is presiding. How do you represent its power over you? Draw another scene in which the problem inner child is quieted. How do these scenes differ? How do you feel when you compare them?

Abstinence from an Indulgence: The Catholic religion has an age-old tradition during the season of Lent (the forty days and nights from Ash Wednesday to Easter) in which religious observants give up something important to them. This small sacrifice is seen as a way to identify with Jesus' suffering as well as a means for purifying the soul.

As an exercise for strengthening your inner grown-up, practice abstaining from an indulgence for a week. Give up something small but significant to you (like chocolate or shopping or caffeine). Notice what it feels like to intentionally deny yourself a pleasure. Stick with it even when you don't feel like it. Recognize each instance of sacrifice as being for the good of your inner grown-up. I don't mean to imply that martyrdom or chronic self-denial should be our goal, simply that the problem child occasionally needs to be reminded that we cannot always have that which we think we need or want. This exercise fortifies the spirit and reminds us that we can survive without every desire being gratified.

In addition you may want to have your inner child write a letter to your inner grown-up asking for help with this. In this letter ask for specific kinds of help and what the inner grown-up can do to encourage you and provide you with alternative activities. For example, if you feel a craving for something sweet you can ask for help to choose something more healthful, or for a distracting alternative like exercise or a movie.

Warning: Your problem inner child won't like this exercise one bit.

Research and Imagine: Research the time of the Pilgrims and the early colonists, or perhaps the pioneers who moved out west in covered wagons. Look for books, both fiction and non-fiction, and/or movies that are steeped in your chosen time period. Not only does learning about history give us a new perspective, but it also can inspire and teach us.

Imagine what it must have been like to start a new life in a new land. Imagine the scenario if your problem inner child were to take over ("But I'm too tired, too scared, too uncomfortable to go on . . .") Bear in mind that the Pilgrims and pioneers were undoubtedly tired and scared and uncomfortable as well. Yet they *persevered* and ultimately founded a great nation. Imagine where we would be if they had yielded to their problem inner children.

Now imagine yourself as a successful pilgrim or pioneer. Imagine triumphing over the obstacles. Feel the strength and determination of our forefathers and foremothers coursing through your own veins. Their courage and fortitude is our cultural heritage and legacy. Let's live up to their promise.

PART

II

Your Inner Grown-up

CHAPTER THREE

The Road to Authentic Adulthood

*What lies behind us and what lies before us are tiny
matters compared to what lies within us.*

—Ralph Waldo Emerson

Josh was only twelve years old and he loved life. He loved
his family; he had lots of friends, and he even had his own
bike and walkie-talkie. But when he went to the carnival in his
town, he was embarrassed and dejected when he wasn't allowed onto a roller-coaster ride because he wasn't big enough.
Big enough. Everything is better and easier when you're big.

So when he came upon a strange carnival arcade game
called Zoltar Speaks and the strange doll sorcerer inside the
booth flashed a sign that read "Zoltar Says Make a Wish," he inserted a coin and made the most natural and sincere wish that
he could think of. He said, "I wish I were big." A card popped
out with the words, "Your wish is granted." Josh didn't notice
that the machine wasn't even plugged in.

So sets the stage for the hilarious 1988 movie called *Big*,
starring the youthful Tom Hanks. The next morning twelve-
year-old Josh awakens in the body of thirty-something Tom
Hanks. The result is a comic adventure as Josh is grown up on
the outside but only twelve years old on the inside. He goes to
New York and is hired by a toy company. His employers are
amazed by Josh's unique insight into toys. He is awed by his
surroundings, spits caviar out at a formal party because it tastes

so "gross," and decorates his apartment with toys, a bunk bed, and a trampoline. He is a little person inside a big body.

After the novelty wears off, Josh realizes that he wants to go home, to have his old thirteen-year-old life back (he'd had a birthday since all this happened). When he finally confesses his true situation to his "girlfriend"—that he is really thirteen—she responds, "Oh, and who isn't? You think that there isn't a frightened kid inside of me, too?" Exactly.

As we've discussed, we all have wounded little children inside of us. And if we allow these little inner people to take charge, we could be in trouble. But before we move onto the Four-Pillar Program of claiming your inner grown-up, I think it's worthwhile to first reflect on the question what *is* authentic adulthood? What are the passages, the developmental stages that should be or could be taking us there? Chronological age alone doesn't seem to be doing it. One friend of mine claimed that she used to date older men because she assumed that they would be more mature. She said with a sigh, "I quickly discovered that age had nothing to do with maturity." Eventually she married a man three years her junior, who is, in fact, quite mature.

Authentic Adulthood

My trusty *Webster's Dictionary* defines "adult" as "grown up to full age, size, and strength: a full-grown person, animal, or plant." Well, that doesn't seem to be adequate, as we've already determined. *Webster's* defines "authentic" as "genuine, real, true." Ah, now there's some food for thought. What distinguishes a genuine, original, "real" adult, from a kid in a big body?

The cynics among us would say that being a "real" adult is akin to becoming more and more imprisoned—trapped by inevitable obligations and bills, by middle-age spread and hair loss, by ties and panty hose and fallen arches, that the road to authentic adulthood is all downhill. I once heard a lecturer tell his audience, "When childhood dies, the corpses are called adults." But I would say that attitude needs a little readjustment.

Sometimes we look for the credentials of adulthood to reflect authenticity—things like a suit, briefcase, job, home, car, spouse, credit line. Acquiring these grown-up accoutrements, for many of us, are like rites of passage into the mysterious land of adulthood. Unfortunately, some of us feel like we're playing dress-up, only looking the part but feeling inside like thirteen-year-old Josh from *Big*.

Sometimes we look for how emotionally "detached" people are from their own parents to determine if they are an adult. Have they "separated" emotionally, physically, psychologically from their parents? Have they chosen their own values and beliefs rather than just accepting hand-me-downs?

Being a "real" adult, however, goes deeper than age or trappings or alleged independence from the previous generation. I would say that a "real" adult has reached a place of peace that comes with a mastering of life, someone who has accomplished the art of living. That means accepting life on life's terms and not forever railing against it—or as one woman told me, "Being an adult means wearing life like a loose garment." What makes an adult true and authentic, the real McCoy versus an imposter, I believe, has to do with the development of four key qualities (which happen to be the four pillars of the inner grown-up): being responsible, mature, loving, and spiritual. Thus claiming your inner grown-up catapults you into the land of authentic adulthood.

I think it's interesting to note that age is not necessarily required to lay the foundation for these pillars. There's no doubt that some children show evidence of having a more developed inner grown-up than many adults do!

More important, I believe that being an "authentic adult" also means that we have developed authority over our lives. Time and again I will make the point in this book that we have the power to choose. A few years ago, "choose your own adventure" books and games were all the rage. In a very real sense, your journey toward authentic adulthood is very much like those books and games. In fact, many psychologists and others encourage their clients to think of their lives as a novel or a screenplay that they are writing. After all, how we perceive the world and our role in it is very much like telling ourselves a story. In other words, we are the authors of our own lives. Why would any of us choose to have our plots turn out badly? How many of us don't view ourselves as the hero?

Transcending Age

Sometimes children become role models to us as we muddle through our adult years, teaching *us* about the nature of adult attitudes and behaviors. Consider Ruby Bridges. Robert Coles, noted author and psychiatrist, wrote a charming children's book called *The Story of Ruby Bridges.* In it, he relates the true story of how in 1957 Ruby, a black girl, and her family moved to New Orleans. In 1960 a judge ordered four black girls to go to two white elementary schools as part of a movement for desegregation. Three of the girls were sent to McDonogh 19, but six-year-old Ruby Bridges was sent all alone to the William Frantz Elementary School.

Coles writes, "On Ruby's first day, a large crowd of angry white people gathered outside the Frantz Elementary School. The people carried signs that said they didn't want black children in a white school. People called Ruby names; some wanted to hurt her. The city and state police did not help Ruby."

Armed federal marshals were sent, however, by the president of the United States to escort and protect Ruby. Ruby held her head high and walked through the crowd without saying a word. The angry mob continued this hateful display not just for weeks but for months. And not only that, the white people kept their children out of school as a means of protest. So every day Ruby came to an empty school, and, except for her teacher, sat alone. But Ruby apparently kept a positive attitude, enjoyed her time at school, and learned how to read and write.

One day the teacher, Miss Hurley, noticed Ruby talking to the mob of screaming people on her way into the school. When Miss Hurley questioned her, Ruby said, "I wasn't talking. I was praying. I was praying for them."

Coles writes, "Every morning, Ruby had stopped a few blocks

away from school to say a prayer for the people who hated her. This morning she forgot until she was already in the middle of the angry mob." The prayer that Ruby repeated twice a day— before and after school—was

> *Please, God, try to forgive those people.*
> *Because even if they say those bad things,*
> *They don't know what they're doing.*
> *So You could forgive them,*
> *Just like You did those folks a long time ago*
> *When they said terrible things about You.*

Can you imagine? Such bravery from a six-year-old. I'm quite certain that many adults wouldn't have such fortitude, such a spiritual attitude of forgiveness, such courage in the face of hatred. I doubt that I would. Ruby was active on all four of the pillars: *responsibility* to attend school and keep up with her studies, *maturity* in terms of her incredible courage and forgiveness, a *loving* attitude toward her enemies, and a *spiritual* strength and connection.

Looks Can Be Deceiving

Just as you might not expect to find authentic adult greatness in a six-year-old girl, you cannot presume to find authentic adult greatness in someone with a position of authority, such as the elderly, a king, an executive director, a corporate president. Some presidents of countries do not always act in grown-up ways! You should not judge a book by its cover.

I have a friend who is teaching her teenage daughter to question authority and not just accept something as right because it comes from an "authority" figure. That's not to say she's teaching her daughter to be disrespectful. Quite the contrary, she's teaching her daughter to be respectful but to use her own judgment and not assume that others are more mature or more responsible than she is just because they are older or hold positions of power.

My friend said, "I think my sixteen-year-old daughter is probably more insightful and emotionally developed than a lot of people with so-called positions of power. I don't want her to be awed by the superficial trappings. Status, money, age—these things don't really mean anything about someone's authenticity. You have to trust your own intuition and your own heart and not be overpowered by what you *think* other people are."

Try This . . .
    List five men or women who you view as being authentic adults. What qualities do they have that you admire? What tells you that they are real grown-ups?

The Origins of Authentic Adulthood

For us grown-ups, the bricks for an authentic adult foundation may or may not have been laid in our childhoods. And a sense of truth may or may not come with status, power, money, independence, age.

Sometimes we require a specific life event, something significant and important and life changing that stimulates us to become authentic adults. It could be an illness or accident that affects us or a loved one. It could be a life transition, some milestone that affects us deeply. It could be a birth or a death that shocks us into a conscious awakening.

The rest of this chapter will look at four such scenarios that stimulate movement to authentic adulthood: death and loss, becoming sober/working a twelve-step program, becoming a parent, and taking a transformational trip. This list is not inclusive. You may or may not have experienced these specific events yourself, but seeing how they can motivate growth in others can stir the potential catalyst within you.

The Lessons of Loss

I mentioned in the introduction that loss is often a motivator for extreme emotional and spiritual growth, the kind of growth that inspires you to be a better person and to savor every moment of this precious life. William was a forty-five-year-old traveling salesman, who told me that he began living when he was thirty-nine—after he began grieving his brother's death.

His brother had actually died two years prior to that from AIDS. But William didn't grieve then. He shut and locked the door on his shame and confusion. Coming from a large Irish Catholic family with a long history of alcoholism, William easily joined in his family's pattern of denial and repression of any "unpleasant" feelings.

But one day something happened to break through his wall of restraint. He was driving along a country road in New England and he began to reminisce about his big brother, Ron. Then he began empathizing with his brother and remembering the ways that Ron had been shunned by their family. Then William began to cry. The tears that had been pent up for the last two years finally broke free. He cried so uncontrollably that he had to pull off to the side of the road.

He told me, "Somehow it came to me that he was showing me the way to my own heart. When I could look at the pain he went through, in our family life and such, once I could empathize with him, I was freed to look in my own depths and sadness. His death had an opening effect on me, and what it did was open up a whole world of the unseen, the possibilities of a spiritual world which had been so closed to me for so long."

This process of a spiritual awakening deepened when the very next year William's father died. He was in touch with, and unafraid of, his feelings from the beginning. He explained:

The story that I'm going to tell you indicated to me that there was so much more to this life than we can see or understand. When he died, he was with my sister, who is very parochial old Irish Catholic. She's from the school that if you don't see it, it's not there. So she was reading to my father, and he was going down fast. She was holding his hand and reading when all of a sudden, she looked at him and he had this incredible smile emanating from him and he was just gazing up. He looked like a five-year-old boy seeing his brand-new bike. Dad was just smiling and reaching up. My sister saw all of this and she said, "Dad, if you want to go, then go . . . go." So he squeezed her hand and he reached up, smiling, and he just died.

I actually had a hard time "grieving" when Dad died because, to me, he saw something, he was going somewhere. This wasn't a preconceived notion in his head, you know. It was really unbelievable. We just knew that he had moved on.

Before Ron and then my dad died, I had no spiritual life at all. But my grief just opened my heart and gave me the ability to look at things and open my mind. It gave me the ability to breathe and have my consciousness raised. Death was a big entrance to all of that.

As a result of his "spiritual awakening," William decided to become a hospice volunteer. Because his whole attitude toward death had been changed, he said that he was no longer afraid of dying and he wanted to help others during that critical transition. He now sees his life as about giving, about being ruled by love. He said:

My wife and children feel a change in me now, too. People who don't know me, or have just met me in the past year or so, think I'm very loving and giving. There's no history of anything else. Not that I was obtusely different from that, but I'm more open now and not as judgmental. This change has opened me to patience. I'm learning from my son and my daughter. I listen to my children more. I'm open to the community. I see myself connected to all those around me. And it also opens me to when people want to take care of *me*. It's a two-way street. I was out of a job four months ago and people were trying to take care of me. That was hard at first, but I have to understand the full piece [*sic*] of giving and receiving.

William knew that for him to change, he needed to be split wide open with something cataclysmic. He needed something that large and powerful to blast open the doors. For many of us, the death of a loved one is that blast.

In fact, it's worth noting that for baby boomers (those born between 1946 and 1964), the death of a parent—which is happening increasingly more frequently and will continue to do so—has an overall sobering effect of forcing baby boomers to realize that there is nobody left standing between them and the grave. Mortality's slap in the face is causing boomers to reevaluate their lives—in short, helping them to "grow up." Consequently many boomers, in the face of becoming "adult orphans," are changing careers, deepening their commitments, connecting to a religion, and in general reshifting their priorities.

Death has the power to teach us about the value of life.

A Life Controlled by Addiction

Sharon began drinking heavily twelve years ago, when she was forty-eight, after her husband left her. Her kids were grown and out of the house, so she drank at home, alone, every night. She knows that she began drinking to cover up the pain of the divorce, but over time it became an addiction and she just couldn't stop.

Eventually she got into another relationship, and he began to comment on her drinking pattern. On the one hand, she knew something was terribly wrong, but on the other hand, she was in denial and felt that she could "control" the drinking. Then one night she had a dream that a voice said to her, "Sharon, you can't drink anymore." It shook her up and she told her boyfriend that she really did need to quit drinking but that she was too ashamed to go to AA (Alcoholics Anonymous). So, she did it on her own and stopped drinking for a whole year.

However, while her alcohol intake may have changed, her attitudes did not. She said:

I know now that what was happening through that year was that I was a dry drunk. I wasn't drinking but my thinking hadn't changed. I felt resentful and sorry for myself and the whole nine yards. You can take the alcohol out of the alcoholic and you still just have ick. An icky person. You really have to change your attitude. There has to be a "you" before you drank, a "you" when you drank, and a new "you" once you get sober. What happens when you change your attitude is that you have a whole lot more energy to reflect, to be introspective, and to not blame others.

Sharon eventually relapsed and started drinking so heavily that she went to a therapist, who immediately recommended AA. This time Sharon agreed. Although she was afraid and uncertain, she went to her first meeting. She sat in the back of the room and a woman sat next to her and said, "You look like you're new. All you have to do is just be here, and by the way, my name is Robin and I'm an alcoholic." Sharon said, "Instantly I just felt like I belonged there; and I have felt like I've belonged there ever since."
She continued,

For me, it wasn't enough to just get sober. . . . Nothing changed inside of me. But with AA, there was an encouragement to change, to grow up. When you're active in the program, there's a nurturing but also a responsibility, a realization that, yes, there may have been reasons to drink, a predisposition to it, it might be in your family—there is a caring for you, but then a "get on with your life" attitude. Both are together. There is no license to *not* get on with your life. You don't get any credit for the victim role; people call you on it.

Maybe it's because being in AA forced Sharon to look at herself honestly, to take a "moral inventory" and to make amends to those whom she had wronged. Or maybe it's because the program also asked her to develop a relationship with a higher power and to develop a daily spiritual practice. Or it could be that the program encouraged her to reach out to other suffering alcoholics. Or maybe it was just the incredible support of the people in the program and the profound knowledge that she wasn't alone in her struggles. Whatever the reasons, AA changed her life. She explained:

> It's a qualitatively different existence that I have now, and the only thing that I can say is different is AA. Peace, centeredness, grounded—I feel all these things now when I didn't before. It might have been a rotten day, but, boy, this is a wonderful life. I'm also more aware of the need for service, of giving back what you've gotten. You have to keep your sobriety number one, but then you stay sober by reaching out to others.

Sharon now does volunteer work in a hospital by playing her flute for the patients. She also helps run AA meetings. And she has a deep and passionate relationship with God nurtured by church, Bible study, and prayer. She didn't have these things to such a powerful degree in her life before AA.

Becoming a Parent

Nothing changes your life quite like becoming a parent. It is one of the most amazing experiences that anyone can possibly have. We are programmed biologically to reproduce; it's how we ensure that life continues on this planet. But having and raising a child transcends mere biology, as it is one of the most satisfying emotional and spiritual experiences that exists in this universe (I guess I'm biased).

Being a parent is demanding, exhausting, exasperating, fulfilling, exhilarating, and joyous. Few things in life are so relentlessly challenging and yet so meaningful. Over and over again, throughout the years, parenting asks you to dance the dance of loving while letting go, of redefining yourself as a person and as a parent, of reconfiguring your marriage and/or other relationships. It's a process that never ends, really, because once you become a parent, you are always a parent.

One mother said to me, "I cannot be strong on my own, but

I can be strong for my children. They bring out a strength in me from some hidden place that I didn't even know existed. I can be strong for their sakes."

Katrina literally forced herself to "grow up" after she had a child of her own. Her daughter's presence gave her the strength and the impetus to do her own maturing. For the first time in her life, she had to truly think of another's welfare before her own and take the focus off of "me, me, me."

She also realized that she was a role model for her daughter and, therefore, had better be the best person that she could be. She told me, "I said to myself I have this child now who's going to look at me for the rest of her life as a role model, and if I don't change who I am—whether it's the unforgiving person or the overreactive person or the controlling person—she's going to pick up on that and just pass it on. I consciously made an effort to look at myself, and I just put my whole heart and soul into wanting to change and improve who I was."

Katrina was not such a bad person, really, but she was over-controlling, which she had learned from her mother. And she was overreactive, which she had learned from her father. And she was unforgiving—of herself. She had had two abortions in her teenage years that she had never forgiven herself for.

She said, "At eighteen I just died. I didn't grow beyond eighteen; I was trapped at eighteen because I felt so guilty. I didn't deal with the things people my age went on to because I was so hung up on what happened. The important things didn't grow the way they should have. But then, when I was thirty-three and my daughter graced my life, I decided to let go of being eighteen and I've had a speed journey ever since to catch up to myself."

Katrina went on a mission of self-forgiveness. She visited with a priest. She read a book on forgiveness. And she came to the realization that she had been young and had made mistakes and bad choices but that that fact didn't need to hurt her for the rest of her life. She had to let it go. She had to *forgive* herself.

For her daughter's sake, she did. She commented, "My daughter is like a mirror for me. She says and does things that are because of my influence. If it wasn't for that little girl, I

What Laura learned at an impressionable time in her life gave her tools that have served her well through the years in helping her to grow up.

But you needn't be just starting your adult life to experience transformative travel. Ann Linnea, at the age of forty-three, paddled Lake Superior in a kayak (that's 1,826 miles!) as a means of reflecting on her life's purpose. She writes about her experience in *Deep Water Passage: A Spiritual Journey at Midlife.* She was looking to connect with her intuitive self. She was looking for some healing, some reenergizing of her life.

She writes, "I think the greatest gift I came away with was the ability to simply go outside in my back yard or a park and know how to be still and to have that presence of the natural world fill me and strengthen me and enable me to go back and do what it is I need to do in my daily life with a deepened spiritual presence." Her journey also gave her the courage to make many important life changes in terms of her family (she got divorced) and her career (she moved and then started her own educational company).

Personal discovery travel is possible to anyone at any stage in the adult life-cycle passage. Whether it's wilderness travel, silent retreat, or adventure in a cosmopolitan city, such a trip can be a vehicle for some intense personal change and can prove to be a stimulant for growing up.

Waiting for the Bolt of Lightning

Not everyone has the "benefit" of a life event, be it blessed or tragic, to instill motivation for growth. If you sit around waiting for some "thing," some upheaval, to launch you on your journey, you could be waiting around most of your life and thus wasting precious time. As one woman told me, "I spent so many years preparing to live and then I decided that I better start because there was less of the candle left." What we're experiencing every day isn't the dress rehearsal for life—it's the real thing.

And it's also worth noting that even if powerful triggers do occur in your life, they may not be the impulse for anything. In other words, for most of us, a trip is just a nice vacation and then we return, unchanged, to our set, patterned lives.

Likewise, some "problem child" parents are so dependent and needy themselves that they look to their children to fulfill their own insatiable needs. And some parents are so immature and irresponsible—for example, deadbeat dads or abusive moms—that although they may love their children on one level, they do not act like loving authentic adults on another.

Similarly, loss is not a passport to transcendence, as many grievers become mired in fear, bitterness, and anger. The danger of loss is that it could lead to a shut-down, stunted emotional world. And, finally, many alcoholics die as alcoholics, or get sober but never change on the inside. The same is true of terminal illnesses and near-death experiences and severe accidents. Even a bolt of lightning in your life is no guarantee that it will jump-start your transformation. Of course, it is possible that the seeds of change are planted in these moments. When we choose to nourish them, they will grow.

How do you actively seek transformation then? How do you grow whether circumstances stimulate it or not? Is it possible to motivate growth by sheer resolve?

Indeed it is possible to will yourself to change, which is where the Four-Pillar Program comes into play. Both the four pillars and the four essential steps (DARE) will offer you a vocabulary and a blueprint for *intentional* growth. All you have to do is make the commitment to yourself. The next chapter will outline the program and its philosophies.

The Authentic Adult in Review

Being an authentic adult doesn't have to do with size or even age, in the end. My son's kindergarten class focuses on a topic each week, such as perseverance, personal best, self-control, cooperation, integrity, patience, and self-confidence. Maybe Robert Fulghum was right when he wrote the book *All I*

Really Need to Know I Learned in Kindergarten. Most grown-ups would do well to focus on such weekly topics.

For some of us, certain life events and/or life passages can serve as a springboard for deep growth and maturation. Loss, recovery, parenting, and travel are but a few examples that can stimulate change.

For the rest of us (most of us) who need a little direction, a little jump-start in our awakening, read on . . .

READING
From *Grow Up! How Taking Responsibility Can Make You a Happy Adult* by Frank Pittman

Adulthood is empowering. Grown-ups know we have the ability to do things, to make things happen, to impact other people. And if we feel powerful, we can get the necessary attention from other people by doing things and saying things that will make them feel good rather than doing what infants do most of the time and adolescents do some of the time: make themselves heard and felt by jarring and disturbing others with noisiness, nastiness, and shock effects.

Adulthood is liberating. Grown-ups can define themselves rather than just pleasing or displeasing those who would define them. Once we are free to do the right thing of our own choosing, we are most likely to do so. And if we know we are doing it, it will have far more power to make us happy.

Adulthood is mellow. Grown-ups have become what they are going to be. The frantic struggle of rapid changes in body and soul is over. The fear and desperation are gone. We have arrived. We are at home in the world. We can relax and go to bed before bedtime without the fear of missing anything.

VISUALIZATION

The following visualization is adapted from an imagery created by Ann V. Graber, known as the logo-anchor technique.

This is an imagery process that asks you to search for an experience rich in meaning, either from the past or from an anticipated event in the future. It is a tool to search for meaning-filled moments in your life, to pinpoint powerful inner resources that can bring about a transformation in an altered perspective or attitude. Dr. Graber claims that the logo-anchor technique is like a short refresher break to inner islands of restoration.

This imagery technique is based on the philosophy developed by Dr. Viktor Frankl known as logotherapy, a therapy based on helping a client find meaning in life. Dr. Frankl survived the concentration camps of Nazi Germany and went on to promote his ideas about the search for meaning.

Begin by getting your body prepared to relax. Stretch your arms high over your head. Then stretch them to your sides, reaching out. Drop your arms, and gently roll your head from side to side. Settle your body into a comfortable position and close your eyes.

Think about the words that you just heard from the reading. What do they make you think of? Did the reading evoke a feeling? Did the reading remind you of any experience from your own life? Take whatever message it is that you need from the reading.

Now bring your attention to your body and where you are in the room. Notice your breath, breathing in and breathing out. Notice the air around you and how it feels on your skin. Listen for any noises that may be near you. Notice any smells in the air. Become *mindful* of your environment and your place in it. Feel the weight of your clothes on your body. Feel the weight of your body on the floor or in your chair. Take three slow, deep breaths. Your consciousness is going on a journey.

Imagine yourself going down a flight of stairs. Down you go, and when you get to the bottom, there is a door. The door opens, and as you go through it, you realize that you've gone back in time. Picture yourself in a situation when you felt very "grown up" and completely capable. Perhaps it was a time of a great achievement, or perhaps it was an ordinary day when you felt totally at peace and full of wisdom. Search for an experience when you felt expansive, confident, and uniquely powerful.

Take this memory and try to envision it clearly in your mind's eye. Where exactly were you? What were you wearing? What were you doing? Who else was there? Take your time and try to remember exactly what it felt like to be in that moment. Were you smiling? Sit with this moment, and remember the inner thrill of knowing that you are on top of the world. How does it make you feel now, remembering and imagining it? The feelings of this moment can be with you at any time that you choose. Sit for a few moments in the silence.

Now, when you are ready, your consciousness returns to your body on a wave of light. Start to sense your body in the room. Feel your body getting grounded and integrated. Wiggle your fingers and toes. Take a deep breath. Start to move your arms and legs gently from side to side. Take another deep breath. Allow yourself to feel a vibrant energy coursing through your body, revitalizing you. I'm going to count from one to five, and when you are ready, after the count of five, you may open your eyes. One . . . two . . . three . . . four . . . five. You may open your eyes.

JOURNAL QUESTIONS

When you were a child, what did you think of grown-ups? Who modeled "grown-up" behavior for you?

When you were a child, how did you *feel* about becoming a grown-up yourself? Were you excited and couldn't wait? What aspects were you most eagerly anticipating? Or were you dreading it and fearful of the process to come? What aspects were you most fearful of?

What kind of grown-up are you now? Where are you stuck? How would your life look different if you were an authentic adult?

EXERCISES

Reading: Read a memoir or biography about someone whom you've always admired, someone who seems to be an authentic adult. Consider men and women, someone alive today or someone from history. Eleanor Roosevelt, Gandhi, Benjamin Franklin, Golda Meir, and Thomas Jefferson are a few suggestions. What do you learn by reading about their lives?

List: Make a list of at least ten things/events/activities/situations that contributed to making you feel like a grown-up. Start in chronological order. Think about each thing on the list. How did each event make you feel? How did you react? How did each event change you, either subtly or dramatically? Which was the most influential in launching you on the road to adulthood? Write an essay about this one and its influence on your development.

Reflection: Write down twenty things that adults can do that children cannot. Isn't it great to be an adult?

Letter: Our career choices are often influenced by others. Write a letter to someone who influenced your choice. Tell them how you feel? If you haven't pursued the field you thought you would, explain why and tell how you feel about your choice.

CHAPTER FOUR

The Four-Pillar Program

Reflect upon your present blessings, of which every man has many; not on your past misfortune, of which all men have some.

—Charles Dickens

One New England autumn day, a college professor friend of mine and I were having lunch and she made an interesting comment about her students in the new semester. She said, "The more I see college-age students coming from difficult family situations—their parents not being grown up—the more I wonder, how *can* they be grown up? We're creating a society where a lot of people simply don't know what it means to be grown up."

That is so true. Many people just don't *know* what it means to be a grown-up. They didn't learn it from their parents, and they're not learning it from cultural resources like books, movies, the Internet, or television. But not having the proper role models is an excuse that only goes so far. Blaming others for your current condition is decidedly un-grown-up.

So, again, if you haven't had a stimulus, a teacher, a role model, or any form of lightning bolt to prod you along the grown-up path, well, that's unfortunate. But now it's time to take matters into your own hands.

Your Inner Grown-up

There is a distinct difference between being a grown-up and being in touch with your *inner* grown-up. Claiming your inner grown-up leads to being grown up. But you can be a grown-up without claiming your inner grown-up. Okay, rather than split hairs here, or quibble over semantics, or get tangled in tongue twisters, let's review what exactly your inner grown-up is. It is simply your highest nature, your best self, your essence that *is* responsible, mature, loving, and spiritual. In other words—and this is key—your inner grown-up *already exists*! You don't even have to develop your inner grown-up; you just have to learn to tap into him. Another way to think of it, is that your inner grown-up leads you into authentic adulthood. Real, genuine adulthood in which you are the authority who rules over your own life.

You may not have seen much of your inner grown-up lately, but he is there, really. Just as your inner child is an unseen yet powerful presence in your life, your inner grown-up has the potential to also be an unseen yet powerful presence in your life. Have you ever felt that you were your own worst enemy, or that you were getting in your own way? When you connect with your inner grown-up, you have a personal advocate who is on your side. Your inner grown-up works for you, helps you out, pulls you out of trouble. It's like your own best friend, working for your best interests. Your inner grown-up is not self-destructive but self-constructive!

It Had to Be You

Everything you have ever needed is right there inside of you, provided by your inner grown-up. Did you ever hear the line in the Disney movie *Aladdin* when the genie (played by Robin Williams) sings, "You ain't never had a friend like me"?— well, that's sort of what your inner grown-up might sing to you. He already knows the answers. She already has all the clues.

Freud, the founder of psychoanalytic thought, might have

called this part of the self the superego (the storehouse of society's conscience, ideals, and values). Eric Berne, the founder of transactional analysis, might have called this part of the self the parent ego state (the nurturing and practical self). Lama Surya Das, author of *Awakening the Buddha Within*, would most likely call this part of the self the Buddha within. The inner grown-up is all of these things and more.

I chose to call this critical aspect of the self the inner grown-up because using the term "grown-up" rather than inner "adult" evokes the child's point of view. It's the child who might recall thinking grown-ups were powerful, smart, capable, dependable, strong. Then those same children discovered that grown-ups were in fact just humans, full of flaws and inadequacies. But perhaps it's the inner grown-up that our children idealized— and it's the inner grown-up that can live up to the promise of that ideal.

Think of what this could mean. Living with our flaws but tapping into the idealized potential—instead of being jaded or cynical or resigned. So often adults compromise and settle, rationalizing lethargy with a shrug since life isn't fair. I grew up my whole life with my mother telling me that "life isn't fair." And I do know that to be true. But should that reality stop us from working to make life better for all? The inner grown-up, being an idealized form of the self, motivates us to do more, be more.

The inner grown-up is plugged into a vast power source, a realm that links the generations. Carl Jung identified what he called the collective unconscious as a reservoir of thought and feeling and truth that is beyond any one particular person, but in fact is available to us all. The collective unconscious is not only fueled by the spirit of all those who are living, but is also filled by the energy of all those who have ever lived. Think of it as the wisdom of the ages, the strength passed down through our genes from our collective human ancestors. I believe that the collective unconscious partially feeds the inner grown-up, thus making it powerful beyond the power of any one person.

Jung and many of those who have amplified his theory also talk about the power of archetypes. Archetypes, as Jung defined them, are patterns that are deeply imprinted in the human psyche and have persisted over time. He found these archetypes in literature, art, mythology, and even saw them expressed in his patients' dreams. In her book, *The Hero Within,* Carol S. Pearson, Ph.D., explores six of the archetypes that she believes are present in every human being. They are the orphan, the innocent, the wanderer, the altruist, the warrior, and the magician.

Your inner grown-up expresses the best qualities of each of the six archetypes, particularly the last three. When we become an authentic adult, when we are fully engaged and have integrated our inner child and our inner grown-up, we embody the best of the altruist, warrior, and magician who exist, and have always existed, in each of us. Claiming your inner grown-up means learning how to access and utilize those dimensions of ourselves.

Part imagination, part conscience, part divinity, part idealization, part ghost, part possibility—your inner grown-up is totally complete. Little did you know that you had this phenomenal resource within you! It is there to influence, shape, mold, inspire, carry, coddle, cajole, guide, direct, and strengthen you. All you need is the key to open the door to get to her . . . she will show you the rest. And the key, I believe, is the Four-Pillar Program. This program simply breaks down your inner grown-up into four component parts for contemplation and for accessibility.

The Four Pillars

The Four-Pillar Program, then, is a new paradigm, an original screen with which to observe and analyze your world. It offers (1) a framework for consciousness, (2) tools and exercises for growing, including the four-step DARE technique to intentionally create change, and (3) shared stories of inspiration and hope. Following the outlines of this program gives you a different way to think and hopefully a new script to follow so that life takes on a deeper, richer meaning. The Four-Pillar Program is designed to help you connect with the vast assets contained within your inner grown-up. Of course, it's not always easy to access your inner grown-up, but with some practice, it becomes second nature.

Central to the whole concept of your inner grown-up are the four pillars of Responsibility, Maturity, Love, and Spirituality. Consider the following lists of attributes. Feel free to brainstorm and come up with your own qualities and add them to the lists. Many of the ideas, you will notice, interweave between the pillars.

RESPONSIBILITY
Duty to the self
Owns own life
Punctuality
Knows right from wrong
Conscience
Volunteer work
Financial security
Civic duties
Environmental respect
Parenting obligations
Honesty/truth
Helps humanity
Connected to the generations

MATURITY
Forgiveness
Gratitude
Cooperation
Courage
Self-esteem
Strength
Empowerment
Delayed gratification
Wisdom
Nonreactivity
Self-control
Consequences
Tolerance

LOVE
Love of self
Aging with dignity
Giving
Selflessness
Compassion
Commitment
Loyalty
Communication
Love of mate/partner
Love of children
Love of seniors
Letting go
Love of the earth

SPIRITUALITY
Connection to a higher power
Centered
Grounded
Aware of blessings
Grateful
Life as purposeful
Death
Faith
Prayer
Grace
Use of talents/gifts
Nature
Spiritual practice

Obviously these are not definitive lists. And as I pointed out, many aspects overlap between the pillars. For example, the concept of being environmentally responsible (don't litter, do recycle, etc.) could fall in the responsibility category, yet it could also be labeled as love for the planet. Or expressing love to a community member in the form of a get-well card could also be considered a spiritual practice of service and thoughtfulness. Or while learning to "forgive" your parents is a key part of maturity, it is also an act of love.

Exactly where each attribute is categorized is not the point. Rather the point is to have a system for identifying certain desired qualities with a direction toward obtaining them.

Common Thread

The four pillars are all different, and yet there is a basic inner grown-up theme threading through them, a pervasive belief that acts as an overarching umbrella.

The primary inner grown-up attitude that links the pillars is that life has meaning and is to be cherished, no matter what the circumstances. Anything, and I mean *anything*, is grist for the mill and fodder for growth. Negatives can be turned into positives. Seeming dead ends often lead to unexpected beginnings. Doors close but windows open. Any situation can lead to soul development, albeit sometimes painfully.

Now this may sound a bit Pollyannaish at first glance, but I'm really not talking saccharine optimism. I understand full well that terrible things—horrendous tragedies and mind-numbing atrocities—do occur. I hear heart-wrenching stories of loss every week in my office.

And yet . . . life does retain its precious value, perhaps even more so because of its fragility. And life is filtered through a perspective lens that alters how we view and ultimately experience any situation.

I recently received a rather corny e-mail from a friend that illustrates the point that everything is about *perception*. You can always reframe a situation to see it as an opportunity to learn or grow. The e-mail read:

I am thankful for . . .

   . . . the mess to clean up after a party
because it means I have been surrounded by friends.

   . . . the taxes I pay
because it means that I'm employed.

   . . . the clothes that fit a little too snug
because it means I have enough to eat.

   . . . my shadow who watches me work
because it means I am out in the sunshine.

   . . . the spot I find at the far end of the parking lot
because it means I am capable of walking.

   . . . all the complaining I hear about our government
because it means we have freedom of speech.

   . . . that lady behind me in church who sings off key
because it means that I can hear.

   . . . the piles of laundry and ironing
because it means my loved ones are nearby.

   . . . the lawn that needs mowing, windows that need
cleaning, and gutters that need fixing
because it means I have a home.

   . . . my huge heating bill
because it means that I am warm.

   . . . weariness and aching muscles at the end of the day
because it means that I have been productive.

   . . . the alarm that goes off in the early morning hours
because it means that I am alive.

All four of the pillars central to claiming your inner grown-up emphasize attitude as an antidote to despair. And attitude leads to action. So, though we cannot orchestrate all that happens to us in life, we can control our attitudes and our actions. Think of spinning gold from straw (as in the story of Rumpelstiltskin) or making lemonade out of lemons. You cannot change the winds of life, but you can learn to adjust your sails! These clichés reflect the perspective of the inner grown-up . . . that life always has possibilities.

A Is for Attitude

It all comes down to one's attitude. Attitude (a belief, a position) is key in terms of all four of the pillars. In fact, you will see "attitude" applied throughout the next several chapters as it impacts each pillar. An attitude of accountability and nonvictimization affects your relationship with *responsibility*. An attitude of strength and gratitude affects your relationship with *maturity*. An attitude of commitment and service affects your relationship with *love*. And an attitude of reverence and faith affects your relationship with *spirituality*. We can't control many and most things in life, but our attitude is in our own hands.

When I was in graduate school in the late 1980s, my supervisor in my first-year field placement, a family counseling center, recommended that I read Viktor Frankl's classic book *Man's Search for Meaning*. I remember thinking that he must be joking, because I could barely get through reading the books and articles that were *required* for my classes. How could I add something extra? But I did make note of the suggestion and some years later finally got around to reading it. I've never thanked that former supervisor for leading me to this book, but it truly is one of the most remarkable, and ultimately inspiring, books that I've ever read.

As I mentioned in previous chapters, Viktor Frankl was an eminent psychiatrist and also a Jew in Vienna in the Nazi era. In graphic detail he recounts his horrific experience in the concentration camps . . . and yet, what emerges are invaluable lessons about the soul's fight for self-preservation, the art of living, and the ultimate search for meaning amidst life's tragedies. His conclusions are the basis for a meaning theory called logotherapy. I mention him at this time because of his reflections on attitude. His enemies could strip him of his clothes and possessions, they could shave his head and imprison his body, but they could not take control of his *attitude*. Dr. Frankl said that "everything can be taken from man but one thing: the last of the human freedoms—to choose one's attitude in any given set of circumstances, to choose one's own way."

Subsequently, his actions were affected and informed by his change in attitude. Amazing. Choice. Choosing your attitude. Choosing your response. One of my pet peeves is when someone says, "I had no choice." There are always choices, even if the choice is to live or to die. It may *feel* as if there is no choice, but upon analysis there is always a choice. And the ultimate choice is to choose your attitude. We live in a world that encourages dualistic thinking, either/or, good/bad, yes/no. What we have to learn is that every situation presents us with multiple options. We simply have to choose which of them to take.

I was once checking out of a hotel when I noticed the following words framed in Lucite right at the check-out counter:

ATTITUDE
BY CHARLES SWINDOLL

The longer I live, the more I realize the impact of attitude on life. Attitude, to me, is more important than the facts. It is more important than the past, than education, than money, than circumstances, than failures, than success, than what other people think or say or do. It is more important than appearance, giftedness, or skill. It will make or break a company . . . a church . . . a home. The remarkable thing is, we have a choice every day regarding the attitude we will embrace for that day. We cannot change our past . . . we cannot change the fact that people will react in a certain way. We cannot change the inevitable. The only thing we can do is play on the one string we have, and that is our attitude. I am convinced that life is 10 percent what happens to me and 90 percent how I react to it. And so it is with you . . . we are in charge of our attitude.

"Wow," I said to the clerk. "That's a great reading; it's so true. Is it possible for me to get a copy of that?" He was happy to oblige and went on to tell me that his boss had put it there because she liked its message. "Of course," he added, "the people who most need to read it and understand it, don't seem to even glance at it. And the people who already 'get it' are the ones who notice and read it."

Then I found the exact same reading on a bulletin board at my daughter's school. "Yes," I thought to myself, "I know. I get it!"

Of course, I'm not saying that cultivating a positive, hopeful attitude is a breeze. It's often much easier to indulge in defeatism and despair, especially if you focus on all the problems and horrors in this world. And sometimes we need to stay in the valley of the shadow in order to heal. In my work with grievers, for example, they must first immerse themselves in the pain of loss before they can move to new levels of growth. I would not necessarily look for a "positive" attitude from someone experiencing acute grief.

And yet, over time it's the grievers with a healthy attitude that tend to grow and transcend. Indeed, one of the four pathways to transcendence in my first book, the "A" in the acronym SOAR, is *attitude*. These grievers allow their attitudes and perspectives toward life, death, suffering, and themselves to change because of their losses. They let death blow the dust off of life. And as a result, they come to behave differently. They *reinvest* in new things (the "R" of SOAR). They start to savor life even in its fragility, because of its fragility. But this happens over time.

My attitude improves if I try to remember that there is much about this life and the hereafter that we don't see and that we therefore cannot possibly understand. In other words, we may not be getting the whole picture.

By the Light of the Moon

My son, who was four years old at the time, and I were driving one night, back from some activity, when he observed the sliver of a moon up in the sky.

"Look at the moon!" he exclaimed. "The moon is so skinny. What happened to the rest of it? Why isn't it round anymore?"

"The moon still is round," I explained. "You just can't see it. We can only see a little sliver of the moon while the rest is in shadows. It has a monthly cycle and . . ." (I was wishing that I could remember my astronomy, but he interjected.)

"I don't think that sounds right, Mommy. Just look . . . the moon isn't round anymore."

"Well," I proclaimed with my maternal wisdom, "looks can be deceiving. Sometimes we only see a small piece of the picture when actually there's a lot there that we just can't see."

He seemed unimpressed. But it reminded me of a good-natured debate I used to have with a friend in college. I was defending the cliché that "every cloud has a silver lining." She would think of horror after horror that simply couldn't have any silver lining to it: earthquakes, wars, murders. My fallback position was usually like the sliver of the moon—there are so many mysteries about how the world works and there's so much that we cannot see. I was still convinced that the worst things in life *can* contain seeds of the best things in life. It just depends on whether or not the seeds take root and grow.

Transcending the Self

One way to nurture those seeds along is to acknowledge that the rest of the moon is there. In other words, to try to see the bigger picture. And if you can't see the bigger picture (and of course we really can't see the whole shebang), then at least try to acknowledge that it exists. In order to be aware of the bigger picture, you have to get out of your own myopic world. You have to transcend yourself.

While many theories, therapies, personal coaching, or other

self-help fads emphasize the self, all attention on "me, me, me," the inner grown-up philosophy stresses getting out of and going beyond "you, you, you." Not to say that you shouldn't take care of yourself, of course—I'm a big believer in self-care—but the focus of the Four-Pillar Program shifts your attention, perhaps subtly for some, perhaps radically for others.

The Four-Pillar Program is predicated on the belief that it is important to rise above oneself, to gain distance from one's life in order to acquire perspective. This includes placing oneself in a historical context, a cultural context, and a generational context. This includes a critical "stepping away" in order to gain clarity—just as you must step away from an impressionist painting in order to more clearly focus on the actual imagery.

P Is for Perspective

In other words, when you transcend the self, you gain a new perspective. One of my favorite images of this reality is the Empire State Building in New York City. I lived in New York for eleven years, and I used to love to go to the top of that building, even when I wasn't playing tourist with a visiting friend or family member. I loved it because when I got to the top, my entire perspective on the city changed. Truly it is a beautiful sight to be up above, perched like an angel watching down from the heavens. The city looked glorious, massive, still, and quiet from up there. And as you can imagine, it didn't always seem that way from down below.

Transcendence alters perspective, which, in turn, alters attitude. The Dalai Lama comments on this fact in his book *The Art of Happiness*, writing:

It seems that often when problems arise, our outlook becomes narrow. All of our attention may be focused on worrying about the problem, and we may have a sense that we're the only one that is going through such difficulties. This can lead to a kind of self-absorption that can make the problem seem very intense. When this happens, I think that seeing things from a wider perspective can definitely help—realizing, for instance, that there are many other people who have gone through similar experiences, and even worse experiences. This practice of shifting perspective can even be helpful in certain illnesses or when in pain. . . . But if you can make comparisons, view your situation from a different perspective, somehow something happens. If you only look at that one event, then it appears bigger and bigger. If you focus too closely, too intensely, on a problem when it occurs, it appears uncontrollable. But if you compare that event with some other greater event, look at the same problem from a distance, then it appears smaller and less overwhelming.

Paradoxically, when you leave the self, you actually become more grounded in the self. Just as it is in giving that you receive. When you transcend the self, you find the true, highest self.

Technique for Transcendence: DARE

The technique central to the application of the inner grown-up concept of transcendence is a four-step process that I call DARE: Detach, Aware, Reorient, Enact/Evaluate. It's a conscious pattern of thinking, a refocusing process that works best when you're in a situation when you feel yourself regressing (retriggered wounded child or problem child) and know you need to grow up. It's based on the kind of detachment that Laura learned from meditation in India, as described in chapter 3, and is essentially a process of rooting out destructive thoughts and behaviors and replacing them with positive, constructive responses. It challenges you to "dare" to break old patterns, to "dare" for things to be different, to "dare" to be a grown-up.

The first step is to *detach*: this means literally to imagine yourself removed from the situation and watching from a distance, either from above, as if you are up on a mountaintop looking down, or sitting back and observing from afar, as if you are watching a scene from a movie on a screen before you. It is important to achieve this level of removal before proceeding to the next step, because only then can you hope to gain some degree of objectivity. I have found that using the movie-screen image seems to work best. See yourself up on the screen, playing out this situation—just kick back in the audience and watch the scene unfold.

Next, become *aware*: notice that you have regressed to a problem child state and ask yourself, "What is going on?" "Where is this coming from?" "What piece of my inner child is getting activated—is it the wounded, dark, or shadow side of my inner child that is dominating?" "What button got pushed that made me go back in time?" Or maybe nothing was activated from the past and you just become aware of how you are acting like a child, a baby. Becoming aware of the situation gives you an opportunity, a *choice* to not be reactive. And if it feels easier, keep yourself up on the movie screen and "watch" yourself becoming aware.

In the third step you acknowledge your feelings but then *reorient*: remind yourself that you are a grown-up and that you can have a different response now. Draw on your inner grown-up resources to find the mature reaction. Ask yourself, "How would my best, wisest, most transcendent self respond?" or "How would I react if I was being responsible, mature, loving, or spiritual?" Maybe you don't know the answer to these questions yet, but sit quietly, have patience, and listen for your inner wisdom to guide you. Ask yourself, "What is a better replacement behavior for this situation?" Ask and listen. And again, if it works more effectively, watch yourself on the movie screen reorienting to your inner grown-up.

And finally, you *enact*: you implement your better response. You act from the inner grown-up position. You behave in a new way. Even when you don't *feel* like it, you still act the grown-up part. The second piece to enact is that after you take action, you should *evaluate* the results: How did the switch work? Was it better to act from an inner grown-up position rather than from an inner child position? How did other people react? How did it feel? Was the new response easy or difficult? Stopping to evaluate the process increases the probability that you will use it again.

If you practice the DARE (Detach, Aware, Reorient, Enact/ Evaluate) approach, you no longer have to be a slave to your problem inner child. You don't have to act on impulse or repeat negative patterns. These four steps give you the power to stop, analyze the situation, and choose an inner grown-up response. These steps, once practiced and used regularly, will anchor you to your inner grown-up.

DARE to Facilitate Change

Let's take a look at how this process can actually work. A thirty-three-year-old woman, Rachel, was eagerly planning her wedding. She had asked one of her oldest and dearest friends, Ariana, to be one of her attendants. Ariana agreed though she was somewhat cool in her response. As the year of planning proceeded, Ariana moved to another town and the women drifted apart. But since they had been friends since grade school, Rachel was not too concerned. She believed that their friendship would endure all changes.

Then as the date approached, the bridesmaid dresses arrived. Rachel called Ariana and left a message for her. No response. Rachel wrote Ariana a letter detailing how hurt she felt. No response. Rachel thought to herself, "Screw her," and concluded that their friendship was over. She inwardly vowed never to speak to Ariana again. Often family and friend lifelong feuds start over just such an incident.

But in practicing the DARE method, first *detach*—I asked Rachel to withdraw herself from the situation and to imagine the entire scene as played out on a movie screen before her; then become *aware*—I asked Rachel to identify how her problem inner child was contributing to this situation and where it was coming from. She realized that she was feeling hurt and abandoned and that she was reacting out of this pain. It reminded her of all the times her alcoholic mother (now deceased) had promised her things but inevitably disappointed her. She knew this pattern only too well. Next, *reorient*—Rachel the grown-up can acknowledge the similar pattern of anticipation and disappointment, but she can realize that Ariana is not her mother. And bearing in mind that a grown-up looks to transcend his or her own perspective, I asked Rachel to consider what Ariana might be feeling. Rachel admitted that as an unmarried woman in her mid-thirties, Ariana might be feeling threatened, jealous, lonely, even frightened of losing their friendship. Perhaps Ariana, operating from her own wounded and scared inner child, was unable to transcend her pain to participate in Rachel's happiness. Understanding this, Rachel could actually empathize with her dear old friend rather than focus only on her own hurt ego.

And then *enact*—armed with the maturity and wisdom of the inner grown-up, Rachel could put aside her hurt feelings. She sought Ariana out yet again, determined to make contact. She approached her with compassion and understanding, not from a place of selfish pride. In the end, Ariana apologized for turning her back and ended up taking her place by Rachel's side during the wedding ceremony.

Finally *evaluate*—Rachel realized that switching from her hurt inner child to her mature inner grown-up really did make a difference and would allow her to keep her relationship with Ariana. In fact, the two are still friends today. Had Rachel stayed stuck in her wounded child self, the two might have remained eternally estranged.

DARE is just a technique to initiate transcendence, the art of getting out of yourself, getting out of the muck from the past. It can work for all four of the pillars so that the internal messages from the past aren't interfering with your ability to be responsible, mature, loving, and spiritual.

DARE Caveats

"Oh sure," you may be thinking, "I'll never be able to do that, certainly not right in the moment of a problem child attack." Well, maybe not at first. There will be plenty of times when you forget, slip, or otherwise regress. Nobody said this technique will come easily or automatically. So don't be alarmed when you have plenty of occasions where you only think of

DARE *afterward*, after you've already acted like a problem child. That's okay.

Practicing the DARE technique requires just that, *practice*. Remember that habits are merely learned behaviors: Bad habits can be unlearned and better habits can be learned. But learning a new habit, that is, a new pattern of relating from your inner grown-up rather than from your wounded child, requires habitual application. Just as I must say "sit" about thirty thousand times before my golden retriever puppy finally understands, I must try the DARE technique over and over and then over again to ingrain this new pattern into my mind.

But if you are more aware, then you're making progress. Also if you can notice afterward and revise the scene in your mind, then you are making progress. Part of the inner grown-up is being mature enough to own your mistakes, make amends where necessary, say "I'm sorry," learn from your mistakes, and try again. It takes courage to admit when you're wrong, but that's the first step in trying to make things better.

Did you ever watch a toddler learning how to walk? She falls and gets up and takes a few steps and falls again and gets up again. Let your inner toddler teach your inner grown-up a thing or two about persistence! So accept that you will fall, and know that you can get up and try again. Each time, you move a little farther on your journey. Have the wisdom to learn from your mistakes, and have the patience to try again. With willingness, patience, and determination, you will grow. The inner grown-up response will become second nature almost without your knowing it. And suddenly it will become your first, automatic response. Almost unconsciously.

Try This . . .

Your journal is an important tool to make you more consciously aware of the DARE technique and to help imprint this pattern in your mind. I suggest that you refer to your journal each morning and each night. Turn the page for some of the sections that might be valuable to keep in your journal:

Daily Life Lessons. Review your day and review what lessons you learned. Keep track of incidents that you either witnessed or participated in during which you saw someone acting from their inner child perspective. Using DARE, trace through the process to arrive at an action plan for making the transition to an inner grown-up response. Sometimes it is easier to see these behaviors in others, but ultimately we need to see them in ourselves.

Goals. By writing down your goals for that day, that week, that month, or that year of your life, you place them more prominently in your conscious mind. Keep in mind that goals need action plans in order to become reality.

Action Plans. Once you've listed your goals (becoming more patient, improving your relationship with a friend or family member, attaining a higher level of fitness) set up incremental stages and deadlines for yourself. Keep in mind that most of your goals can't be accomplished in a single step, but will be met if you think in terms of steps and stages—what can you do each day, each week, each month, to reach that goal.

Once you break a larger problem/concern into smaller more manageable sub-steps, the goal becomes much more attainable. The short-term goals will also help keep you more focused, disciplined, and motivated. Keep track of your progress. Don't forget to include rewards for yourself for meeting those short-term and long-term goals.

Theoretical Underpinnings

The DARE technique is not about unearthing the unconscious or focusing on past traumas. It asks you to only be *aware* of what's happening in the moment, and then it asks you to substitute a different reaction. You can only do this by employing your rational, cognitive (thinking) mind.

In Rachel's case being aware of her problem inner child did link back to a past association, to that of her alcoholic mother. But usually it's not even necessary to know where the problem child behavior is coming from. It might not even be coming from the deep, dark past anyway. The truth is that we all get socked with problem child behavior from time to time (anger, fear, insecurity, anxiety) regardless of our upbringing, just because we're human. It's the cognitive mind, not the unconscious, that needs to be harnessed for help.

In essence, the DARE technique and indeed most of the Four-Pillar Program are influenced by a school of psychology called cognitive therapy, developed by Dr. Aaron Beck. Dr. Beck departed from his psychoanalytic roots when he came to the conclusion that it was thought distortion, not unconscious conflicts, that were central to his client's problems. Furthermore, it is thoughts that lead to behaviors. Thus in order to change behaviors, one must change thoughts.

I believe that thoughts influence behaviors and that thoughts can be changed! Attitudes and perceptions can be modified, and behaviors will change accordingly.

Likewise, a school of thought called solution-focused therapy has influenced my thinking. This therapy stresses solutions of the future, not problems of the past. It helps people imagine their lives as unstuck and then create the goals and scripts for getting there. Two techniques from this school are included in the "Exercises" portion of this chapter, and the previous "Try This" section was based on these approaches.

Another extremely influential theory on my own work that I mentioned earlier is logotherapy, devised by Viktor Frankl. Logotherapy is an existential approach to life that stresses the search for meaning as an important human undertaking. Logotherapy is not concerned with self-actualization or even self-focus, but self-transcendence. It emphasizes personal choice, free will, the noetic dimension (life of the spirit) and attitudinal change as therapeutic concepts.

So while I understand that the past has an influence and that unconscious thoughts will prevail, they do not have to have absolute control. Perhaps now is the time to cut the fuel line to their energies. The inner grown-up knows how to honor yet override the past. Let her exercise her power.

However, having said this, I also understand the value of

deep healing on many levels, even the unconscious level. So the Four-Pillar Program includes a component to reach those lower recesses of the mind. The visualizations in particular, as well as the readings and many of the exercises, take the healing to that deeper level.

I think of singing as a metaphor for this. Singing is my passionate hobby, and through my classical training I have learned that the muscles in my throat respond to my thoughts. So if I'm going for a high note and think scary thoughts (like I'm going to crack on that high C), my throat closes up. But if I think about technique such as coming above the note and landing on it, or opening my throat, or if I distract my worries by focusing on the text, I'm generally fine. But as important as the mind is in influencing the sound, it is the breath from below, the ultimate support from the diaphragm, that really anchors things.

Similarly, while thoughts and mind tools are key to this program, it is the whole picture, moving from the mind to the heart to the gut, being anchored deeply, that heals on multiple levels.

Tapping Inner Grown-up Resources

So if your inner grown-up already exists intact, our task becomes finding ways to access the treasures. One quick and easy way is to use affirmations. In the first session in my workshop I pass out the following affirmations. I ask the participants to reflect on these and to write them down in their own handwriting as well. I invite everyone to add their own personal affirmations to the mix. I also suggest that they say the affirmations out loud every day as a means to start internalizing them.

I am a grown-up.
I can handle this.
I can get through this.
I am responsible, mature, loving, and spiritual.
I know that I am powerful and courageous.

I have all that I need to manage this.
I am filled with faith, not fear.
I have inner resources of incredible power.
I am connected to divine strength.
I can DARE to live my life differently.

I can *detach* from this situation, become *aware* of what's really going on; I can *reorient* to my inner grown-up, and I can *enact* in a new way! *Evaluate* that!

One woman came back the next week and shared her experience of going to see an acupuncturist for a back ailment. After the needles were inserted, she was not in any pain and yet, when she was left alone in the room, she began to panic. "My back is full of needles!" she told herself. Her heart rate began to accelerate and she was on the verge of yelling for the acupuncturist to get the needles out and quick, when suddenly she remembered the affirmations.

She began to chant them in her head—remembering some, making up others—reminding herself that she was a grown-up and that she could manage this, and that she had a reservoir of internal strength from which to draw. It calmed her down, allowing her to cope with the situation and to relax into the moment.

Try This . . .
Make a list of your own affirmations, words that resonate for you. Write them down in your journal. Read them every day. Soak yourself in the words. Absorb them into your being. Believe them.

Playing the Part

Another way to initially jump-start your relationship with your inner grown-up is to "act as if." You may have heard of this concept, sort of a "fake it till you make it" philosophy. You literally plan to spend around fifteen to thirty minutes each day pretending like you're totally in touch with your inner grown-up. You are exceedingly responsible, mature, loving, and spiritual in those moments. Really *feel* the part. How does it feel to walk, talk, and listen when you're aligned with that inner grown-up? Do you look different, sound different, behave differently? Do others notice any change? Think of yourself as an actor or actress taking on a new part. Immerse yourself in character, that is, your inner grown-up.

I was working with a fifty-five-year-old woman who had an acrimonious relationship with her stepdaughter. For a myriad of reasons, they just couldn't get along. My client, Sara, was throwing a big party for her husband, and naturally the stepdaughter was planning to come. Before the party Sara was starting to nervously anticipate the tension that was sure to escalate between her and her stepdaughter. But instead, Sara decided to make a change and work with the "act as if" concept. She decided to pretend that there was no tension between them. She decided to come from an inner grown-up position and be pleasant and cordial and hospitable to her stepdaughter. The result? The party was relatively stress free. I wouldn't say that they're destined to become the best of friends, but Sara was proud that by "acting as if" there was no trouble between them, suddenly there wasn't.

If you practice doing this exercise every day for several weeks, you just might find that you're actually "acting" less and less. In other words, the inner grown-up starts becoming internalized. She becomes less of a character to play and more of a reality to claim.

Try This . . .
   "Act as if" exercise, but begin slowly. Begin with just five minutes at a time in which you use your imagination to deal with a real problem—either a situation you encountered in the past or one you might face in the future. Visualize yourself responding in the most authentically adult manner possible. Then

act as if you are completely self-confident, secure, peaceful, mature, and so on. Think from this perspective, feel from this perspective, act from this perspective. Try it at home to begin with, in a safe environment. During these five minutes, you are your future self; you are aligned with your inner grown-up. Feel yourself into the part. Try it when you are alone. Try it when others are around you.

The next week try it for ten minutes at a time. Take your act on the road, so to speak, by trying it at the office, in the grocery store, in a committee meeting. Respond to people as the grounded, centered, self-assured grown-up that you wish to be and already are deep down. It may feel completely awkward and fake at first, but keep acting even though you haven't integrated those feelings yet. Keep at it, deliberately and mindfully. You will start a snowball into motion that will carry you forward with its momentum.

Then add more time to your acting practice and start using the technique in times of crisis or stress. Pick a challenging situation, like Sara did with her stepdaughter, and see what a difference it can make.

Notice that what begins as artificial acting becomes easier with practice. The more you act a certain way, the more you begin to actually feel the part. And the more you feel the part, suddenly you are no longer acting. What you sought becomes ingrained within you.

Symbols of Your Inner Grown-up

Let's return to the Four-Pillar Program. Remember in chapter 1 I mentioned that I ask participants in my support group to bring an object that represents/expresses/symbolizes their inner child. Well, I also eventually ask them to bring an object that symbolizes their inner grown-up.

Again, you see a wide variety of things that people bring in. One woman brought in the lyrics to "Amazing Grace" and another brought in a rosary—representing their spiritual natures.

Others have brought in datebooks and Filofaxes and Palm Pilots—representing their responsible natures. One man brought in a tile that represented the house he was remodeling—a grown-up task that represented his mature capacity. Another woman brought in a picture of her two children, who she says have taught her the true meaning of love.

These are the images that can remind us of our strengths, our potentials, our place in this world as grown-ups, and our power to influence and make a difference in the world in which we live.

At the end of the group session, I give each member a small polished stone, a piece of rose quartz as a symbol of their inner grown-up. Because it is a rock, it is strong. Because it is polished, the ragged, sharp edges (of the past) have been smoothed and softened. Because it is "rose," it represents a blossoming nature, always striving for more growth. I encourage them to carry this rose quartz to remind them of their inner grown-up and all its power and potential.

Try This . . .
Select an object that represents your own inner grown-up. Look at it. Hold it. What does it tell you about you? What qualities does it possess that are a reflection of your best self?

The Program in Action

It might be helpful to see how one woman utilized the program's resources to connect with her own inner grown-up for the first time in her life. Agnes was a sixty-two-year-old woman who entered the Claim Your Inner Grown-up support group with some trepidation. She had never been in a support group before and seemed initially guarded. She told the group that she had been a victim most of her life, helpless and powerless and always looking for answers.

Agnes, like so many of us, had a difficult childhood. While it was punctuated with some pleasant moments, she received heaps of criticism from her parents. She learned to doubt herself, and like many women of her generation, she believed she only mattered as a wife and mother. So she married a highly critical man when she was young, since that's the dynamic to which she was accustomed. And she had three children in rapid succession without really ever knowing what she was doing or why.

When her husband became physically abusive and when she became physically ill, Agnes finally mustered the incredible strength to leave him. She said, "I realized how sick I was and that the marriage was the cause and that if I didn't leave him, I was going to die. We had this so-called 'perfect' life—a beautiful house and beautiful children, but there was nothing I could do to please him. He was an abusive tyrant and I had to leave."

But leaving came with a price. In the 1950s divorce was relatively unknown, and she described feeling like a social pariah. Also she had to struggle financially and take jobs as an unskilled laborer to try to make ends meet. Nothing came easily to her as she struggled as a single mom with three children. She felt victimized by life.

Eventually, after her children were grown, she married a much older, wealthy man. But, not surprisingly, he too was emotionally abusive. Their relationship was complex, with many happy times as well as times of strife. After fifteen years of marriage, he died unexpectedly. And in the four years since his death, she has been in a legal battle with her stepson contesting the distribution of her husband's estate. This battle had been consuming her inside and out, socially and financially, for the past four years. Again she felt victimized by her life circumstances.

In our second group session together (the sesssion on Responsibility), Agnes became visibly upset. As she reflected on being responsible for her own life, she seemed confused and agitated. Listening to the others sharing their own experiences, she began to cry. At the end of the session she bolted.

The next day, just as I was planning to call her (I was afraid that her feelings might have frightened her and that her internal resistance would cause her to leave the group), she called me. And not unexpectedly, she announced that she wished to withdraw from the group. When I asked why, she retorted, "I think I'm much older than everyone else in the group and that I just don't fit in." I noted that she was in fact the oldest in the group, but only by a few years. I inquired if her reluctance had more to do with the topic of responsibility and that perhaps it had hit a nerve.

At that she began to reflect on how she had gotten upset in the session and that she wasn't used to feeling upset and that maybe it had touched a vulnerable spot within her and that maybe, yes, she did need to look at this issue in her life. And lo and behold, by the end of our phone conversation, she agreed to remain in the group.

In the next four sessions, Agnes worked diligently. She completed all the homework assignments, wrote in her journal, joined in the visualizations, shared openly in the group, and took her growth seriously. She employed the DARE steps both to diffuse the power of her problem child and redirect herself toward her inner grown-up. This technique reminded her to leave the familiar place of pain and victimization and to stay squarely on track to claim her present power. One of her reorienting phrases that helped her was, "I live on Miller Street now [her current residence] not Kenwood Avenue [her childhood address]."

At the last session she came in wearing a bright lime green sweater and skirt (previously she had worn drab colors and baggy pants). She looked glorious. Everyone commented on her appearance, her lightness, the sunniness emanating from her eyes.

She revealed that she had dropped the court battle—which was basically over anyway, but she just finally decided to "let go" of the fight, literally and metaphorically. If was as if a lightbulb had gone off—one of those rare and precious "aha" moments—when she finally got it from the inside out that she alone and nobody else was responsible for her life. She said that firing her lawyers felt like losing twenty pounds. She did indeed seem visibly lighter and freer.

After the group ended, Agnes told me that to her amazement she felt tremendously better. She said, "I'm so glad that I followed through and stayed with the group because I feel powerful, power in myself really for the first time ever, as a person. I never felt power in my life before. I felt abjectly victimized most of my life. But I didn't know how to change it; I didn't have a clue."

Working the Four-Pillar Program helped her claim her power. She said, "I always felt the answers were from outside, and that was something that finally in this group I learned—that really the answers come from within, that the answers aren't outside of us after all; they're inside us. And I also learned from the group that I had to take *responsibility* for my life and that meant taking responsibility for the estate and the outcome and working or not working. That was a huge step for me."

She continued, "No longer do I think that my children are going to solve my problems. That was a big one. I had really leaned on them through the years to help me solve my problems, to make me feel better. I hadn't even realized that I was doing that, they were so willing for so many years."

Agnes expanded her range in all of the pillars. For spirituality, she told me that her faith got sharper and deeper and that she started attending a new church since our group. For maturity, she found courage where previously she had none and realized that she needed to find a job to support herself whether she liked it or not. It had to be done as an extension of responsibility for her own life. Her life is about possibilities now, not just about limitations.

As for love, she is learning to have a new appreciation for herself and who she is, including how old she is. She noted:

I've always looked at my getting older as a force against me. I no longer do. I see it now as something that I accept and love and rejoice in. There's a wisdom in being older that you don't have when you're younger. There's more gentleness in your living. I am a grandmother, which is entirely a nice role, giving and loving and joyful. And I have a tremendously great friendship with each of my children now and their spouses. I don't fight my aging anymore. And I look at myself in the mirror and I think I am beautiful. I choose to see that it's wonderful. My memories are no longer a chain around my neck. I looked back this time and I let the inner child grow up. Finally, I became a grown-up.

Wow. Pretty profound stuff. Agnes will need to continue to work on these issues, no doubt. But she's made the most important step—the step of analysis and honest appraisal and the desire to change. For me, seeing her grow was an incredible gift. I was so proud of her ability to stick it out and get to the other side. No one said growing is easy. Our built-in comfort with homeostasis and familiarity will always challenge change, even positive changes. But Agnes showed that persistence and willingness do make a difference, and that giving the Four-Pillar Program a chance yields results.

The Idealized Grown-up

You may protest, "This inner grown-up stuff is sounding too ideal, too unattainable." True, no one is perfect. Because the inner grown-up is your highest and best self, it is unrealistic to think that it can always be functioning. Humans by their nature cannot be perfect.

And yet, it is something to strive for. It *is* in our nature to believe in growth and self-improvement. And we can most certainly get glimmers of our best self—of that potential—on a regular basis.

This program provides tools for you to take charge of your own life. It puts control into your hands so that you don't sit around hoping that life will make you grow up. It emphasizes how to relate to your life in an active rather than a passive manner, offering resources for claiming your own power.

You can watch from the dugout if you want, but someday you just need to go to bat and take a good, hard swing. It's time to play the game, for real. Batter up!

The Four-Pillar Program in Review

Your inner grown-up is inside, fully formed, ready to work for you. You don't need to develop or create him, all you need to do is find access to him. The Four-Pillar Program gives you the keys, including the four-step DARE key.

The program is about improving your attitude, which leads to active change. The program is about gaining a new perspective, looking at situations in a new light. The program offers stories of hope, exercises, and tools, such as affirmations, symbols, and "acting as if," that touch on all levels of the mind and soul.

READING

An aging Hindu master sent his apprentice to put a handful of salt in a glass of water and then to drink it.

"How does it taste?" the master asked.

"Bitter," spit the apprentice.

The master laughed and then asked the young man to take the same handful of salt and put it in the lake. Again he asked the apprentice to drink it. The master asked, "How does it taste?"

"Fresh," replied the apprentice.

"Do you taste the salt?" asked the master.

"No," answered the young man.

The master replied, "The pain of life is pure salt—no more and no less. The amount of pain in life remains the same, exactly the same. But the amount of bitterness we taste depends on the container we put the pain in. So when you are in pain, the only thing you can do is to enlarge your sense of things. . . . Stop being a glass. Become a lake."

VISUALIZATION

The following visualization, like the visualization from chapter 3, is adapted from an imagery created by Ann V. Graber, which she calls the Journey to Your Interior Castle to meet with your higher self. She describes your higher self as "the part

of you that personifies the best elements of your being; it is
that unique individuation of divinity which finds expression
through you."

I have adapted her journey to the interior castle as a visualization to meet your inner grown-up. Be open to allowing any
image to come to mind. This will be an important meeting.

Get yourself into a relaxed position. Close your eyes and follow the natural rhythm of your breath. Reflect, for a moment,
on the words that you just heard from the reading. What do
they make you think of? Did the reading evoke a feeling? Did
the reading remind you of any experience from your own life?
Take whatever message it is that you need from the reading.

Now, take a deep cleansing breath. Imagine yourself going
down a flight of stairs. Down you go, and when you get to the
bottom, there is a door. The door opens, and as you go through
it, you realize that you're going on an adventure. Imagine yourself in a meadow. It is a warm and sunny day and you see
many wildflowers all around you. You feel the warmth of the
sun on your skin and you feel a light breeze lift your hair.

Before you lies a bridge, a bridge leading from tangible
reality into the land of higher consciousness. On the other side
of the bridge is a gate, a gate to the crystal city. You enter and
find yourself on an avenue walking through the crystal city. All
around you are amazing sights and sounds. The sun glistens
on the crystal buildings. You walk along filled with awe and
wonder.

You can see at the end of the avenue a large castle made of
crystal and gold. It is a wondrous place. As you approach the
castle, you are allowed into the gates and you climb a large
staircase. At the top of the staircase is a door. You open the
door to discover a gorgeous ballroom adorned with sumptuous
ornaments, all glass and gold. At the end of the ballroom you
see an orb of light. You feel drawn to the light and begin to approach it.

As you get closer to the light at the end of the ballroom, you
see that it is your inner grown-up standing in the ray of light.
You recognize at once that this is your higher reality. Allow
whatever form to take shape that needs to take shape. You may

see yourself resplendent in golden robes, with a crown, like a majestic king or queen. You may see yourself as a witch or wizard. You may see yourself as a wizened crone or a worldly gypsy. Perhaps you even see your inner grown-up as an exalted beast or animal. Your inner grown-up welcomes you with a smile and joyously greets you. This is a sacred encounter.

You smile at your inner grown-up, who smiles in reply. She then reaches into a crystal vase and produces gold "grounding" dust that she sprinkles onto your head. You immediately feel yourself grounded and rooted at the base of your spine, solidly attached to your reality and your inner strengths. You reach out your hand to touch that of your inner grown-up's, and as your hands touch, you feel an electric shock that courses through your body. You feel your body filled with a sort of light and energy that makes you feel revitalized.

Ask your inner grown-up now what it is that you need to know, do, or change, so that you can live a life with harmony and purpose. Wait for an answer. An answer may appear right away in the form of a knowing, or a visual or auditory impression. Or perhaps an answer will appear for you at another time. Be still and quiet and listen for any communication from your inner grown-up.

After a while you will know that it is time to go. Thank your inner grown-up for your visit, knowing that you can return at any time. You turn to exit the palace through the ballroom, down the staircase, and out the castle gate. There is light emanating from the corners of your clothes. You feel energized and complete. Walk back down the avenue, through the crystal city, until you come to the gate at the bridge. Walk through the gate and cross the bridge back into the meadow.

Now, when you are ready, your consciousness returns to your body on a wave of light. Start to sense your body in the room. Feel your body getting grounded and integrated. Wiggle your fingers and toes. Take a deep breath. Start to move your arms and legs gently from side to side. Take another deep breath. Allow yourself to feel a vibrant energy coursing through your body, revitalizing you. I'm going to count from one to five, and when you are ready, after the count of five, you may open your eyes. One . . . two . . . three . . . four . . . five. You may open your eyes.

JOURNAL QUESTIONS

Which pillar is the most developed for you already? Why is this one easy for you?

Which pillar is the most challenging for you now? Why is this one so difficult for you?

Which of the four DARE steps is the easiest for you already? Why?

Which of the four DARE steps is the hardest for you now? Why?

The Miracle Question: If you went to bed one night and then woke up in the morning and your "problem" (i.e., where you are stuck in your life) was gone, how would you know it? How would your life look differently? How would others know that your problem was gone? How would you act differently?

Scaling: On a scale from 1 to 100, with 100 being the ideal person that you can be, where are you on the scale? What would life look like if you were higher on the scale? What things can you do to get you higher up on the scale? What are you afraid of?

EXERCISES

Transitional Object: Carry a stone in your pocket to represent your inner grown-up. The stone can be of any color that you choose. You may find the stone on a beach, forest, or road. Or you may choose to purchase a stone, like rose quartz or amethyst. Let it remind you of your solid strengths as an authentic adult.

Letter: Write a letter to your inner grown-up asking him what he has to tell you, how you'd like him to be a part of your life. Then, write a reply letter back from your inner grown-up to your present adult self, responding to your thoughts and questions.

Picture: Create a picture of your inner grown-up. You met her in the visualization, now recreate that image, or the feeling of that image on paper. You can use paint, pastels, textures, fabrics, whatever you feel like. (Again, this is not about your talent as an artist. Make it literal or abstract, free flowing. I used to completely freeze up at the thought of drawing or painting. Once I was in a prayer group and our final group together was a painting session. I nearly skipped it because I think of myself as severely artistically challenged. But I went grudgingly—since my inner grown-up told me to go!—and I let myself relax. We listened to music and we let the spirit move us. In fact, we became like children, freely expressing ourselves with paint. I actually loved the experience. This is an example where your inner child—who isn't afraid to draw or paint—can help you reach your inner grown-up.)

Inner Grown-up Survey

(Modified from an Al-Anon Family Group questionnaire, 1984, abridged, as printed in Charles Whitfield, *Healing the Child Within* [1987])

This survey is a tool to help assess where you're getting stuck, what you need to work on, and which of the four pillars will require the most attention for you.

Circle the word that most applies to how you truly feel.

1. Do you seek approval and affirmation?

    Never   Seldom   Occasionally   Often   Usually

2. Do you fail to recognize your accomplishments?

    Never   Seldom   Occasionally   Often   Usually

3. Do you fear criticism?

    Never   Seldom   Occasionally   Often   Usually

4. Do you overextend yourself?

Never   Seldom   Occasionally   Often   Usually

5. Do you have a need for perfection?

Never   Seldom   Occasionally   Often   Usually

6. Are you uneasy when your life is going smoothly? Do you continu- ally anticipate problems?

Never   Seldom   Occasionally   Often   Usually

7. Do you feel more alive in the midst of a crisis?

Never   Seldom   Occasionally   Often   Usually

8. Do you care for others easily yet find it difficult to care for yourself?

Never   Seldom   Occasionally   Often   Usually

9. Do you isolate yourself from other people?

Never   Seldom   Occasionally   Often   Usually

10. Do you respond with anxiety to authority figures?

Never   Seldom   Occasionally   Often   Usually

11. Do you feel that individuals and society in general are taking ad- vantage of you?

Never   Seldom   Occasionally   Often   Usually

12. Do you have trouble with intimate relationships?

Never   Seldom   Occasionally   Often   Usually

13. Do you cling to relationships because you are afraid of being alone?

Never   Seldom   Occasionally   Often   Usually

14. Do you often mistrust your own feelings?

Never   Seldom   Occasionally   Often   Usually

Other questions to consider are:

15. Is it difficult for you to relax and have fun?

    Never   Seldom   Occasionally   Often   Usually

16. Do you find yourself compulsively working, eating, drinking, or seeking excitement?

    Never   Seldom   Occasionally   Often   Usually

17. Have you tried counseling or psychotherapy yet still feel that "something" is wrong or missing?

    Never   Seldom   Occasionally   Often   Usually

18. Do you frequently feel numb, empty, or sad?

    Never   Seldom   Occasionally   Often   Usually

19. Is it hard for you to trust others?

    Never   Seldom   Occasionally   Often   Usually

20. Do you feel a lack of fulfillment in life, both personally and in your work?

    Never   Seldom   Occasionally   Often   Usually

21. Do you have feelings of guilt, inadequacy, or low self-esteem?

    Never   Seldom   Occasionally   Often   Usually

22. Do you find that it is difficult to visit your parents for more than a few minutes or a few hours?

    Never   Seldom   Occasionally   Often   Usually

More questions to ponder:

23. Do you lose your temper?

    Never   Seldom   Occasionally   Often   Usually

24. Do you often make decisions based out of fear?

    Never   Seldom   Occasionally   Often   Usually

25. Do you fear becoming a failure?

    Never   Seldom   Occasionally   Often   Usually

26. Do you believe that other people are responsible for the condition of your life?

    Never   Seldom   Occasionally   Often   Usually

27. Do you have difficulty asking for what you want from others?

    Never   Seldom   Occasionally   Often   Usually

28. Are you afraid of commitments?

    Never   Seldom   Occasionally   Often   Usually

29. When you think about your mortality, are you afraid of dying?

    Never   Seldom   Occasionally   Often   Usually

30. Do you doubt that your life makes a difference in this world?

    Never   Seldom   Occasionally   Often   Usually

If you answered "occasionally," "often," or "usually" to a majority of these questions, then it's time to claim your inner grown-up.

CHAPTER FIVE

Pillar I—To Dream
the Responsible Dream

*The best years of your life are the ones in which you
decide your problems are your own. You don't blame
them on your mother, the ecology or the President.
You realize that you control your own destiny.*

—Albert Ellis (founder of rational emotive therapy)

We were in a session and Jason, a thirteen-year-old boy, told me that he couldn't wait to be a grown-up because then he could do whatever he wanted whenever he wanted. He would be free.

I replied, "Grown-ups can't do whatever they want. They can't leave their jobs, run red lights, kill people. They have responsibilities, obligations to society."

The teenager responded, "Oh, yes, they can do anything as long as they don't get caught. If you're a smart grown-up, you can do whatever you want, whenever you want."

Isn't it ironic that grown-ups remember childhood as a time of unparalleled freedom and yet here was a young man yearning for the independence that he anticipated in adulthood—and seemingly not respecting the limitations to those liberties. I understand his position (sort of)—I couldn't wait for the perks of adulthood either, and, hey, I live in New Hampshire, a state whose motto is "Live free or die." Perhaps this mantra made sense during the American Revolution, which gave birth to the phrase, but do such libertarian sentiments reflect a grown-up perspective now?

Grown-ups have a lot of privileges, of course, but the reality is that these freedoms come with a price tag: *responsibility*. When you act responsibly, you do what's right, what's expected. And you do it because you know it's intrinsically the right thing to do, not because someone (the government, the law, the landlord, your boss) is telling you to do it and watching to make sure that you do. The inner grown-up acts in a responsible manner, accountable to his duties because such behavior is morally correct. Think of your inner grown-up as your own personal Jiminy Cricket, the animated conscience from *Pinocchio*, sitting on your shoulder telling you how to conduct your life.

There are several levels of responsibility that are worth examining. The top level has to do with basic responsibilities in life—with money, the future, time, and the people in your life. The middle level (the core) has to do with responsibility to and for yourself, for the outcome of your own life. And the final, perhaps deepest level has to do with your responsibilities to others beyond the small sphere of your immediate existence. These levels are familiar to the inner grown-up. She can navigate the terrain easily for you—just tap into her resources.

The Basics

I just got them in the mail—credit card access checks. Oh boy! Listen to what I can do: Have immediate access to cash! Start those spring home improvements early! Take that long overdue vacation! Great, but didn't they forget to mention that I would actually have to *pay* for these things eventually with my *own* money, at a high interest rate, of course.

Plastic money . . . monopoly money . . . pretend money . . . buy anything you want . . . don't worry about actually paying for it. Credit cards have played right into our national fantasies of having all the things we want right when we want them. Did you know that the average credit card user has eleven cards?! Did you know that more than 50 million households carry high-interest credit card debt with more and more Americans going bankrupt every year? Did you know that a huge percent-

age of lottery winners are actually plagued by money management problems *after* they win?

When you think about being a responsible grown-up,
money responsibility is pretty high on the list. Skills like paying the bills, paying them on time, paying taxes, saving money
for the future, not spending beyond our means—these are all
things that a grown-up should be doing. And in the end, fulfilling grown-up responsibilities rewards you with a very gratifying soul satisfaction. But how many times after a tough week
at work have you thought that you owed yourself a reward of
a new pair of shoes, a sweater, or some other treat? We should
treat ourselves well, but responsibly well, avoiding later long-
term problems.

A grown-up should also be responsible about life and death
management, like estate planning: having a will, choosing
whether or not to have a living will, appointing a guardian for
the children. Of course, in order to do this, you have to admit
your mortality. Grown-ups can and should face the fact that
they're not going to live forever. Some of us still seem to think
and act as if death is an option.

And a grown-up should be responsible about time management, as well, especially punctuality. When people are chronically late, something is going on unconsciously, something
vaguely resentful. Being late (on a regular basis) is a passive-
aggressive act that is both disrespectful and arrogant. Grown-
ups show up where they are supposed to when they are
supposed to, at the appointed hour.

And finally, a grown-up should fulfill his emotional obligations to his family members—taking care of the kids, visiting or
providing care for elderly parents, staying in touch with the in-
laws. Perhaps especially the children . . . when you sign on to
raise another human being, you need to actually do it, not
pawn that responsibility off onto some stranger. The true and
responsible grown-up is dependable, true to his word, reliable,
and emotionally available.

But most of this you know already. Sometimes you succeed
in being responsible with your money, with your time, with
your family, with your promises, and sometimes you fall a bit

short. All of the above-mentioned aspects of responsibility are important—vital for the true inner grown-up—but I'd like to take us a bit deeper into the topic of responsibility. I'd like us to go beyond the obvious and to settle on the more obscure level of what responsibility for the inner grown-up really means, the deeper core of analysis—that is, *that you, and nobody else but you, are responsible for your life.*

This Is Your Life

Life is made up of your own choices; to a certain extent, you make your own luck. In other words, the most vital and critical aspect of responsibility is truly understanding that one's locus of power is within. That means that *you*—not your parents or your spouse or society—are responsible for the condition of your life. *You* are responsible for your happiness, and *you* have created your life. No matter what tragedies have befallen you, no matter what kind of abusive childhood you survived, that is not license to spend the rest of your life hosting a pity party for yourself. Now I'm not trying to be harsh, but some people do need a kind of metaphorical slap in the face.

Isn't it ironic that we live in a culture of the "self," worshiping self-government, self-actualization, self-discovery, self-improvement, self-aggrandizement, and yet . . . when it comes to the bottom line of who is responsible for your life? Well, certainly not the self! Quick, pass the buck.

We indulge in a popular victim mentality. It is always easier to blame someone else for our circumstances. You did it, not me. But in doing this, we give our power away—to our bosses, our spouses, our parents, our children, our pasts. The very "self" that we are so enamored with becomes diminished.

Benjamin Disraeli said, "We are not creatures of circumstance. We are CREATORS of circumstance." What that means is that we may not be able to control everything that is done to us, but we can, and should, control how we respond to those circumstances. The inner grown-up is intent on claiming and keeping his or her power.

Good-bye, Victim—Hello, Adult

Julie was a fifty-year-old classical singer, aikido instructor, and lecturer about conflict management. About fifteen years ago, Julie attended a lecture on conflict resolution. She was working in real estate at the time and thought she might be able to pick up some useful tips, as her life was conflict ridden. In that lecture Thomas Crum, author of *The Magic of Conflict*, demonstrated some aikido techniques and how the philosophy of working with attack energy could be integrated into other aspects of life. Julie was hooked. Now she practices aikido and lectures on the topic herself.

Julie said, "In aikido, we say that the attack is a gift of energy, and if we see it that way, we can actually use the energy to our advantage." In other words, when a martial arts "attack" comes her way, she takes that energy, uses it, and redirects it in a way that has a positive outcome. Apply this principle to life and you see that your quality of life doesn't depend on what happens to you; it's what you do with it that makes the difference. You cannot change people or situations, only your relationship to them. And when conflict comes, rather than blocking the energy, you take it, change it, and rechannel it.

Imagine seeing the "attacks" in our lives as gifts of energy. Imagine looking for the opportunity in conflict, asking, "What can I learn from this?" This concept is the opposite of victimization and is the essence of the inner grown-up responsibility for the self.

So Julie began to apply these principles to her life. And consequently two primary relationships changed profoundly. She explained:

> I've been married for twenty-five years. There was a time about ten years ago when I was at a crossroads. Up until that time I thought, more or less, that my husband should be the way that I thought he should be. Then one day, it was just like waking up and I thought "Geez, this is a pretty nice guy. Why don't I appreciate where he is instead of trying to put things on him and have expectations that he has not got for himself. I'm just creating conflict here. What do I really want?"

And so I practiced the two principles of curiosity and appreciation. Curiosity about the conflict—what about this should be of interest to me? Instead of trying to get rid of it and resisting it, I invited the energy in by being curious about it. And then appreciating the other people in the conflict and where they're coming from, in this case, my husband. It means I can appreciate where he's coming from and what his good and wonderful qualities are. I don't know, that realization changed my life that day.

Julie took the energy from her husband and responded to it differently. She no longer tried to change him. She found that she wasn't as annoyed by him; instead, she became curious and appreciative—taking "conflict" energy, detaching from it, being curious, and then appreciating what she became aware of. Her husband did not, in fact, change at all, but she changed how she related to him and that's what made the difference.

Julie knows how hard it is to live with and implement this thinking. When she gives a workshop on conflict resolution, she usually starts by saying, "Raise your hand if you think that you can make the other person in the conflict actually change." And usually people are timid and nobody raises their hand. Then she prompts, "Raise your hand if you try anyway."

Every day you have a choice in how you want to respond to others and to the conflicts that arise in your day. Every day you have an opportunity to notice when you're reverting and then make a new choice. Over time the new habit starts to take over. "You know it's a new habit when it becomes as unconscious as the old one," she said.

Just as with the "act as if" technique that we discussed in the last chapter, when you practice a new behavior and keep practicing it, it eventually carves a new pattern into your mind. Repetition and reward has always been a time-honored method for behavioral training. How else do you train a bear to dance? Now I'm not suggesting that we're mere circus animals, of course, merely that we, the human animal, can *train ourselves* to develop new behaviors. Though the desired behaviors may feel awkward at first, over time, with repetition and with the re-wards that they bring, they become natural habits.

Julie also applied her newfound wisdom to her relationship with her mother. Although she didn't have an abusive child-hood, it was still fraught with the normal amount of American dysfunction. Julie said, "I had the usual hang-ups with my mother, mostly that she was kind of a figure not having much power. I learned all my acquiescing behaviors from her." Julie continued:

> It all started when a friend of mine was in a situation where she was having a hard time with her mom and didn't like her mom at all. Another friend of mine knew this friend's mom and really liked her a lot. I just saw the juxtaposition. I had always seen this mom in one friend's eyes and then I saw her in this other friend's eyes. And I thought, "Wow, I bet that happens with my mother. I bet some people really like her."
>
> So I told myself, "My mother has a lot of friends. People seem to like her. What if I were her friend? I'd probably like her; she's a neat lady." So I decided to practice being her friend instead of her daughter for a while. Then I stopped expecting maternal things from her. It changed our relationship. I decided to appreciate what she can give and what *is* rather than living in the disappointments from the past.

Ironically, once Julie no longer expected maternal emotions from her mother, once she relaxed and became her mother's "friend," then her mother actually began to behave in a more maternal manner!

Julie learned how to reframe conflict in her life. She changed her attitude. She decided to see conflict not as a personal per-secution but as an opportunity for growth. She confirms that her quality of life is better, that her life flows more freely, and that, as a result, she turned her life of work into a work of art.

A New Attitude

Claiming the power of your responsibility also means re-framing your perspective in order to stop casting blame.

Blame. Many of us love to blame others for the condition of our lives. It is so tempting, so satisfyingly easy. I once had a sixty-six-year-old woman seek bereavement counseling with me regarding the death of her husband. They had been married for forty-one years . . . a very long time.

When I see someone for bereavement counseling, I try not to make assumptions about how the client is feeling or what the relationship that they are mourning was like. Most people jump to the conclusion that the person is sad,—"Oh, how sorry I am that your husband died; it must be so lonely and sad for you." Well, not necessarily. Many of the people I see are experiencing "complicated" bereavement because they have feelings that make them uncomfortable. They don't know how to process some feelings such as guilt, anger, hatred, and even relief.

When I first saw Myrtl, I knew she was a woman who had held emotions inside for most of her life. She had a strained demeanor, a fierce look in her eyes that reflected repressed anger—lots of it—and resentment. In our first session, she confessed her secret to me, a secret that few people were privy to—her marriage had been a misery for thirty-one out of the forty-one years. A sham.

Why? Because her husband, Harry, had slept with another woman ten years into their idyllic marriage, when they had three children at home and another one on the way. And Harry continued to enjoy his dalliances for the rest of their marriage. Myrtl looked at me with all sincerity and proclaimed, "That man ruined my life."

Here was a woman telling me that her life had been virtually wasted and that it was all because of *him*. Does that sound like the inner grown-up road of taking responsibility for your life? Well, of course, I didn't tell Myrtl that, not right away. I listened; I questioned; I gathered her history; I empathized with her betrayal.

After that first affair, their relationship was tense, fueled by sarcasm, cutting comments, and lingering resentments. Yet she had stayed in the marriage. She had stayed all those years for the children's sake.

"I had four children to raise and no marketable skills. Where was I going to go? What would I have done to support us? I was trapped," she said. "And the children didn't know about their father's infidelity. I wanted to preserve their relationship with him."

But why did she stay with him after the children were grown? Because she was used to her own private hell and wasn't really sure anything else would be better, she told me.

In my work with Myrtl, I tried to help her move away from her position of victim. I tried to help her forgive Harry, not for his sake, but for her own. I tried to help her look at the past in a new light. I'd like to say that we were successful on all fronts, but thirty-one years of thinking does not change with ease.

But what we did accomplish was important. Myrtl never could use the word "forgive" with Harry, but she did cut the tie to his power, and that was a huge step for her. She could accept that he no longer needed to ruin her life anymore. She could admit that she was responsible for her life now and that since he was dead, she might as well get on with things and not blame him for the quality of the life that she had left.

She also, at my urging, began to do volunteer work in her local library. Reading had always brought her pleasure and helped her get beyond herself. She said she had always loved the escape of good fiction. She even began to tutor some children at the library, helping them to learn to love reading. And while she released emotion pent up over the course of thirty-one years, she even came to admit that there were some good times with Harry.

Over the course of several months, Myrtl's entire affect changed. Her eyes no longer fired darts of hatred. She actually smiled in a way that eased the lines of resentment that creased her complexion. She seemed lighter. She laughed out loud as she described her work at the library.

I was proud of Myrtl. She no longer gave him an ounce of power. He may have ruined her past, in her mind, but he couldn't ruin her present. All of her power that she had so freely given away now came flooding back to her. And it seemed to give her youth. When we had our last session together, she looked years younger.

My hope for Myrtl is that she might even release Harry's hold over her past. Perhaps that will come with time, perhaps not. But she did understand that her life was now firmly in her own hands, her responsibility, with no one else to blame.

DARE to Change Your Attitude

Of course, a death does not release everyone into responsibility. Most of us must claim our life responsibility firmly in the presence of those to whom we are most in danger of giving our power away. That's when we must work extra hard to claim our own strength. The DARE technique, when practiced regularly, can help with this ongoing awareness.

Recently my family and I went on a spring ski weekend and my attitude took an abysmal turn down into the gutter. Considering that I hadn't skied in over six years, coupled with the fact that I don't even particularly like the cold, I was pretty much in a problem child state by the time I got to the top of the mountain. I was sore, complaining, frustrated with my awkward heavy boots, and when I fell in some powder and couldn't get up, I just exploded. My problem child came out all over the place as I wailed to my husband, "I can't believe you made me come here! I can't stand skiing and I don't want to be here and this is all your fault."

Uh-oh. Red flag. Bells and whistles went off in my head. Once I heard myself place the blame onto him, I knew I was over the top. Being there may have been his idea, but it was *my* responsibility to agree and to follow through and to be out on the slopes. He didn't make me fall. I, as a grown-up, am responsible for my life.

Fortunately, my husband, being a very patient man, let me rant and rave for a while until I got back up on my skis and came to my senses. Realizing that I needed to claim my inner grown-up, I quickly swung the DARE technique into gear. (My actual children, by the way, had great attitudes!) First, I *detached* from the situation and imagined myself up on the ski lift looking down at this woman screaming like a lunatic. Then I became *aware* of what was happening, that my whining problem child was totally out of control, or in control as the case may be. Then I *reoriented* to the present by recalling that I'm a grown woman and that I do have the resources needed for dealing with this. My inner grown-up surveyed the situation and told myself that I simply had to get down the mountain. I had the skill to do so and I might even have fun in the process. The only other way down the mountain was via ski patrol, which would have been ludicrous. And finally, I *enacted*. I chanted a mantra in my head of "Just do it, just do it," and I skied down that mountain. I didn't stop to think about my sore legs or the cold wind on my face. I did occasionally look up to notice the exquisite beauty and to be thankful for such a gorgeous scene. And after I finally got down, I *evaluated* and realized that when I made the switch, when I claimed my inner grown-up, I felt worlds better. I apologized to my husband for acting like such a baby. And in fact, I actually went back up the mountain again!

So while you may know on every level that attitude is everything, that sneaky, whiny, pouty, intolerant, and impatient problem child will keep coming home to visit. The best that you can hope for is that the visits are short and infrequent.

The Power of Others

In the final analysis, responsibility is related to power. On the slopes, I decided to take back my power. Every day we have that choice. Where is your power? Do you own it or do you give it away to others? Where is the source of your sense of self-worth?

Brian was a forty-two-year-old man who was beginning to claim his power after all these years. He told me that all his life he had felt like a puppet, owned and operated by those around him.

He would look to others to tell him he was doing a good job. He would look to others to tell him he was funny, smart, and an okay person. These are things he didn't believe in or experience internally. And he was devastated by negative comments.

After several months of therapy, he was more inclined to say, "I'm okay no matter whether anyone tells me so or not." He knows that this message needs to come from within. Even though he didn't grow up with this message, his inner grown-up supplies it now. For each of us, this new voice is possible. Listen for it. Believe in it.

Of course, we are all influenced by other people's ideas. It is natural to be shaped and molded by the input of people around us. And of course, we are all sensitive to other people's approval. I'm the first one to respond to praise and compliments. I love them. But do I need praise to feel whole? No. Do I require compliments to validate my existence? No.

Outside approval should be more like an ice-cream sundae. It's great and it's delicious, but it isn't necessary for survival. Other, healthier alternatives exist. Your nutrition for the self, your mental vitamins need to come from within you, not from outside. You are responsible for your self-esteem and your sense of self-worth—others can only contribute to them on a very superficial level.

And likewise, negative input from others (like people telling you that you're not smart enough or attractive enough, like parents telling you all your life that you're inept or stupid or fat) should not still be controlling how you feel about yourself. Cut through the negative interference. Being too dependent on others for defining who you are, either positively or negatively, makes you far too vulnerable—like a child. You are a grown-up now. *You* decide how you want to define yourself. *You* claim responsibility for your self-worth. You don't need to be controlled by other people's opinions, whether good or bad.

Claiming your inner grown-up also means that you do not resort to being a chameleon, that is, changing who you are to fit the expectations of who you are with. You don't need to spend your life acting the parts that other people script for you. If you do that, your very core gets lost in the process. Owning your power means being true to who you are no matter what other people expect.

Learning to claim your power, independent of outside forces, I'll admit, can be a huge challenge. It's a journey, and the journey takes time. If you've spent years sending your power out via express mail, it will be quite an adjustment to learn to hold on to it. But I'm confident that you can learn this if you keep an open and willing heart.

The Power of You

Admittedly it is hard to acknowledge your inner power if you feel essentially rotten to the core. You have to have a healthy sense of self to believe in your power. You have to heal enough to come to see that your core, the center of your being, is beautiful.

Life really is a work of art, and you are the artist of your life. What kind of artist are you? If everything in your life spins out from your relationship with yourself, it's time to own and honor all that you are. I use the "core" collage exercise to help people get in touch with themselves. I ask people to collect words and images from magazines, catalogs, or any other source and glue them onto poster board to create a collage that reflects their essence, the core of who they really are. I instruct, "Go to the center of you and what your life is about. Reflect this creativity in a collage."

I'm intentionally vague about what the "core" is because I want people to interpret this concept in whatever way is meaningful to them. There simply is no right or wrong way to complete this exercise. Even so, many people have some trepidation about completing this task.

A woman in one of my groups looked fairly horrified when I made this assignment for the following week. She muttered about how she's not artistic and she wouldn't have time and on and on. I asked her to just give it a try. To my surprise, the next week she came in with a huge poster board filled on both sides with beautiful words and images. She also was surprised at her willingness to fully engage in the project, especially given her initial resistance. She said, "You know I wasn't crazy about this, but once I got started I just couldn't stop. I couldn't believe it when I ran out of room and had to turn to the other side! It made me feel so good and helped me see that I feel a lot better about myself than I thought I did!"

Often people are initially skeptical, claiming that it sounds simplistic or even stupid. But they persist. And they usually bring back masterpieces. Some people are struck by the beauty of their collages. It can be a very powerful experience to try to capture the core of *you* on paper like this. You may see parts of yourself that you had forgotten about.

Or you might see parts of yourself that have been lying dormant. One woman created a lovely collage of beautiful images— open doors and sunlight and butterflies and rainbows. But she claimed that if people who knew her saw this collage of her core, they would be surprised. Why? Because she wasn't living from that place of beauty. Much of the wholeness, much of her passion reflected on the paper, was not getting translated into her actual living. She was shocked, in fact, to see that so many key aspects of her core were totally inactive in her life. For the moment, that is . . . I told her that it's never too late to live from that place.

Other people struggle with images and realize that they need to work on loving themselves. If more images emerge that reflect damage or distress, then it may be time for healing the core. One woman's collage focused heavily on food, weight, and exercise issues. Her comment was that this was one key aspect of her core that eluded her. She had struggled for years with her weight, with her choices about food and exercise. She said, "If I could get a handle on this area of my life, if I could use food in a way that honors the essence of who I am, which is not what I'm doing now, then I will know that I've grown up."

Now is that time, for her and for all of us. The healing comes with awareness and openness. The power comes with acknowledging that our core is beautiful and honoring it accordingly. It is in our core where our inner grown-up resides, where we make contact, where we connect with all that is possible. Our inner grown-up knows that the core really is glorious. And connection to this vibrant center can fuel a life of meaning and passion. Believe.

Try This . . .

Make your own "core" collage. Use images and words from magazines, catalogs, books, papers that reflect the essence of *you*. Consider your interests, your roles and goals, your history, but also the core of who you are, that is, symbolic representations of your soul. Cut them out and glue them onto poster board. Let your creative impulses dictate how the images should be arranged. Feel free to add to the piece with paint or other design elements. How do you feel about this experience? What does your collage say about you and your life? Are you living from this place?

An alternate extension of the collage, suitable for all but especially for those who truly cannot get the hang of the collage, is to bring in an object that symbolizes their inner core. This, too, can be a way of getting in touch with a deeper level of the self. One woman, for example, brought in a rose, symbolizing her blossoming nature, though not ignoring the occasional thorn. But perhaps my favorite example of this was a woman who simply brought in a sparkling golden cord, a two-foot-long bit of trimming that she had purchased from a fabric store. She quietly told the group, "This says it all. This cord is strong and solid, glittering gold. When I meditate, I envision this cord as my core, right at my center. It empowers and comforts me."

I would also note that reading about these exercises is *not* the same as doing them. There is an awakening that occurs in the process of searching for images, making selections, and creating a visible sign of your interior, of your soul. Until you actually do it, it is hard to understand. So I would invite you to really try them—you have nothing to lose and everything to gain.

Try This . . .
    Find an object that represents or symbolizes your inner core.
What does it say about you? Put it in a place where you can see
it often. Connect with its power.
    I encourage people to keep their collages or their "core" ob-
jects in a place where they are readily seen. I ask people to reflect on them often, to hold the images in their mind's eye when
they meditate, to absorb these hopeful, healing images into
their unconscious. Just looking at these tangible reminders, visual cues, helps encourage empowerment.

Designing Your Own Life

Once you begin to heal, once you recognize your core for
its beauty, then you can claim your power, your responsibility.
Then you recognize that if your life isn't what you want it to be,
you *change* it. No one else is going to do this for you. You are
the designer of your life.

If you're not happy in your work, then change your work. If
you don't like where you live, then move. If you don't have
enough friends, then make a plan for improving your social
network. And if you have friends that drag you down, then
make some new ones.

This may all sound too simplistic, and perhaps it is. I know
that it's not so easy to move or to find a new job or to make
new friends. But I believe in possibilities, not traps. I believe in
making things happen, not complaining incessantly. I believe
that when you take a positive approach to making your life
what you want it to be, when you harness your responsibility,
then miraculous things can happen. It may take awhile, but you
can certainly set the ball into motion. Remember that these
long-term goals can only be met when we make an action plan
of incremental steps toward achieving them. Set your sights.
Take the steps.

Connecting to an energized core helps you know deep down

in your bones that this is possible. You have the power, and the responsibility, to shape the life that you desire.

Understanding your essence—loving and appreciating your core and accepting responsibility for your own life—is a huge step. But you cannot stop there. The last level of responsibility, the deepest level, is to shift your focus from healing and concentrating on the inside to turning toward the world at large. You have many responsibilities to our world, not just to yourself.

Beyond the Self

If your world, in the final analysis, begins and ends with your core (no matter how golden it is) and all that is involved with your small sphere of existence—paying the mortgage, buying the kids spring clothes, planning the vacation, going grocery shopping, landing the next promotion, preparing dinner, worrying about this or that—then your world is narrow indeed.

Beyond your corner of the sky exists a world of others, a world of the hungry and the oppressed and the downtrodden and the frightened, and they need your help. One individual's life is connected to the whole—or as the early-seventeenth-century writer John Donne put it so poetically, "No man is an island, entire of itself; every man is a piece of the continent, a part of the main."

The problem is, we live in an age of entitlement. Many of us feel "entitled" to perks, privileges, to having whatever we want when we want. In fact, we're usually much more concerned with what we are entitled to rather than with what we might actually be responsible for.

Our society is big on rights—the Bill of Rights, patients' rights, the rights of dying people—but where is our Bill of Responsibilities? John F. Kennedy urged us to reflect on our role in the world when he urged us to, "Ask not what your country can do for you—ask what you can do for your country." He turned rights upside down, asking us to look at our obligations.

We have a responsibility to reach out to others and to help those in need. In the eighteenth century, every house had two fire buckets near the front door so if your neighbor's house was burning, you filled your buckets with water and went to help. In the nineteenth century, if your neighbor needed a barn built, there was a neighborhood barn raising and everybody helped.

Obviously the world works differently now, but what have we lost in the process? How many of your neighbors' names do you even know? And beyond your neighbors, beyond your immediate community, how do you touch the lives of people "out there"? How are you making a difference?

Sure, you think, nice concept, but I'm too busy, too overburdened, and I have nothing to give. I'm not responsible for "those" people. (And no single snowflake in an avalanche ever feels responsible for the destruction it has wrought either.)

Simply put: We do have a responsibility to give back because that's how this world improves. Lyndon B. Johnson, another great American president who pushed us to be more responsible, was fond of quoting from the Bible, "To whom much is given, of him shall much be expected." He and his wife, Lady Bird, raised their daughters to consider community service as a regular and expected part of their lives.

Now clearly, on a surface level, it would seem that some of us are "given" more than others. But I'm not just talking about rich people needing to give back. And I'm not just referring to the privileged, the comfortable, the beautiful people. We all, regardless of our socioeconomic status, have been given much. We all have many blessings if we choose to look with fresh eyes—whenever we experience good health, a great night's sleep, the smell of freshly cut grass, the taste of a home-cooked meal, the glow of a rainbow, the sound of children's laughter, the unexpected smile of a stranger. Are not all of these things great blessings?

The gift of being alive on this planet at this time in history is our blessing. And with this blessing comes certain holy obligations. Those in the Jewish tradition are called to perform "mitzvahs," or acts of service. Because we are alive, we are called to our holy obligations.

Good Fortune Obligates

The inner grown-up knows and lives the expression that Albert Schweitzer coined, that "good fortune obligates." We all have good fortune in our lives, despite the apparent circumstances. And we all have something to give, no matter how seemingly small the gift.

On December 28, 1997, the *New York Times* reported on the death of Max Uzewitz, a penniless Polish Jew when he came to America in 1913. In his will, he left $5,000 to his great-granddaughter Nancy Lublin, a twenty-four-year-old New York University law student. With her legacy, Nancy began Dress for Success in the basement of the Greenwich Village Methodist Church.

Dress for Success is a nonprofit organization that helps low-income women make "tailored transitions" into the workforce. That is, each client receives one suit and accessories when she has an interview, and another suit when she lands the job. Potential clients are referred from homeless shelters, domestic violence shelters, job training programs, and ESL (English as a second language) programs. Nancy urged well-dressed New York women to give up some of their business clothing and challenged wealthy companies to donate handbags, shoes, and suits.

Since its inception Dress for Success has thrived and expanded, opening in over fifty cities in America, Canada, and Europe. Furthermore, they have suited over twenty thousand clients. The suits symbolize the organization's faith in every woman's ability to succeed, and indeed their clients have.

Where did Nancy get the idea? She said, "I'd been to interviews; I knew that getting dressed for an interview was a nightmare. And when you think about what it is for women coming from a homeless shelter, or a prison, or coming to this country as the land of opportunity, without any money, that must really be terrible!" Besides, "Poppy Max always said that when life smiled on you, you should share your good fortune."

It's all about spreading the good, sharing the wealth. When you live from a place of abundance and giving, you experience a world of richness. When you live from a place of greed and scarcity, you experience an impoverished world.

The Decline of Personalism

The inner grown-up asks that we move beyond personalism. Personalism refers to that cultural phenomenon of rights over responsibilities, freedoms over commitments. It peaked in the 1970s as a movement of doing what feels good in the personal pursuit of happiness (you know, the "me" decade).

Ironically the focus on self-fulfillment missed a fundamental reality: fulfilling responsibilities to the family, the church, the community, the country, the world, actually does *feel good*. It is the ultimate paradox because in the end anything allegedly "altruistic" feeds the soul and the self and leads to personal gratification and fulfillment, which was the goal of personalism in the first place!

The inner grown-up knows that we are all connected on this earth, now more than ever before by technology, truly making this "a small world after all." The inner grown-up sense of responsibility moves beyond the person, reaching out to the greater world.

Finding Your Way

I know that you're busy and stressed and overwhelmed. Believe me, I know. Okay, it's not always possible to go to Latin America with Habitat for Humanity to build a home for the homeless. Okay, it's not realistic at this time to make your pilgrimage to India to carry on Mother Teresa's work. It's not an option to help the street children in Romania at this time. And money is scarce, so you're not writing out big checks right now.

Maybe, you conclude, you are not so fortunate and therefore cannot give back. Maybe it is a time of great personal challenge. It's true that there are times in our lives when we have seemingly nothing to give. Grievers in acute grief, for example, generally cannot reach out to others. Someone who is desperately ill, or desperately poor, or desperately depleted in some way is probably not too focused on how to give to others.

But there will come a time when these people are in a position to give. There will come a time when the well has a fuller supply from which to draw. And there may be glimmers of giving even in the moments of emptiness—a smile, time, attention, simply a personal presence.

You can find something to do to enrich this world. Don't give in to your many excuses. Check your local newspaper for ideas. Call social service agencies and ask how you can help. Volunteer with your family members. For example, I wanted to involve my children with me to do service both because I wanted them to have the experience and also because I didn't want to take time away from my family while doing volunteer work. So, I decided to take my three children to visit a nursing home once a month. The kids play games with the residents during their activity hour. Not only do the residents love it and I feel good about it, but my children are learning important lessons as well—and they have fun.

I was giving a lecture once about the benefits of outreach, and a gentleman asked me, "What about an elderly person who is at the end of life, who can't get around, What can he do?" An excellent question, I thought. And I responded with the message that I took from the best-selling book *Tuesdays with Morrie*, that there can be meaning in life up until our last breath. We all have something to give, even at the end. Maybe this gentleman could write condolence cards after reading the obituaries. Maybe he could tell stories to preschoolers about what life was like when he was a child. Maybe he could record an oral history on a tape recorder for his descendants.

I don't have all of the answers, but I encourage people to be creative. If you are breathing, you have something to give, somewhere, to someone. Whatever your circumstances, don't underestimate your potential for influence. Anyone with a core as golden as yours has something to share.

The Weight of the World

Of course, the problem with accepting your responsibility to improve this world is that it can be construed as an overwhelming, tremendously burdensome task. In the enchanting 1998 modern Cinderella remake film called *Ever After*, the prince is told by his mother, the queen, and by his future princess, "You were born to privilege and with that comes specific obligations." This prince had spent his life feeling trapped in his gilded cage, oppressed by his rank and title. He felt the burden only of his station in life and failed to see the opportunity that his privilege afforded him.

But then, as his beloved's perceptions influenced him, he came to see new possibilities. He said, "I used to think that if I cared about anything, I would have to care about everything, and I'd go stark-raving mad, but now I found my purpose." His purpose became to create a public university that would offer a good education to all people, regardless of their socioeconomic status.

It is true that if you feel responsible for *everything*, you could feel overwhelmed and powerless. Save the Whales, the Sierra Club, Mothers Against Drunk Driving, Save the Children, Red Cross, UNICEF, United Way, World Wildlife Fund, March of Dimes, World Hunger Relief, American Lung Association, Alzheimer's and cancer and diabetes and head injury groups, and on and on. Where could you possibly draw the line? How can you fix the world?

There is a Jewish story and practice called *tikkun* that illustrates how we don't have to save the whole world or take up every cause to make a large impact. When God created the world, his divine light was stored in sacred vessels. But the vessels couldn't contain the power of the light within them and they shattered, showering divine sparks or fragments on the earth. These divine sparks are also contained within each of us.

The world became chaotic. The responsibility of each Jew is to retrieve the divine shards and restore order to the earth. Fulfilling one's duties, giving, helping others, being truthful and ethical—all of these good works (*tikkun*) help restore order to the divine realm. But more important, *tikkun* is a collective task and no one good deed is done in isolation, for redeeming one person is to redeem the world. One person's responsibility affects the outcome of us all.

My father, an attorney in Texas, recently was on a business trip to Guatemala and had the occasion to visit an orphanage there. He was moved in such a way that he could not remain silent. He reached out with a letter to his clients to raise money for this orphanage, to improve the plight of these precious yet pitifully impoverished children. I said to him, "But what about the orphans in Romania and China and Russia, what about all of them?" He said, "I can only help one child at a time, and that is enough. It's more than were helped before." Yes, it's one life at a time, one more than had been helped before.

Responsibility as Codependence

Another warning about responsibility is that the concept could be construed as a call to take care of everyone else, a kind of codependence (which is an overused word, I know) or an "I have to take care of you" attitude. Codependents gain their identity by having others be dependent upon them. That's how a codependent gains strength—by being responsible for everybody else. That's not the kind of responsibility that an inner grown-up fosters.

You cannot be responsible for someone else's life, for their sobriety, for their health, for their emotional state, for their well-being. I have a client who feels responsible for her brother's suicide. This raises the age-old question from the Bible regarding Cain and Abel, "Am I my brother's keeper?" I believe the answer is yes and no. Yes, you are your brother's keeper to the extent that you need to reach out to your brothers and sisters across the world to improve the condition of this planet, even if just by one little bit. But no, you are not your brother's keeper because you cannot keep your siblings safe, sober, healthy, or even alive. They need to claim their own inner grown-ups on that score.

Responsibility as Self-blame

One last point that I'd like to make about responsibility: Just because you are responsible for your life does not mean that you are responsible for everything in your life. There are those who believe that you, with your infinite power, have created everything in your life, good and bad, that there's no such thing as randomness or other people's free will. I do believe in the mind-body connection, but I don't believe that you can necessarily give yourself cancer, for example. I don't believe that you consciously or unconsciously cause a drunk driver to rear-end your car. You cannot blame yourself for everything. Having an overly inflated sense of responsibility in life can be as damaging as having no sense of responsibility in life.

The truth is that bad things do happen to good people. They just do. And they will happen even if you have the right thoughts, the best positive attitude, the correct calm mind. Perhaps we'll never understand the playing out of life's circumstances. Was it fate? meant to be? God's will? But I'm fairly convinced that being responsible doesn't mean that you can control everything that happens to you or to others. I'm not even sure God controls everything that happens to us.

The root of the word "responsibility" is *respond*. You are responsible only for your response to what life throws your way. You don't necessarily do the throwing. You cannot control the forces of life, but you can control your response. That is your responsibility.

So let your inner grown-up emerge to see your core as something beautiful and sacred and golden. Let your inner grown-up create a life that is responsible and accountable with money, time, life, and death. Dare to let your inner grown-up move you into a life that matters, that reaches out and touches the lives of a few or many. Take your core and spread its influence far and wide. The inner grown-up knows that taking on responsibility, with all its pleasures and challenges, is the route toward true freedom and empowerment.

The Responsibility Pillar in Review

Grown-ups have an obligation, a duty to be responsible with their time, money, actions, and plans for the future. But even deeper than this reality is the the inner grown-up's awareness that each individual is responsible for his own life and happiness. Owning responsibility for the self means that you cannot blame others for your circumstances or your mental, physical, and spiritual health.

Casting off blame has the ultimate effect of liberation. Free and unfettered, you can claim your true power. Owning the core of you helps you establish this authority within your own life.

Being responsible for your own life eventually needs to shift to seeing how you can be responsible to others in need, to our earth, to the world. Like a domino that falls, setting off a chain reaction, your acts of goodness will shift the energy in the universe.

Being responsible, however, means also knowing your limitations. You are not obligated to save each and every soul on the planet. If you feel overly burdened, then the weight will be an albatross. The inner grown-up knows how to find the balance and to walk the line between being responsible and letting go.

READING
"Autobiography in Five Short Chapters"
by Portia Nelson

1. *I walk down the street.*
    There is a deep hole in the sidewalk.
    I fall in.
    I am lost . . . I am hopeless.
        It isn't my fault.
    It takes forever to find a way out.

2. *I walk down the same street.*
    There is a deep hole in the sidewalk.
    I pretend I don't see it.

I fall in again.
I can't believe I am in the same place.
    But, it isn't my fault.
It still takes a long time to get out.

3. *I walk down the same street.*
    There is a deep hole in the sidewalk.
    I see it is there.
    I still fall in . . . it's a habit.
      My eyes are open
      I know where I am.
    It is my *fault.*
    I get out immediately.

4. *I walk down the same street.*
    There is a deep hole in the sidewalk.
    I walk around it.

5. *I walk down another street.*

VISUALIZATION

Begin by getting your body prepared to relax. Stretch your arms high over your head. Then stretch them to your sides, reaching out. Drop your arms, and gently roll your head from side to side. Settle your body into a comfortable position and close your eyes.

Think about the words that you just heard from the reading. What do they make you think of? Did the reading evoke a feeling? Did the reading remind you of any experience from your own life? Take whatever message it is that you need from the reading.

Now bring your attention to your body and where you are in the room. Notice your breath, breathing in and breathing out. Notice the air around you and how it feels on your skin. Listen for any noises that may be near you. Notice any smells in the air. Become *mindful* of your environment and your place in it. Feel the weight of your clothes on your body. Feel the weight of your body on the floor or in your chair. Take three slow, deep breaths. Your consciousness is going on a journey.

Imagine that you are like an onion, covered in layers and layers. We are going to begin peeling the onion, separating one layer off at a time. Take off the first layer, which represents your physical appearance, the outward expression of you—your height and your hair color and your weight and your clothes. These things are not the real you.

Next peel off another layer that represents your job, a job that is perhaps your calling in life or is perhaps just a way to pay the bills. It is not the real you, either.

Next peel off layer after layer representing your roles in life: wife, husband, sister, brother, mother, father, daughter, son, friend, grandchild, grandparent, boss, employee, entrepreneur, board member, client, patient, volunteer . . . all the roles that you assume in your family, in your life. These roles are part of you, but they are not the real you, either.

Keep peeling off aspects of you—your interests, your hobbies, your talents—until you are stripped bare to the core of who you are. What do you see? What do you find there? What does your core look like, feel like? Is there a color? Is it solid or flowing or sparkling? Is it opaque or translucent? Sit with this core for a few minutes and bask in its energy.

Gradually, begin to add the layers back to your core. Bring back the roles, the identities, the qualities that define you in your life. Add back layer upon layer until you are a full onion again.

Bring your attention to the center of your being within these layers and imagine a golden light there, an orb radiating a holy glow. The light begins to expand to fill your body, and as it does, your body begins to feel lighter and more buoyant. You feel so free that you could almost float. You rest for a moment in this feeling of illuminated weightlessness.

Now, when you are ready, start to sense your body in the room. Feel your mind and body getting grounded and integrated. Wiggle your fingers and toes. Take a deep breath. Start to move your arms and legs gently from side to side. Take another deep breath. Allow yourself to feel a vibrant energy coursing through your body, revitalizing you. I'm going to count from one to five, and when you are ready, after the count of five, you may open your eyes. One ... two ... three ... four ... five. You may open your eyes.

JOURNAL QUESTIONS

Core Question: Do you experience the truth that happiness lies within you, independent of people, situations, and circumstances? Expand on this idea.

What is the worst thing about being a grown-up?

What is the best thing about being a grown-up?

Where do you give your power away? Or to whom?

If you had experienced the perfect childhood with perfect love, how would your life be different now? What's holding you back from making your life that way now?

EXERCISES

DARE Thought System: Look often for opportunities to practice this thinking. Be aware of how it can be applied to the responsibility pillar. Identify a regression and then detach, become aware, reorient, and enact/evaluate. Notice this week and fill in:

SITUATION	DETACH	AWARE	REORIENT	ENACT
What happened	Pull back	How I was regressing (inner child)	Remember that things can be different now; I am a grown-up	How I did change or could've changed thoughts/ behaviors
				EVALUATE How did it work?

Credit Review: Obtain a copy of your credit history. Are you proud of it? Does it reflect the person that you are? What can you do to improve future credit history, if necessary? Cut back to one credit card, consolidating all of your debt, and start paying off the debt on this one card.

Make a Will: If you haven't already done this, now is the time. Consult with a lawyer and get your estate in order, no matter how old you are.

Volunteer: Preferably once per month or more. Find someplace, somewhere, something you care about enough to get involved in. Assess your time availability and the needs of the organization. Consider the arts, nature, the needy, community events, and so on. You can always find excuses about not having enough time. But there's enough time to watch TV or chat with friends, right? Consider volunteering with a friend, a buddy, or with family members. You make time for your priorities. Fulfill your duty to society and make volunteering a priority.

CHAPTER SIX

Pillar II—From Here to Maturity

*Look well into thyself; there is a source of strength
which will always spring up if thou wilt always
look there.*

—Marcus Aurelius

It was an ordinary afternoon when Shirley's four-year-old daughter was whining loudly for her mother to come turn on the television. Shirley said, "You know how to do that; you can do it yourself." Then her daughter whined for a drink of water. Then she whined for a blanket.

Shirley's father (who had divorced Shirley's mother years ago) was visiting from out of town and commented on the scene he was observing. "You know that's all about control. It's a control issue. I guess she learned that from you, which, of course, you learned from your mother. You are like your mother in many ways."

Pow. Shirley felt that comment like a ton of bricks. You see, Shirley's mother had abused prescription drugs, had been in and out of psychiatric hospitals, and often had left Shirley abandoned both emotionally and even physically. Shirley's worst nightmare in becoming a mother herself was the fear that she would be like her mother. So for her father to say this was a true slap in the face.

Her reaction was immediate and visceral. Her heart began to race; her face became flushed. She became hysterical and screamed, "I am nothing like my mother," as she ran upstairs crying. Shirley was having a major retriggering problem child moment. First of all she was reacting with shame to her father's perceived "critical" voice. And secondly she was reacting to the fear button that was pushed for her—fear that she would end up becoming like her mother.

Once she got up to the bathroom to compose herself, she splashed water on her face and said to herself, "I don't have to react like this. I can do this differently." Then she applied the four-step DARE technique to withdraw and switch to a better space. She *detached* from the situation to see what had happened. She became *aware* of the fact that he had pushed an emotional button that caused her to react in an immature, regressed, wounded child manner. She *reoriented* to a position of power and strength by summoning her inner grown-up and using affirmations to remind her of her mature energy.

And then she *enacted*: she was ready to go and talk with her dad from a grown-up position. When she came back downstairs, she was able to have an honest conversation with her father about how she had reacted and why. And he, in turn, apologized for his comment and went on to praise her mothering skills. Upon *evaluating*, she said, using the inner grown-up approach left her feeling closer to her father when at one point in time such a scene would have led to several weeks of estrangement.

Learning how to make the switch from problem child to inner grown-up takes mindfulness and practice. It may not be easy, but it is possible to do. No doubt the retriggered wounded child is a simpler role to play, in some ways, because it is so familiar and so comfortable. And it is a natural part of our human emotional makeup to revisit problem child feelings, no matter how grown-up we are.

Mastering the problem inner child is a key component to the inner grown-up and is the heart of maturity.

The Foundation of Fear

During the first session of my inner grown-up support groups, I mentioned that I have each participant write down three problem child qualities that hold them back in life. Then we pass around these index cards in a ritual called the silent witness. The beauty of this exercise is that people realize they are not alone in struggling against their childish demons. What amazes me is that approximately 80 percent of the time, fear tops the list.

Fear is a problem child quality that affects us when we're children and likewise when we're adults. Our fears change, of course, from fear of the dark and monsters, to fear of failure and loss, perhaps. Fear simply is an ongoing reality in our lives. But it doesn't have to control us. We can learn to live with it.

In a charming children's story by Katharine Holabird called *Alexander and the Dragon*, Alexander is afraid of the dark. He comes down to breakfast and tells his family that there is a dragon under his bed and that he can no longer sleep in his room.

"Hmmm," says Alexander's father. "There are only two things you can do with a dragon. You've either got to scare it off or make friends with it."

Alexander goes on to first fight the dragon, but then befriends it. "I made friends with the dragon under my bed and it's not scary at all," Alexander tells his parents that evening. "The good thing is," adds Alexander, "I'm not afraid of shadows anymore and I don't even need a night-light."

Our goal is not to expunge problem child reactions from our lives. That is an exercise in futility. But we can also make friends with our fears, coax them into the light of day, to discover that they are not so overwhelming after all.

When I was a child, if I was afraid, I used to sing these words from the Rodgers and Hammerstein musical *The King and I*: "You may be as brave as you make believe you are."

Amazingly it really did work. This is a perfect example of the "act as if" exercise from chapter 4. Our emotions as well as our behaviors are influenced by our mental outlook. Change the mental outlook and you change the behaviors and then eventually the feelings. Thus, you "make believe you're brave" and start acting as if you really are brave, and eventually you come to feel brave. Many of the inner grown-up techniques are essentially about changing negative self-talk.

Courage Is for Cowards

Courage is acting *in spite of* fear, not with the absence of fear. If we wait for the fear to disappear, we may possibly be waiting around forever. The trick is to forge ahead, even *with* the fear.

Bill Cuff, Ph.D., a professor in New Hampshire, conducted his doctoral dissertation research on courage. He interviewed people from a variety of categories looking for themes of courage in facing adversity. His findings confirm that courageous people live with lots of fear, they just choose to act despite that fear.

Dr. Cuff identified a three-stage model that was consistent across the board. Stage 1: anticipation; stage 2: immersion; stage 3: resolution. He writes, "The first stage is characterized by a strong sense of anxiety or fear around the impending decision to act. Part of this stage is the willingness to acknowledge and tolerate these feelings rather than avoid and deny them. This process seems to involve accepting a feeling of vulnerability which accompanies a loss of safety and moving through it."

Stage 2 (immersion) is jumping into the situation despite the fear. And stage 3 (resolution) is a feeling of pride and strength for having taken the risk. Facing the fear is part of what makes the courageous act so courageous. The inner grown-up knows how to do this.

The Courage Within

Buddhist teachings comment on *bodhicitta*, which means "awakened heart" or "courageous heart." The Buddha claimed that everyone has *bodhicitta*—it's inside us, even if we're not connected with it. Traditionally, *bodhicitta* is compared to a diamond that's been buried in mud for thousands of years. At any point, you can slog through the mud and uncover it, discovering a perfectly beautiful jewel within. Everybody has this courageous heart, but not everyone has the courage to do the work to claim it.

One of the ways Buddhists work to claim their courageous heart is by a meditation technique called *tonglen*. When I first read about *tonglen* in an incredible book called *Awakening Loving-Kindness* by Pema Chodron, I was amazed. I had often heard or read about the kind of technique where you breathe in goodness and light and positive energy, and you breathe out the stress and the negativity and the badness. That had always made sense to me. But *tonglen* asks you to do quite the opposite. You breathe in pain and misery and suffering and fear, and you breathe out joy and well-being and goodness. In Chodron's words:

> The essence of tonglen practice is that on the in-breath you are willing to feel pain: you're willing to acknowledge the suffering of the world. From this day onward, you're going to cultivate your bravery and willingness to feel that part of the human condition. You breathe in so that you can really understand what the Buddha meant when he said that the first noble truth is that life is suffering. What does that mean? With every in-breath, you try to find out by acknowledging the truth of suffering, not as a mistake you made, not as a punishment, but as part of the human condition. With every in-breath, you explore the discomfort of the human condition, which can be acknowledged and celebrated and not run away from. Tonglen puts it right on the line.

In other words, you willingly breathe in the pain and suffering of the world. Then, on the out-breath, you breathe out joy and pleasure and feelings of goodness and peace. We often wish that life could be only the out-breath experiences, but, of course, life is both realities.

In the *tonglen* practice, you cultivate a courageous heart by keeping it open to inevitable suffering. And you cultivate a loving heart by blowing the gifts of joy and delight back out into the universe. What an interesting concept, really. It asks you to accept that suffering and pain exist, that fear and problem child qualities and dark baggage from the past exist, will always exist . . . but then it asks you to also accept that there is goodness and strength and joy, and that these are possible to have as well. And that not only are they attainable, but that they should be shared with others and thus multiplied. A Native American saying echoes this: "Sorrow shared is halved. Joy shared is doubled."

The inner grown-up is reflected in the practice of *tonglen*. It is rooted in the transcendent possibilities of the out-breath, but it does not deny the realities of the in-breath. The inner grown-up chooses courage in the face of fear.

But I Don't Want to Do It

But I don't want to breathe in pain—that sounds terrible. And I don't want to be brave even when I'm afraid—it's too hard. And I don't want to make the bed or clean the kitchen—I'm too tired. Let's face it, sometimes it's just plain easier to be an immature kid. I am working with a twenty-seven-year-old young man who was raised by a mother who believed in pampering her sons. She always did their laundry, made their beds, cooked their food, and picked up after them. John never lifted a finger, never had a chore to do, but also never experienced a sense of personal power in contributing to the household or of taking care of himself. Thus he became a highly dependent person.

John grew up to marry a modern woman, a woman of a different generation who had no intention of running a household on her own while also working full-time. John consciously knows that he should help out, share household chores . . . but John says that he's lazy. He'd much rather come home from work and crash on the couch for some relaxation while his wife serves him—who wouldn't? He knows he's not living in the 1950s, but he can't seem to break the chain of sloth. His barely unconscious mantra to himself is "But I don't want to do it."

Sure, it's so much easier to have his wife do stuff—even if she's yelling at him and griping and complaining but ends up doing it anyway because John just won't help. The problem is that John is weakening his marriage by holding on to his immature, lazy attitude. The mature inner grown-up knows that there are consequences to action and inaction. Who knows how long his wife will continue to enable him? Perhaps her threshold of tolerance will soon be reached.

His attitude is not unlike that of my children, who on occasion whine to me, "But I don't *want* to do my homework," or "I don't *want* to practice the piano," or "I don't *want* to brush my teeth." And I answer with sanctimonious maternal maturity, "There will be plenty of things in life that you won't want to do, but you just have to do them anyway. That's what grown-ups do."

Likewise, John has a lot of things in his life that he'd rather not do, but his inner grown-up knows that he needs to act. What I'm trying to teach John, and also my children, is that it honestly doesn't matter whether you want to help out or not— you just should. Sure, you have choices, but the mature choice is to do this, whether you *feel* like it or not.

Maturity—the art of being fully developed as a human being—is about finding your strength, pushing through the resistance, transcending yourself, and doing what you have to do (whether you want to or not) because it simply has to be done. Of course, for that to happen, you sometimes have to bend your emotions to the will of reason.

The Will of Reason

We live in a society that practically worships the free expression of emotion. And emotions are wonderful; they're marvelous. They lift us to great heights. They drop us to deep lows. Life would be very dull without them, right? True, but I would argue that emotions can be crippling. And though it may seem controversial for a therapist who freely encourages emotion in her office (I have a tissue box beside every chair) to criticize feelings, I'd say that I equally encourage reason with and even *over* emotion, when appropriate.

Contrary to popular opinion, it is the indulgence of emotions that accounts for much unhappiness in our society. Emotions blind our logic. Emotions can twist our common sense into un-recognizable shapes. And it's usually irrational emotions that keep us stuck in the problem inner child state.

Emotion tells me that I was hurt in my childhood and now I have low self-esteem. Reason helps me shake off the past and claim my current power. Emotion tells me to have an affair. Reason keeps me committed to my marriage. Emotion tells me to harm another out of anger. Reason prevents me from acting impulsively. Emotion causes me to buy the dress even though I cannot afford it. Reason reminds me of my budget. When you are ruled by your emotions, like a pinball you bounce from one feeling to the next. Reason keeps you grounded. Reason, one might be so bold to speculate, makes civilization possible.

I'm not saying that emotions should be squelched, sup-pressed, repressed or even banned . . . simply that they should not be allowed to run rampant. Just as a child needs bounda-ries and limits, our own emotional lives need containment at times. Reason helps you respond rationally rather than react impulsively. The inner grown-up knows how to take command of out-of-control emotions with a healthy dose of thought management.

Thoughts, like our bodies, can easily get out of shape. Think of the inner grown-up as implementing a regime of thought "aerobics." Highly toned thoughts focus on what is possible, on what needs to be done, on harnessing power not poison. If you work on it, you can let go of weak thoughts (thoughts that tell you you're no good, thoughts that remind you about what you don't have) and strengthen them with strong thoughts (thoughts that tell you you're wonderful, thoughts that focus on what you do have).

That's essentially what the four-step DARE system (Detach, Aware, Reorient, Enact/Evaluate) is about, identifying problem-atic thinking and behaving and substituting more acceptable and healthier thoughts and behaviors (fueled by the inner grown-up). It's about imposing free rational will over irrational feelings that threaten to take control. It's about jolting yourself into the present and diffusing the power of the past. Again, this kind of inner thought training takes time to implement, but it leads to a mature ability to have reason prevail over emotion when necessary.

Roadblocks to Maturity

There's one problem with all of this emphasis on thinking and reason and thought control and self-talk—you can feel something in your head but not in your heart. You can sustain that for a while perhaps, but not indefinitely. As I mentioned with singing technique, you can control the vocal cords with the mind, but you have to have the support from below, the sustaining breath from the diaphragm. Similarly, you need to eventually absorb into your being the messages that move south from the head to the heart to the gut. That's when a belief becomes truly integrated, unconsciously embedded.

A woman in one of my support groups told me that when she was a child and she asked her mother, "What is a grown-up?" her mother replied, "It's just people who 'act,' that's all, just people who are 'acting' grown-up." I replied, "Acting may be the first step, but it can't end there. Eventually, the reality of being a grown-up needs to move farther, from the head to the heart."

The "act as if" technique, my singing the song from *The King and I* to "make believe you're brave, and the trick will take you far"—these things work because you begin by acting, but then something else happens. Over time you integrate the act. It moves to a deeper level, and suddenly the thing that you are pretending is no longer an act. It becomes reality. Remember: Your inner grown-up is already there inside of you, fully formed—you just need to connect with it. And your inner grown-up is not a fraud. Your inner grown-up helps you to feel authentic by absorbing the "act" from the head into the heart and soul.

Of course, the "act" doesn't always move south, not for everyone. Some people can't seem to absorb and integrate and own what they pretend. I think one of the chief interfering obstacles for preventing something from moving into the heart is that the heart is preoccupied with something else—with blame and guilt and self-denial. And that's where forgiveness comes into the picture. You need to forgive in order to clear a space in the heart for absorbing new growth and opportunities.

The Journey to Forgive

Beginning the journey of forgiveness, and working hard to make the journey progress, is an important foundation point for the maturity pillar. Forgiveness probably will not come in a moment of epiphany. More likely it is a process that develops over time. And for many of us, forgiveness is a daily choice. Forgiveness does not mean condoning any abusive or cruel behavior. But it does mean letting go of your attachment to the events of the past.

Every so often you read in magazines stories about amazing forgiveness: the mother who forgives the man who murdered her daughter, the man who forgives the drunk driver who made him a quadriplegic. And you read these stories and think perhaps, "Are these people crazy? Or are they saints? Are they for real?"

Yes, they are for real. Holding on to hatred, obsessing about revenge strategies, keeps you tormented and stunted. People who forgive already know on some deep level that holding on to resentment and grudges is like clutching a hot coal. Your intention is to hurl this burning block at the object of your wrath, but you only end up searing your own hand. When you don't forgive, you invite toxic energy into your life.

An extremely helpful book for anyone working on the issue of forgiveness is Robin Casarjian's *Forgiveness: A Bold Choice for a Peaceful Heart*. Her subtitle alone highlights why forgiveness is so important—it leads to a peaceful heart. Forgiving another frees the spirit and expands the soul. Forgiveness is not for the other person, forgiveness is for you, for *your* peace of mind. And as Casarjian points out in her book, forgiveness is a decision; forgiveness is an attitude; forgiveness is a way of life.

A Personal Odyssey

I was working with a client, fifty-year-old Felicia, who told me that she had a dream in which her mother (who had been dead for twenty years) asked for her forgiveness. Felicia's mother had been a difficult woman—always critical of and verbally cruel to Felicia. Managing the problem inner child who had been so influenced by this mother was one of our focal points in therapy.

I asked Felicia what she thought of the dream. "Oh," she replied. "No way am I going to forgive my mother. I'm not going to let her off the hook. She can rot in hell for all I care." I replied, "Maybe forgiving your mother would let *you* off the hook."

After that, our work together took a turn. Although initially resistant, Felicia was soon open to the idea that forgiving her mother was not for her mother's sake, it was for her sake. Forgiving her mother would unburden her own heart, would unlock the chain that bound her in problematic ways to a past that held her tightly in its grip.

So Felicia agreed to be open to the process of forgiving her mother. She was skeptical but open. I first asked Felicia to write a list of all the ways that her mother had hurt her through the years. Then I asked her to write a list of all the ways that her mother had been a positive force in Felicia's life. (You can imagine which list was shorter!) All the while we were discussing Felicia's mother and the kind of upbringing that had made this woman the cruel and critical mother that she had become. In seeing the malevolent forces that shaped her mother (i.e., an abusive and alcoholic mother of her own), Felicia began to broaden her perspective just a bit and come to understand how her mother had internalized the negative influences of her own upbringing.

Then I had Felicia write an open letter to her mother describing her feelings, pouring out her heart and soul, and trying to move in the direction of forgiveness. It took her several weeks to actually complete this letter, but once she did, she came into her next session and reported, "Well, I'm getting there. I haven't totally *forgiven* her yet, but I think I am *forgiving* her. And I am feeling a bit lighter." I asked her to write to her mother again, staying with the theme of forgiveness.

For Felicia the process lasted several more months before she finally got to a place where she said, "Yes, I have forgiven my mother and I do hope that she is released from purgatory, or wherever she is stuck. I want her to be free because now I am, too." What incredible growth. And what a privilege for me to see it happen. Felicia could respond from a generous heart now, one that wanted freedom not only for herself, but also for her mother.

And furthermore, after forgiving her mother, she noticed that her problem inner child wasn't misbehaving as much. Now, if she received a slightly negative or critical comment from a colleague or friend, she no longer spiraled into despair. She didn't see herself as the child being persecuted by the parent. She could respond as a grown-up and not feel that her core was being violated. Forgiving her mother freed her on many levels.

Forgiving Your Parents

One of the hallmarks of maturity is being able to forgive your parents. Perhaps they did nothing more than demonstrate their flawed humanity—they didn't express their love enough or in the right ways; they didn't attend your third-grade recital; they never came to a single one of your baseball games; they weren't home when you returned from school. Or maybe they got divorced, drank too much, hit you with a belt, or worse. The list of grievances can be large or small, but each list is relative. No one had perfect parents. Accepting them for who they were, with all of their own limitations and frailties, knowing that they did the best job they could at the time given their circumstances—that is what forgiveness is about.

Marsha was a forty-eight-year-old woman whose father sexually abused her from the time she was eight until she was twelve. Marsha worked with me in individual therapy for about a year on issues of loss and forgiveness. In that time, she struggled to understand her own wounds. She struggled to forgive her father, whom she still sees semiregularly. And she struggled with letting her own children come to know their grandfather in a limited way. And while she made tremendous progress emotionally, she still felt a certain weight around her neck when it came to forgiveness. She struggled with forgiving someone for something that is essentially unforgivable.

When Marsha heard about the Claim Your Inner Grown-up group, she signed up hoping to work on more personal growth. When I asked her to write a letter to whomever it was she needed to forgive (and, of course, she chose her father), acknowledging all of her ambivalence in the process (knowing that she would not actually mail the letter), and then to write a "reply" letter from him to her (written by her own hand), she was able to reach another level of letting go. She commented to me, "Something shifted. What appealed to me most about writing these letters was the belief that there was a certain peace that could be achieved, *for me*. It wasn't just that he deserved to be forgiven or that I don't deserve to be mad at him because I do, but that there could be a forward leap to that idea of peace, for me. And the writing and the expressing . . . well, the peace did begin to happen."

Forgiveness happens in degrees. It is a process. What Marsha's father did was unacceptable, no matter what his own background was that led him to that place. There are no excuses for behavior that will always be considered unacceptable. But Marsha didn't have to burn herself with the coal anymore. She could just let it go. The attachment was released and consequently she, too, was released.

One aspect of this for her was that through the letters, she came to realize that her father was more than just a weak and injured man who did despicable things. He was also the man who took her out for ice cream, who held her hand when she was sick, who made her laugh when they watched sports together.

In the end, no one is all good or all bad. Reality exists in shades of gray, especially in the world of the inner grown-up. Very few things are, in fact, all black or all white. Most people are a mixture, a melding of many wonderful and not so wonderful qualities. The inner grown-up looks for and honors the gray in life. Marsha acknowledged more of the gray in her father, and it helped to make forgiveness possible.

It's critical to realize that you can do forgiveness work whether the person you need to forgive is alive or dead. And even if they are alive, a cathartic "meeting" does not need to happen. The entire process can be done internally, intrapsychically. Remember the process is not for the benefit of the other person; it's for your own benefit.

Try This . . .

Write a letter to whomever it is that you need to forgive (whether they are alive or dead—you will not mail these letters). Begin by discussing your feelings toward them; list how they have wronged you; what they have, in fact, given you; and if possible, write in the direction of forgiving them. How does this make you feel?

Write a response letter from that person to you as well. You are, in fact, writing the letter from them to you. But try to really imagine what they might say to you. Feel their reply. Get out of your own way and let their words flow through your fingers and onto the paper. See what comes up. How does this make you feel?

Forgiving Yourself

Once you've forgiven your parents for all that they did and didn't do, it's time to look around. Is there someone else? A sister, a brother, a child, a friend? How about you? Do you need to forgive yourself for something you did or didn't do?

Sandra began attending a grief support group at her local

church after her seventy-eight-year-old mother died. Sandra
grieved the loss of her mother with relative ease. They had always had a good relationship. She missed her mother terribly,
but she was comforted by the fact that her mother had lived a
good, long life. Therefore, what came up for Sandra during the
sessions was unexpected. She heard another woman mourning
for the loss of her son. And as Sandra listened to this woman's
poignant grief, her own pent-up tears began to fall.

Sandra had also lost a son, two sons in fact, but not to death.
Sandra had lost her sons twenty years before to a messy divorce, and they had only now, just months before, reentered
her life.

Sandra had stayed in a physically and emotionally abusive
marriage because of her sons. She had endured years of snide
remarks and insults and sporadic violence, even in her sons'
presence. Her husband at the time was so forceful in his hatred
of women in general and her in particular that he was beginning to brainwash his two sons into siding with his opinions.
Sandra felt scared and alone. She also felt weak and knew that
he would eventually kill her, even as he had already killed her
spirit . . . almost.

Through the help of supportive friends and a guiding therapist, Sandra planned her "escape" and eventually moved out
of the house, taking her possessions and leaving good-bye notes
for her sons. The courts branded her a mother who abandoned her children and awarded custody to their father. After
that, there were years of struggle, years of reaching out to her
sons and having them slam the door in her face, years of
rejected phone calls. But she never for one minute stopped loving them.

She tracked where they went to college, had friends of hers
gather information concerning their whereabouts. She continued to write letters and make phone calls, but they were always
vehemently rejected and ignored. At times she would lose track
of her sons and not even know whether they were alive or
dead. She shuddered to think what their father must have said
to build a wall around them so great that neither time nor distance could scale its heights.

When Sandra came to see me, these boys had both, seren-dipitously, reentered her life. Though they each lived far away, finally the great wall seemed to be coming down. For her, it was a miracle. How do you bridge the gap over twenty years of silence?

My first assumption was that she would be working on for-giving them, forgiving them for rejecting and abandoning her. But when I asked her about that, she commented, "Oh, no, it's not them that I need to forgive; it's *me* that I need to forgive."

She still needed to process the fact that she had left them all those many years ago. She needed to come to a place of peace and accept that she had done everything she could to reestablish contact with them through the years. She needed to understand that the past had played itself out the way that it needed to.

Several things happened to help her with this process. As she told me her story, as she reviewed the past, she was moti-vated to go through some old boxes and found her diary from those trying years. Through reading the lamentations of the desperate woman she was at that time, she began to have more compassion for the difficult situation she had been in. At that point, I asked her to write a letter from her current self to her self of twenty years ago. And the second piece to that was hav-ing her self-of-the-past write to her self-of-the-present.

Sandra found this exercise remarkably freeing. Somehow it allowed her to view herself with more kindness and com-passion. She saw that while she did have a choice, she did what she felt had to be done at the time to save her very life. She had no idea that the boys would turn on her afterward. But even then, she understood the pain that motivated their behaviors.

In a short time, Sandra was able to forgive herself and move on. Since then she has visited both of her boys in their respec-tive homes, has hashed out with them feelings held for more than twenty years, has made her apologies (as have they to her), and she is now setting about the business of having a re-lationship with them from this moment on.

Try This . . .
If you need to forgive yourself for some transgression, then write a letter to yourself about it. Write about your guilt, how you failed. Write to that self of the past who made a mistake. Have your past self write back to your current self, as well. See what there is to learn.

Fuel for the Future

Perhaps it's not a specific event that needs to be revisited; perhaps it is just the way you were—and sometimes still are—that brings a sting of remorse to your eyes. Maybe you have a history of a bad temper, or a past of drinking too much, or a record of being terribly self-centered, or maybe you never made your peace with someone because you were always so angry and blaming and resentful, but you're working on that.

So you can continue to berate yourself for all that you did or didn't do, but self-flagellation seems to serve little purpose. Or you can say, "Yes, I was that way; I did and said those things, and I'm not too proud of them. But I can use that as my inspiration to make things different. I can 'dare' to change. I can make sure that I don't treat people like that anymore. I can use that as fuel to change my future."

Carol is struggling with these concerns now. She spent years blaming her father for her life. She gave her power away to him and wasted many years because she behaved so caustically toward him. Meanwhile he recently died unexpectedly, and she is filled with guilt and regret. While she needs to process those feelings, she also needs to remember her mistakes to ensure that she doesn't fall into the same trap again. If she just ends up treating her friends, her husband, in the same manner, then she learned nothing from her mistakes with her father. The experience will have served no purpose. Or she can use what happened as insurance that things will be different.

I grew up in Texas and a familiar expression is "Remember

the Alamo." I didn't actually know what that meant for years until I got a bit older and realized that the Texans *lost* the battle of the Alamo to the Mexican army. But they use that loss as a motivator. "Remember the Alamo" means remember and work together for success so that next time we will win.

Carol now has a choice of how to interpret her previously childish behavior with her dad. She can make herself miserable with it, or she can forgive herself and resolve to do better next time. She can resolve for change to occur as an honor to her father's memory.

Each of us always has a choice in how we want to interpret information. We can choose to berate or forgive ourselves. Each of us is worthy of forgiveness because, I believe, at the core, we are essentially good. Think back to the core collage exercise in chapter 5. At the core, at your center, in your soul, you are good and golden. You may make mistakes and do awful things, but you are worthy of forgiveness, just as others are. Be gentle with yourself.

The Wisdom Within

When you forgive yourself and others, when you let go of suffocating resentment, you move into an expanded space. You recover and perhaps even enlarge your spirit. When forgiveness becomes a part of who you are, you are freed emotionally. Then you are able to get a new perspective, are able to tap into a vast storehouse of mature inner resources. The inner grown-up is wise beyond your wildest dreams, but you cannot unlock the door to this wisdom if your heart is preoccupied with emotional turmoil.

Jean Houston is a sparkling leader in the field of human potential. She is known for her many inspirational books, lectures, and workshops that help people access what is possible. In essence, I believe, she helps people get in touch with their inner grown-ups.

In a mental health professional magazine, I was recently

reading an article about Houston and her work. She tells a story that is aligned with inner grown-up wisdom:

One day, when she was 8, she went with her father to deliver a script to the famous ventriloquist Edgar Bergen. As they entered the door of his hotel room, Bergen was immersed in a serious philosophical dialogue with his dummy, Charlie McCarthy, who, to make the scene even more peculiar, was clearly the instructor.

When Bergen realized that Houston and her father were in the room, he looked up a little sheepishly and explained that the conversation was not a rehearsal for their act, but a discussion with Charlie, the wisest person he knew. "When he answers me, I have no idea where it's coming from or what he's going to say next," said Bergen. "It is so much more than I know."

Hearing Bergen's explanation of the conversation with Charlie as an exchange with another source of wisdom within him made a deep impression on Houston. "At that moment," she recalls, "my skin turned to gooseflesh, an electric hand seemed to touch mine. I suddenly knew that we all contain so much more than we think we do. The image came to me of a house with many floors, and I saw that in ordinary awareness we live on a shelf in the attic of ourselves, leaving the other floors relatively uninhabited and the basement locked."

I just love this example of inner wisdom. Edgar Bergen was impressed by Charlie's wisdom; but Bergen *was* Charlie McCarthy. And yet he was attributing Charlie's wisdom to some unknown, outside source. I would propose that it was his inner grown-up that was fueling Charlie. The inner grown-up is connected to wisdom that is beyond us and yet within us. You must listen quietly to hear its voice. But if a puppet will help you hear the sage perspective within, then by all means get a puppet!

Aging Gracefully

While the inner grown-up can supply us with wisdom at any age, wisdom often is associated in many cultures with aging. Our elders are supposed to be wise, having gained a perspective that only living over a long period of time can provide. So why do we spend vast amounts of money and resources trying to reverse or at least delay the inevitable aging process? Why are wrinkles acknowledged with horror rather than reverence? Why do men and women lie about their ages, lopping off decades if they can get away with it?

The inner grown-up is not afraid of aging or of approaching the twilight years. The inner grown-up mature perspective *embraces* aging for its unique delights, certain challenges, and enhanced perspectives. You might think of the mature inner grown-up as a partial inner crone, an inner elder who is content to mine the riches of each and every particular stage of life.

I once read about a group of women in California who call themselves the Red Hat Society, a club whose membership begins at age fifty. These women dress in red hats and purple dresses (inspired by a poem called "When I Am an Old Woman" by Jenny Joseph), go out to tea, and revel in their graceful aging. The point of the group is to make the most of where they are in life, to celebrate the joy and wisdom of growing older.

Aging certainly brings about real issues of sickness and limitations and mortality, but the inner grown-up looks at aging realistically, seeing the process as a natural friend and not as the enemy. Seen in this light, aging is a unique passage of precious proportions, a gold mine of potential perspective that is usually unavailable to the young.

Try This . . .

Develop a ritual to celebrate your aging. You can do this by yourself, or with others of a similar age. Think about ways to honor the aging process and rejoice in the graceful passage of time. Come to see the signs of aging as a symbol of a life well lived.

Finding Meaning in the Past

When you are in touch with your inner wisdom, when you see life from a bigger perspective, you have the opportunity to get a new handle on the past. You can take on the mature perspective of "What does this situation have to teach me?" "What can I learn from this?" "How does this piece fit into the overall puzzle of my life?" "Where is it leading me that I otherwise wouldn't have gone?"

Essentially, the past does have the power to influence the present, but also the present can ebb backward to affect the past. When you put a new spin on the past, cast it in a new light, see it from a wiser perspective, you actually alter its potency.

For me, this was perhaps most evident with my parents' divorce when I was twelve years old. Of course, I was in the generation where seemingly everyone's parents were divorcing. But being part of a statistical trend did not make it any easier.

When my parents divorced, my world was irrevocably shattered without my consent. Nothing was the same. I changed schools. We moved to a smaller house. My weekends were now filled with "visitation" privileges. And I didn't take well to the unwanted changes in my life. I was a preteen and I was angry (never mind that I might have been angry anyway by virtue of being a preteen).

It took me years to work through the anger and resentment that I felt first toward my father, then later my mother. It wasn't an easy adolescence in many ways. And my anger continued sporadically well into my young adulthood, even twisting its way into my life in the form of an eating disorder.

But many years later, as I went through my own process of forgiveness, I learned to *reinterpret* my past. I could see that the divorce served some useful functions in my life, after all. The usual research indicates that children of divorce are prone to a similar fate. But in *Innocent Victims*, Thomas Whiteman draws on his clinical experience to identify four key ways that children with divorced parents have an edge over children from two-parent homes: (1) children of divorce are often more sensitive to other kids and their problems; (2) children of divorce tend to be more mature and responsible than their peers; (3) children of divorce are often better able to put life's experiences into perspective; and (4) children of divorce tend to be motivated to succeed in marriage.

Based on those criteria, you can easily trace how it came to be that I'm a grief counselor and psychotherapist. No wonder I'm now writing about the topic of my inner grown-up and am devoted to my marriage—it's all because of my parents' divorce! The formative loss occurring during an impressionable time developmentally may, in fact, have molded me into the kind of person that I have become. And for this, I can say that I am grateful. I wasn't always able to say that.

Can you reinterpret your past? Can you see how it led you down a road that you otherwise might not have traveled? The question then is not "Was my past pleasant?" but rather "Can I see meaning in that part of my life?" And if not, if it hasn't led you to a better place, can you change the navigation to get you on a better path? Are you willing to search for the meaning now? It is never too late to reroute the course.

Recasting the Past

Carly was a thirty-five-year-old woman who came to me for individual therapy because she wasn't experiencing deep joy in her life. She suspected that this was largely because she had never deeply grieved the loss of her mother, who died when Carly was only five years old. She had never been encouraged to grieve as a child. Children are often shielded by well-meaning adults who don't understand the importance of feeling sorrow and loss.

But Carly lost more than her mother. In essence she lost her father, too, since he became consumed by his own grief and withdrew emotionally from his children. Carly recalls feeling protective toward her father, knowing how fragile and limited he was emotionally. Compassionate as she may have been, the bottom line is that her needs went unmet.

When I asked Carly to bring in an object representing her inner child, she brought a prayer card from her mother's funeral. In fact, her mother's death had become the defining event in her life, an excuse for everything about the past and the present. Carly reasoned that she didn't really know how to love because she never knew a mother's love; she couldn't really be a good mother herself because she had never learned mothering. After all, she lost her mother when she was five . . . shouldn't that explain everything?

In my work with Carly, I tried to help her see that her mother's death may have been a momentous event, no doubt, and that it certainly has and will continue to affect her forever; however, it does not have to be *the* explanation for Carly's life. Carly's life is now Carly's life. The time came to dethrone the wounded five-year-old whose pain and devastation had controlled Carly's life for the past thirty years. Now was the time for Carly to claim responsibility for her present and her future from a position of personal power.

I felt that Carly's work didn't need to focus on nurturing, or even disciplining, that abandoned five-year-old wounded inner child. She had actually had way too much attention and control over the past three decades. Instead, I felt that Carly's work needed to essentially focus on her inner grown-up. I asked her first to begin to view herself as more than just a woman whose mother died when she was five. Clearly there is more to Carly—her identity and her life—than just this fact. I asked her to notice and list the ways in which she is, in fact, a wonderful mother. I wanted her to claim some of her strengths and dynamic energies.

And I also, later, asked her to shift her focus away from herself, to transcend herself by giving "love" gifts to her husband and her children. Not only did they notice her altered behavior; they loved it! They felt inspired to reciprocate the love in an intentional way. The whole dynamic of the family switched from tension to supportive love.

Over the course of several months of struggling with these issues, Carly did begin to loosen her grasp on her victim status. She described feeling less vulnerable, less wounded, more loving, and more joyful. Certainly Carly will always carry a sad legacy with her and will be influenced forever by her early profound loss, but she is now more in touch with her own power and obligation to shape her life.

And furthermore, Carly is starting to understand that who she is now, including the wonderful loving qualities that make her unique, such as her compassion and her strength and her sensitivity, exist *because* of her mother's death. So her early experiences were the mold that made her who she is today and that includes the positive characteristics as well.

If you can see your childhood experiences as being responsible for more than just damage, then you can revise your relationship to your past. Pain from the past actually paves the way for strengths of the future. You have to broaden your perspective to see how the pieces of the puzzle fit together. By making that connection from the present to the past, you can actually paint a whitewash over past pain. It did have a purpose. Thus while you can't change what happened specifically, you can change how you respond to it now and how you weave it into your life generally. In that way, you can rewrite the past. We will discuss this possibility further in chapter 9, the chapter on integration, which explains how your inner grown-up can help your inner child put together a new puzzle.

Mature Acceptance

Maturity for the inner grown-up means accepting life on life's terms, relaxing into life. This means that you cannot always be happy. Bad things will happen. Suffering is inevitable—it's part of the human condition. And maybe even the bad things and the suffering are not all that they seem to be. Make peace with the shadows. There is so much that we cannot see, cannot know. Maturity quietly and gracefully accepts impermanence, change, loss, aging, even death as integral parts of life. Listen to your own inner words of wisdom. They might say something like this:

- Trust and let life flow.
- Put it in the river, that is, release your concerns, let them flow away where they will.
- If your stocks go down, don't jump off a bridge. Put it in perspective.
- Bend with the wind. It is the willow that bends and survives. It is the mighty oak that snaps in the strong wind.
- Cultivate a calm and quiet confidence.
- Trust in the universe.
- Let life unfold.
- Be patient and persistent and then let it go.
- Be tolerant of opinions that differ from your own.
- We are all connected.
- *Que será, será*—whatever will be, will be.
- All things are as they should be.
- When God closes a door, somewhere he opens a window. Look for the window.
- Accept. What you resist, persists.
- I have everything I want because I want everything that I have.
- Grant me the serenity to accept the things I cannot change, the courage to change the things I can, and the wisdom to know the difference.

Listen for your own inner voice of wisdom and courage and forgiveness and acceptance. Listen for this voice. It is there inside of you. Access is available. Be still and listen. This voice will help you in times of trial and tribulation. This voice will guide you and sustain you. It is the voice of power, strength, love, and divinity.

The Maturity Pillar in Review

Your inner grown-up is courageous. He knows how to face fear and to act anyway. There is a deep reservoir of strength and courage inside of you.

The inner grown-up knows how to act even when she doesn't want to or doesn't feel like it. Her reason is able to overrule her emotion when necessary.

The mature inner grown-up is able to forgive, knowing that doing so frees the self. Not forgiving the self or another individual shackles you with a heavy weight, leaving you stuck. Often it is forgiving your parents that enables you to release the mature self.

The mature inner grown-up realizes her wisdom within and knows that this gift continues to grow and expand with age. The inner grown-up does not fear aging, even in a culture that worships youth.

The mature inner grown-up sees how all strands in life weave a beautiful textile. He accepts life on life's terms, with its suffering and its joys. He acknowledges that his own strand is a valuable piece to the total tapestry.

READING
From *Awakening Loving-Kindness* by Pemo Chodron

There is a story of a woman running away from tigers. She runs and runs, and the tigers are getting closer and closer. When she comes to the edge of a cliff, she sees some vines there, so she climbs down and holds on to the vines. Looking down, she sees that there are tigers below her as well. She then notices that a mouse is gnawing away at the vine to which she is clinging. She also sees a beautiful little bunch of strawberries close to her, growing out of a clump of grass. She looks up and she looks down. She looks at the mouse. Then she just takes a strawberry, puts it in her mouth, and enjoys it thoroughly.

Tigers above, tigers below. This is actually the predicament that we are always in, in terms of our birth and death. Each moment is just what it is. It might be the only moment of our life, it might be the only strawberry we'll ever eat. We could get depressed about it, or we could finally appreciate it and delight in the preciousness of every single moment of our life.

VISUALIZATION

Begin by getting your body prepared to relax. Stretch your arms high over your head. Then stretch them to your sides, reaching out. Drop your arms, and gently roll your head from side to side. Settle your body into a comfortable position and close your eyes.

Think about the words that you just heard from the reading. What do they make you think of? Did the reading evoke a feeling? Did the reading remind you of any experience from your own life? Take whatever message it is that you need from the reading.

Now bring your attention to your body and where you are in the room. Notice your breath, breathing in and breathing out. Notice the air around you and how it feels on your skin. Listen for any noises that may be near you. Notice any smells in the air. Become *mindful* of your environment and your place in it. Feel the weight of your clothes on your body. Feel the weight of your body on the floor or in your chair. Take three slow, deep breaths. Your consciousness is going on a journey.

Imagine yourself going down a flight of stairs. Down you go, and when you get to the bottom, there is a door. The door opens, and as you go through it, you see a rushing stream. You also see a large raft nearby and, without fear, you step into the raft and launch yourself into the rushing stream. You allow yourself to lie back and feel the current carrying you down the stream. The water is at times slow and meandering and at other times faster and fiercer. You flow with the river, without fear. You rest in total trust and complete abandon.

After a time the raft comes to a stop, and you sit up to find that you are in the middle of a beautiful clear lake. You dip the fingers of your right hand over the right side of the raft into the cool water. As you do so, you imagine all the negative, unforgiving, hostile, fearful energy that occasionally is in your body streaming out of your fingertips and into the right side of the lake. Your body feels emptied of all immaturity.

Next, you dip the fingers of your left hand over the left side of the raft into the cool water. As you do so, you imagine strong, wise, forgiving, peaceful, reasonable energy wafting up into your fingertips and filling your body. Your body feels full of maturity.

And finally, you dip your right hand back into the water, returning all the centered, peaceful, rational, and mature energy to the water, releasing it to the river of life where it can be shared and multiplied.

Eventually, the raft floats back to the edge of land and you easily jump to shore, pulling the raft along with you. You feel rested and at peace. It is time to return to the realm of consciousness.

Now, when you are ready, your consciousness returns to your body on a wave of light. Start to sense your body in the room. Feel your mind and body getting grounded and integrated. Wiggle your fingers and toes. Take a deep breath. Start to move your arms and legs gently from side to side. Take another deep breath. Allow yourself to feel a vibrant energy coursing through your body, revitalizing you. I'm going to count from one to five, and when you are ready, after the count of five, you may open your eyes. One . . . two . . . three . . . four . . . five. You may open your eyes.

JOURNAL QUESTIONS

Core Question: Who is it that you need to forgive? What's stopping you from forgiving this person?

What holds you back in your life?

When was a time that you felt fully aware of your courage, your strength, your wisdom?

How would your life be different if you lived from a place of reason with and over emotion? How would *you* be different?

When do you become "uptight" or "stuck"? How is it possible to let yourself flow more freely with the river of life?

How do you feel about your own aging? How do you celebrate birthdays—with joy or sadness? Is aging a frightening
prospect for you? What do you fear the most about it? How
can you embrace rather than run from it?

EXERCISES

DARE Thought System: Be aware of how this affects your maturity pillar.

Practice using the four-step process in your daily interactions.

Notice this week and fill in:

SITUATION	DETACH	AWARE	REORIENT	ENACT
What happened	Pull back	How I was regressing (inner child)	Remember that things can be different now; I am a grown-up	How I did change or could've changed thoughts/ behaviors
				EVALUATE How did it work?

Write a Story: Write your life story using the language of fairy
tales: evil queens, magic wands, flying horses, enchanted
witches. Start with "Once upon a time . . ." and finish with an
ending to the story that you choose. Give yourself the power to
reenvision your life and its possibilities.

Finding the Inner Grown-up Voice: This world moves so
quickly, at such a dizzying pace, that we sometimes forget that
it is possible to slow down and be quiet if we just schedule this
in as a priority. We manage to brush our teeth and shower
every day (or most days), right? All of us need to carve out time
for a daily ritual of silence. This is a sacred meditative time to
be still, to be quiet, to listen to that inner voice.

For a minimum of five minutes every day (preferably fifteen

minutes or more), go to a place where you can be alone and silent. It can be at your desk at work, with the door closed. It can be at home, outside, wherever. Get comfortable and then be quiet and still and listen for that inner voice of guidance, wisdom, courage, reason, capability. Listen for that voice; it is there. You don't have to do anything, visualize anything, say anything, though it may be helpful to focus on your breathing. Just give yourself an opportunity to listen to the inner voice every day, for at least five minutes.

You may not hear anything at first. You may find the exercise silly even. Think of calming the waters in your mind, making the surface still and clear so that you can eventually see below into the depths, waiting to see what will emerge. Be patient and persistent (mature qualities), and you'll be amazed at the subtle shifts that will eventually occur. Be still and listen.

CHAPTER SEVEN.

Pillar III—All You Need Is Love

The heart that goes out of itself gets larger and fuller.

—Horace Mann

On Mother's Day this year, the senior high youth group led our church's Sunday services. The topic was, appropriately, "Love." They sang songs about love, read poetry about love, and shared their personal essays about love. It was wonderful to hear the voices of teenagers today. And I found that the voices hadn't really changed all that much from when I was a teenager. There were a few youths who spoke about love in terms of their crushes, the latest guy or gal who they liked, maybe even loved (puppy love, that is).

One young woman spoke about how much she loved her dad. Another talked about how much she loved her mom. Several reflected on loving their friends, on loving the church, on loving God.

Think about how many kinds of love there are: there's romantic love—the thrill, the ecstasy, the rush and romance that's the bread-and-butter of most of our movies, music lyrics, advertising campaigns, and novel plots. There's parental love—poignant and complex love for our parents who loved and sometimes failed us, and for our children, whom we in turn have loved and sometimes failed. There's love for our pets, our siblings, our friends; love for our neighbors, our community, our nation, our earth.

I once heard that the Eskimos have dozens of different words to describe kinds of snow; the Greeks had several words for love. For us, there is but one word: *love*. It's the word that a mother might say to her newborn, and it's the same word that a teenager might say in terms of how he feels about pizza.

They say that "love makes the world go 'round." But unfortunately love sometimes also leads to jealousy, violence, murder, even war. And the loss of love leads to the most painful devastation of all—a broken heart. Love causes much joy and much suffering in our lives.

This Thing Called Love

When I was a child, one book that I was fond of was *The Giving Tree* by Shel Silverstein. I always thought it was a sweet story about love. I never realized the complexities of its message until I became an adult.

The story is about the relationship between an apple tree and a boy. The boy loves the tree and the tree loves the boy. The boy spends hours and hours swinging from the tree, climbing the tree, and resting in the shade of the tree. But, as is the way of life, the boy grows up and moves away, and the relationship between them changes.

The boy returns one day and the tree, who is so happy to see the boy that her branches quiver, cries, "Come play with me." The boy, now a man, says he doesn't have time to play; he must make a living now. The tree offers her apples for the boy to sell to make his living. The boy takes her apples and leaves.

The boy returns but needs materials to build a house. The tree offers her branches to the boy. The boy takes them and departs again. Next time when the boy returns, he needs a boat in which to sail away. The tree offers her trunk for him to make a boat. Each time the boy returns the tree is filled with happiness to see him. And each time she gives the boy something of herself that he takes, and then he leaves.

Finally, the boy returns as an old man. The tree, which is

now just a stump, apologizes that she has nothing left to give. The old man replies that all he wants is a place to sit and rest. He sits on the tree stump. And the tree is happy.

When I reflect on this story now, it seems to be about a boy who selfishly takes and takes and takes with no regard for the tree who loves him. And the tree continuously gives and gives and gives, in a codependent manner, with no thoughts of replenishing herself, until she is left with virtually nothing.

This cannot be a model for healthy love. Obviously, there are different ways of expressing love, different dynamics in experiencing love. Some people love in a way dominated by their inner children, while others find that their inner grown-ups primarily navigate them through love's waters.

Inner Child Love

The inner child is needy. Plain and simple. There's nothing inherently wrong with this—think of infants whose every need must be met by their caretakers. Think of toddlers and young children who are utterly dependent and vulnerable. This kind of neediness is developmentally appropriate.

However, childish love asks that its own needs get met first. Thus, if as an adult you are seeking love from an inner child position, you will be looking to others to be filling you and defining you and fixing you. Sometimes you will seek this from your friends, or from your partners and spouses, or even from your own children. Without meaning to, perhaps, your experience with love will be "And what have you done for me lately?"

This inner child position may be appropriate temporarily when you are sick or vulnerable, but the problem with this type of love is that it is insatiable. No one can fill your every need as when you were an infant. And furthermore, it is not their responsibility. In the end, inner child love is selfish and self-centered, just like the boy in *The Giving Tree*.

The other potential pitfall of inner child love is that it is often rooted in fear—fear that you don't deserve it, fear that you will lose it, fear that there won't be enough to go around, fear of rejection, fear of intimacy, fear of vulnerability, fear of self-disintegration or losing your identity, fear of commitment.

So while you might initially think of inner child love as pure and sweet and simple, the lurking problem child areas loom large, indeed, for all of us.

Inner Grown-up Love

Inner grown-up love means letting go of fear and insecurities, choosing to risk loving in spite of the dangers. Loving from the inner grown-up perspective also means looking at how you can *give*, how you can share and spread love and compassion to others. This love is less concerned with what you need but instead with what you can give, just like the tree in *The Giving Tree*. There is a Nepalese saying that encapsules this idea poignantly: Remember that the best relationship is one where your love for each other is greater than your need for each other.

Grown-up love is altruistic, with no ulterior motives. It is about genuine concern and affection for someone else. But, of course, no one can be all selfless, or else, like the tree, there will be nothing left but an old stump. I'm not advocating total self-denial or self-sacrifice. There needs to be an integration of giving and receiving, of offering and taking. Inner grown-up "giving" love needs to be balanced with the inner child "taking" love. You need both.

I once heard Elisabeth Kübler-Ross, the guru of death and dying, tell her audience that two of the most important lessons in life are to learn to love and to learn to be loved. You cannot continue to offer gifts if your well has run dry. Replenishment is about receiving—it is easier to give love when you have first been filled with love.

That replenishing love may come somewhat from others, which is natural, but that love also needs to come to you, from you. You need to love yourself first. It all begins right at home, in your own heart. Loving yourself really is the foundation, the starting point, for if you cannot love yourself, you really cannot love others either. At least not in a grown-up way.

On Loving You

In the 1984 movie *The NeverEnding Story*, the hero must pass through two gates on his quest to save the empress and the world of Fantasia. The first is a gate guarded by two giant sphinxes who can see straight into your heart and can tell if you feel your own worth. If you do not feel your own worth, the sphinxes will destroy you. Even the fancy knight in stunning armor is vaporized because the sphinxes could tell that he didn't really feel worthy, not in his heart of hearts. The second gate is a magic mirror in which you must face your true self. The old man tells the hero, "Kind people find that they are cruel, and brave men discover that they are really cowards. Confronted with their true selves, most men run away screaming."

What would happen to you? What would the magic mirror reveal about how you really feel toward yourself? Would the sphinxes destroy you, or do you feel your own worth?

Perhaps you've been told somewhere along the line that self-love is arrogant and selfish and conceited. Maybe just thinking about it makes you feel a little squeamish. There are those who can look in the mirror every morning and say to themselves, "I love you." Are you one of those people? Or does the very idea make you squirm?

A woman once told me that self-love is a little bit like baking a cake. If you didn't start off with all the correct ingredients, for example, if you somehow didn't get the "eggs" when you were a child, then after the cake is baked, you can no longer put the eggs in. Some things you just cannot go back and add, after the fact.

An interesting analogy perhaps, but I think this is a negative and defeatist image. Think of the inner grown-up as the eggs, or at least an egg substitute. You don't need to go back and add the missing ingredients. Remember that the inner grown-up has been inside you all the time. All you need to do is gain access to it. If you didn't grow up believing in yourself, if you weren't appropriately lauded with praise and affirmation, if you didn't get the parenting that helped you believe in yourself, it's not too late to give that to yourself now. You must learn to love yourself, no matter how hard it is, no matter how awkward it might feel, and no matter how uncomfortable it is. For if you cannot love yourself, you cannot genuinely love others.

Being self-centered and egocentric is also not the same thing as loving yourself. In fact, many people who are the most puffed up with bravado and self-interest are masking a deep insecurity about their own self-worth. Truly loving yourself means that you can honestly appraise yourself and appreciate your strengths and your flaws. You also genuinely cherish who you are and what you have to offer.

Think about it. You come into this world alone, traveling down the birth canal, just you and yourself. And when you leave this world, it will be alone. Even if there are people beside you holding your hand as you take your last breath, you are crossing that threshold between life and death on your own; your loved ones aren't crossing with you. You need to be your own best friend. You're all you've got in some ways, and while you will have help from people along the journey of life, you are your own common denominator through the years.

Try This . . .
Make a list of twenty things that you love about yourself. Choose qualities that make you unique, special, and lovable. How hard is it to complete this list?

The Loving Power of the Inner Grown-up

Kathy attended one of my support groups and was clearly lacking in self-love. When I asked the group the question "Does your life reflect that you love yourself?" she laughed out loud and said, "That's easy, no, no, no. My life reflects more of a self-loathing." She could easily trace the sources of her self-loathing to her upbringing with a narcissistic, alcoholic father and a passive, disinterested mother. Knowing this didn't make it any easier for her to overcome, however.

She told me that she could never understand the concept of self-parenting from the inner child movement. "People would tell me to 'parent' myself, but I didn't know what that meant. My only experience with parenting was about neglect and abuse."

But then we did the visualization in which you meet your inner grown-up. You may remember this from the visualization at the end of chapter 4, when you went through the crystal city and into the crystal palace and met your inner grown-up. For Kathy this was a very powerful experience. She said, "I can't believe it. She was so powerful and self-confident and gorgeous. She was wearing a lavender suit, of all things. And I guess she must be a part of me because I did summon her, after all. Is she really inside of me?"

I assured her, "Yes, that anchored woman you just connected with is your very own inner grown-up. And you can go back and visit with her anytime you choose. She's always there. She's inside of you. She can help you start to love yourself."

"What do you mean?" inquired Kathy. "She can actually help me learn to love myself?"

"Yes," I responded. "This week do the meditation on your own, meet with her and let her hug you and even hold you, the current you or even the child you, and see what happens."

Well, the next week Kathy came to the group and she was glowing. She was wearing makeup for the first time since we began meeting (which for her meant attention to her appearance). She had on a beautiful lavender sweater, and she sported a wide smile. She fairly burst out of the seams to share with the group that a "miracle" had occurred. She had had another meeting with her inner grown-up, several in fact. And she had allowed her inner grown-up to comfort her, to hug and hold her, to "parent" her in a way that she hadn't understood until now.

"I honestly feel like something incredible has shifted in my life. I've never felt this way before. I really have found something inside of me, something that *is* me, that can bring me a measure of peace and self-confidence." She went on to say that she saw some hope now, some possibility that she could learn to love herself, could learn to see herself and her capabilities in a new light. "I feel like life is opening up to me now, and at fifty-four I'd say it's about time."

Remember loving the self is accepting you for who you are, flaws and all. No one is perfect, and even with years of therapy or years of reading self-help books, you still will not be perfect. We all feel inadequate at times, overwhelmed and awkward and "less than" . . . but that doesn't make us any less lovable. Forgive yourself for all of your imperfections, and embrace the entire package of who you are. Let your inner grown-up mirror for you how special you truly are.

Once you learn how to love yourself (which is an ongoing process), or even once you just take the first steps down that path, then your heart is full and free to share the love with others. Just as in the responsibility pillar you moved from focus "within" to focus "without," the love pillar asks you to do the same. Begin by turning inward and learning to love yourself, then use that love to transcend yourself.

Some Enchanted Evening

Seemingly everything in our society conspires to make us desire the incredible, the *ultimate* love: romantic love. We long for the buzz and the thrill and the high and the obsession of real romance. We search, sometimes our whole lives, for the perfect mate, the person who will make all of our dreams come true. And if we cannot find this perfection, we feel cheated and empty. Unfortunately, almost everything we are led to believe about "true love" is a myth!

Myth #1: You can (and should) fall in love at first sight.
I admit it . . . I bought into this theory, having been raised on classic songs from the Rodgers and Hammerstein version of love: From *Cinderella*, the lyrics "Ten minutes ago I saw

you . . . You gave me the feeling the room had no ceiling or floor." Or consider from *South Pacific*, the lyrics "Some enchanted evening, you may see a stranger across a crowded room."

Who can resist such expectations? Actually, I don't believe in "love" at first sight, though I certainly believe in "attraction" or even "lust" at first sight. And I don't believe that heart-fluttering love can or even should be sustained. Much of what we imagine falling in love to be hooks right into our inner child selves: immediate gratification, magic dust and fireworks, impulsive fusion fantasies. True love is not instantaneous. It must develop, deepen, evolve over time. Only time can produce a rich, mature love that is fortified with age. But the movies don't tell you this.

The inner grown-up enjoys the time
it takes for love to develop.

Myth #2: When I fall in love, the hole inside me will be filled and I will be complete. I will have found my other half.

If you expect all of your needs to be met by your beloved, you will be profoundly disappointed. And I've got more news for you, you don't need someone to fill in your other half because you are completely whole to begin with! Furthermore, the essence of true love isn't about having your needs met anyway . . . it's about meeting the needs of someone else whom you love.

I once listened to a local radio call-in program and a woman wanted more love in her life from her husband. He ignored her, she said. The host basically said something to the effect that if she wanted more love from her husband, she should be giving him more love. The paradox is that when you treat your husband in a loving manner, then he will feel loved and will begin to treat you in a more loving manner. You change first.

The inner grown-up knows how to
reach out to others and to love them.

Myth #3: True love will last happily ever after . . . with little or no effort.

The truth is that a great relationship doesn't just "happen" on its own. In fact, the foundation of love is fairly fragile as it ebbs and flows. People fall out of love almost as impulsively as they fall into love. That's why staying committed to a relationship is what is of ultimate importance (provided that it isn't abusive or dangerous).

I once heard a woman say, "Love is not a word. Love is not a feeling. Love is a decision." That's a pretty extreme notion. I happen to believe that love is all three of these things, but I think the extremity of her statement proves an important point, one that we often forget in an age when divorce is as common as ice cream in summer.

We *decide* to love. We *choose* to stay committed. Now, if we're talking about the ultimate commitment, that of staying in a marriage or other monogamous relationship, you have to understand the truth that you will not always *feel* loving toward this person. However, this is irrelevant. The point is that you stay committed because you made a covenant; you are devoted to working it out. There will be times when you look at that person across the breakfast table and wonder, "What exactly did I see in him, anyway?" or "And why exactly did I marry her?"

Nobody ever tells you going into the wild ride that this will happen occasionally. But it does, and you have to ride it out like surfing a wave. It honestly doesn't matter whether you still get butterflies when they walk in the room. Most likely, you won't. But you made a commitment and the inner grown-up knows how to honor that commitment.

Of course, you are probably thinking of a million excuses and reasons that certain commitments should be broken: abusive marriages, loveless marriages that never rebound, and so on. There are certainly exceptions to every rule, but, by and large, I believe that love requires us to keep commitments, even when the love doesn't *feel* so great. Remember from the last chapter, reason over emotion. Reason tells you to stay committed, work it out. And when you do, the love grows.

I once had a client start therapy because she was mourning the death of her second husband. Then she volunteered

that she had been the instigator in divorcing her first husband, the father of her two sons. I asked, "Why did you divorce
him?" The answer was not that he was abusive or cruel or hateful. The answer was not that he was adulterous or alcoholic or
chronically irresponsible. She simply said, "I didn't love him
anymore." And then she followed that with "It was probably
the most selfish decision that I ever made, and in many ways, I
regret doing it, especially since it had such a terrible effect on
my children."

Just because you feel like you don't love someone anymore
is not a sufficient reason to break the commitment. Wait awhile.
The love will most likely come back. Love ebbs and flows.
Love feels intense and then distant. Love wavers and is unpre-
dictable. Why? Because it is rooted in *feeling*. But reason can
overrule emotion. Reason honors commitment. Plug into your
inner grown-up and let her rational, committed self weather all
of your storms.

Another woman I know who was grieving the loss of her
husband, whom she had been married to for thirty-one years,
told me, "One of the thoughts that brings me the greatest consolation during this sad time is that I know we fulfilled our commitment to each other. I can rest deeply in that knowledge." For
her, the fulfilled commitment was testimony to their love.

Commitment and the fulfilling of the commitment honors
love, grows out of love, and even transcends love as it brings a
serenity to the soul.

The inner grown-up knows how to fulfill commitments.

Covenant to the Self

Likewise, being committed to yourself (your health, well-
being, serenity) is key to being committed to another. How you
treat yourself is intimately connected with how you treat others
and also how they learn to treat you.

How you love yourself will be the template, the model for not only how you can love others but how they, in turn, love you. Cherie Carter-Scott says in her informative book *If Love Is a Game, These Are the Rules*:

How you perceive and treat yourself is exactly how others will perceive and treat you. Every day you unconsciously show and tell people how to treat you without ever uttering a word. Since you are your own primary caretaker, others look to you for guidance on how much love you require. You give them the cues; you dictate how people speak to you, how they treat you, what they think of you, and what they expect from you. Whether you are conscious of doing this or not, you are the one who establishes the model of how others relate to you.

That's why it is so important to love yourself, because it demonstrates how others might love you as well. If you set a good example, others are sure to follow suit. For example, some people demonstrate love to themselves by taking care of their health, pampering themselves with massages and hot baths, taking "mental health" days and mini-vacations. Some people respond to "gifts" and shower themselves with fresh flowers, shopping sprees, and inexpensive trinkets.

Others know that human contact and communication are essential to feeling loved, so they schedule interesting activities and make plans with friends in order to fill that need. Others find that solitude and contact with nature fills the bill, so they make a point of scheduling hikes and camping trips to soothe the soul. The point is that the inner grown-up knows how to love the self in the ways that she needs to feel loved. Are you committed to taking care of your own love needs?

You have to activate your inner grown-up in order to fulfill your own love needs. The trouble is that with love, the inner child frequently gets involved, and usually from a problem child perspective. Claiming your inner grown-up might be just what the love doctor ordered. Let's look at how the four-step DARE technique can keep the problem child at bay.

DARE to Love

Edith has lived a sad and difficult life. She endured a child-hood of extreme physical and emotional abuse. Her father was a violent alcoholic and her mother was emotionally distant. As an adult she had a terrible marriage that was a strain for years, though she finally got divorced. And then when she was in her forties, she lost her eighteen-year-old son in a tragic accident. There is a sadness in Edith's eyes, and she battles depression. Yet she has rebuilt her life in a positive way. She has a deeply sustaining relationship with God and practices her faith in the community of a church. And recently she has entered a new loving relationship.

The gentleman whom she is dating has his own baggage, of course, including the fact that he just ended a thirty-year mar-riage. They are proceeding slowly and yet it caught her off guard when he announced to her one day, "You know, I don't love you." Now imagine how such a remark would injure. We can only guess his own protective motivation. He went on to assure her that he cared deeply about her and that he wanted to continue their relationship. But Edith was wounded to the core. She had never felt loved as a child, and given her back-ground, this comment was just too much to absorb. Her retrig-gered wounded child reaction was to flee. And initially that's exactly what she did. She refused to take his phone calls, avoided him at all costs, and decided never to see him again. In other words, Edith didn't call on her inner grown-up at first. She didn't search for any tools to help her manage her feelings. She reacted from her pain and she retreated. In many ways, it is just easier and more familiar to luxuriate in the problem inner child reaction.

Eventually he managed to contact her and asked, "What's wrong? What happened? Can we talk about it and fix it?" And that's when she came out of her cave and began to analyze what was happening. Realizing that she wasn't happy in the cave anyway, she resolved to work this situation out in a differ-ent manner no matter how difficult it might be to do so.

With the help of the DARE technique, Edith was able to first *detach* from her pain and distance herself from the situation. She sat down in a quiet place, and she closed her eyes and imagined watching the entire situation on a movie screen.

Then she became *aware* of how his comment had struck a vulnerable chord originating from her childhood. She thought about her abusive parents, who made her feel like a nuisance, an inconvenience. She was aware of a piece of herself that felt unlovable. She thought about how extra-vulnerable and sensitive she had felt since her son died.

And then, still sitting in a quiet place with her eyes closed, she *reoriented* herself to her inner grown-up. She consciously affirmed that she *is* a lovable person despite what anyone told her when she was growing up, despite what this new man in her life had implied. She reviewed her own list of affirmations, reminding herself that she is a grown-up. She called upon divine powers, reminding herself that God loves her for who she is. She spent a moment visualizing her inner grown-up in the crystal palace who hugged her and sprinkled her with "grounding" dust. And finally she imagined her golden core, which for her, as she imagined it, was thick and strong, like a rope.

And as she employed all of these techniques, she finished by *enacting* that, yes, she could react differently to his statement. She could "change the channel" and not operate on automatic pilot. So she called him, talked with him, and shared her feelings.

Edith also sought, from a position of maturity, to understand *his* position, recognizing his own fears and insecurities. And as they talked openly, they came to a mutual understanding about their relationship. He was able to understand that his comment was a reflection of his own inner child fear, and she was able to understand that his comment certainly was not an indication of whether or not she was lovable. By *evaluating*, she realized how grateful she was to come to this new place of peace. She learned that the old buttons didn't have to get pushed in the same way, or at least didn't have to control her responses. To date, they are still seeing each other regularly, respecting each other's feelings, and letting the relationship unfold in its own time.

*   *   *

Romantic unions, however, are not the only love relationships studded with minefields. All relationships offer opportunities for both great joys and great pains. And the inner child is
prone to surface in them all.

From the Child to the Parent

The Bible tells us to "Honor thy father and mother." For
some of us that is easier to do than for others of us. But as our
society continues to live longer, with the life expectancy statistics creating new categories of life-span development, we children are also becoming parents to our parents. For many this is
a strange and bewildering turn of events. Our inner child says
that the parent is supposed to take care of *us*.

Francine was a thirty-five-year-old woman who was no
stranger to hardship. When she was twenty-nine, after having
been married for only three years, she was unexpectedly thrust
into the role of young widow when her husband was killed in a
hunting accident. Francine's world, understandably, fell apart.
She was shattered, but over time she began to pull her life together. She told me, "After that tragedy happened, I had new
eyes to see. And what I saw is that when everything gets taken
away from you, love is the only thing left. Nothing could kill
the love that I continue to have for my husband. Love is what
really matters."

So when she heard that her mother was diagnosed with
Alzheimer's disease, she instantly knew that she would become
her mother's full-time caregiver. To do that, she left her job and
her home in California and moved back to the East Coast, her
childhood home. Her other sisters were unwilling and unable
to make such a sacrifice. But Francine did this out of love. She
explained, "When you love someone, you help them. You do
anything for them in their time of need."

Francine has been her mother's caretaker now for several
years, and it is not easy work. She brushes her mother's teeth;
she dresses her mother; she does all the things for her mother

that her mother once did for her. Coping with such an abrupt role reversal is difficult, but Francine finds that she can do so when she stays rooted in love.

Francine does not view her efforts as grudging sacrifice or with a sense of martyred pride; she genuinely feels good about her choice to care for her mother. She said, "I always felt love from my mother—she modeled that for me. And now I'm giving that back. I feel stronger and more peaceful, deeply peaceful, because of it." The love you give out in your life will come flowing back to you.

The inner grown-up knows how to love selflessly.

From the Parent to the Child

I once read a novel in which the main female character was such a narcissistic mother that I was thoroughly repulsed and had to stop reading the book. Although the daughter was in need, the mother could not give to her because she was so overly preoccupied with what people would think about *her*.

And I often come upon articles proclaiming "fatherlessness" (deadbeat dads) as America's number one social problem. These seemingly unconcerned and irresponsible fathers fail to keep their commitments to their offspring. They put their own selfish needs before their obligations. The consequences are dire, indeed, as father absence has been linked to violence, teen pregnancy, delinquency, and a host of other social ills.

Raising a child is an ongoing commitment whether you *feel* like doing it or not. When you bring a child into this world—and remember that child entered planet earth at your invitation, not his own—you have a responsibility to that child. The enduring bond should be based on love, but at the very least it should be honored out of commitment.

Parenting should be done to meet the child's needs, not your own. When you become a parent to fill your own needs, you're already off on the wrong foot. It's dangerous when teenagers idealize having a baby. They think, "Oh, won't it be fun to be needed. Won't it feel good to have my own baby doll to take care of and make me feel important."

You shouldn't have a baby to make you feel older, to make you feel younger, to fulfill your own unmet needs, to save your marriage, or to enhance your self-image. Having a baby, raising a child, is not about your needs.

Pure parental loving is an act of total self-transcendence. That's why your inner grown-up is always happy for your child, wants the best for your child, and is not jealous of them if they excel or surpass you in some way. I do believe that pure parental love is the most holy of all loves, perhaps because it mimics what God himself must feel for us, his children.

When I had all three of my children christened, this is what the ministers read from Kahlil Gibran's *The Prophet*:

Your children are not your children.
They are the sons and daughters of Life's longing for itself.
They come through you but not from you,
And though they are with you yet they belong not to you.

You may give them your love but not your thoughts,
For they have their own thoughts.
You may house their bodies but not their souls,
For their souls dwell in the house of tomorrow, which you
cannot visit, not even in your dreams.
You may strive to be like them, but seek not to make them
like you
For life goes not backward nor tarries with yesterday.

You are the bows from which your children as living arrows
are sent forth.
The archer sees the mark upon the path of the infinite, and
He bends you with His might that His arrows may go swift
and far.
Let your bending in the archer's hand be for gladness;
For even as He loves the arrow that flies,
So He loves also the bow that is stable.

But of course, we are human. We are, at times, narcissistic. We cannot love perfectly because we are not perfect people. Our egos get in the way of our parenting. Our own inner child self-gratification and dependency needs get triggered. And our own issues and fears of loss are hovering ever presently.

Being a parent is always about letting go, always about loss, always about redefining the relationships between you and this baby, you and this toddler, you and this preschooler, you and this elementary school child, you and this adolescent, you and this young adult, you and this grown-up. Change is the only constant. You have to be willing to negotiate a delicate balance of holding on and loving while simultaneously releasing and letting go.

I wrote an essay entitled "Where Did My Baby Go?" because, in many ways, I was bereft that my first daughter was growing up and in some senses the person she had been before simply no longer existed. I almost felt betrayed. That baby that I loved so much, that round-faced, bald, and smiling toothless wonder child had evaporated. She had turned into a walking, talking, demanding little bear. Eventually that little bear disappeared, too, and evolved into a fully self-sufficient grade school virtual preteen.

But that's what parenting is . . . it's savoring each stage and moment for its own particular joys. The stage will pass. This person will metamorphize into a new being, and you'll be left racing to adapt to the changes. But through it all, you as a parent are there to support their growth. They have not been summoned to provide your growth—that might be a welcome by-product, an extra perk as payback for all the diaper changing and sleepless nights, because more than likely parenting will cause you to grow in tremendously wonderful ways, but that is not the primary reason for being a parent.

*The inner grown-up knows how to
commit to and parent a child.*

Beyond yourself, beyond your lover and your parents and your children and your family, there is more. There are your neighbors to love.

Thou Shalt Love Thy Neighbors

In my church a woman asked the congregation to give food for delivery to local food pantries. We did it for a few months, and it felt wonderful. It felt wonderful not only to buy an extra jar of spaghetti sauce knowing that I would be bringing it for the collection, but it also felt wonderful to see other people bringing their jars on the appointed Sunday. It seemed that the total of us became larger than the sum of our parts.

But when that woman moved to California, nobody took her place to organize the collections. At first I noticed this development and thought to myself, "That's too bad. I miss those collections." Then it really began to bother me, and I asked the ministers about whether we were going to continue the collections. They replied that nobody had volunteered to take the project over.

"Hmmm," I thought. And then, "Oh, no, I couldn't possibly get involved with that. My life is too busy. My 'plate' is too 'full.' " I found a dozen excuses to not get involved.

But then I began to think about love . . . about loving my neighbors, about helping those in need, about how "good fortune obligates." So along with another interested church member, I decided to formally organize the Help Your Neighbor Drive.

It has turned out to be the simplest, easiest volunteer work possible, but with maximum impact. Each month you simply pick a local social service agency, ask them what they need (one or two items works best), inform your group about the collection date and item (through the newsletter or bulletin board or other group communication tool), and then collect and deliver on the appointed day. It's a breeze.

It becomes more than just bringing mittens to give to the Salvation Army. It becomes about joining with others to make a difference. It becomes about personally impacting lives that are, for the moment, less fortunate than your own. It becomes about loving your neighbors.

I challenge anyone reading these words to do the same. Anyone, anywhere, can organize such a drive. You don't have to belong to a church to start such a program. Start it at your work. Start it with any club or social organization. There's nothing worse than sitting around knowing that you should be helping but are not sure how, or feeling that you don't have the time.

Make the time. Find little ways to help. Take action. It will make you feel better. And don't just get motivated during the holidays. Think about giving all year long.

You can go beyond collections and deliveries, of course. Consider touching the actual lives of your neighbors in need, such as through a mentoring program or a big sister/big brother program, a hospice, a hospital, a nursing home, a homeless shelter. Then think bigger. What about faraway neighbors? What about sponsoring a child in need in a foreign country? What about making donations to those suffering from natural disasters, wherever they might live in the world?

Once your heart begins to expand, the expansion is limitless.

*The inner grown-up knows that
we are all truly connected.*

Try This . . .
   The next time a new neighbor moves into your neighborhood or into your apartment building make them a coffee cake or homemade cookies and deliver them with a smile and a welcome. It will blow them away and will make you feel terrific!

The Ripple Effect

Every summer my family and I vacation on a small, secluded lake in New Hampshire. And every summer one of my favorite activities is to kayak into a still cove and sit there, soaking in the beauty of nature. I dip my finger into the lake's cool waters, and the entire composition of the surface is suddenly changed as the single point from my finger creates ripples that continue to expand and spread. I put my paddle in the water and the fish and waterfowl around me are immediately affected. I make an impact, however subtle, on the environment around me.

Which is why an important expression of love is to understand and honor this intimate connection between ourselves and the environment. Thus, we need to protect our natural resources, make a commitment to "reduce, reuse, recycle," as my son's preschool song says. The Native American culture exemplifies how we should honor and bless our Mother Earth, giving thanks for her bounty and respecting her limitations.

Something else happens when I'm in this kayak on the lake. Every so often a powerboat or even just a canoe passes by, and always the impact on me is enormous. Within a few minutes of their passing, I am suddenly rocked by the waves generated in their wake. I am struck again by how intimately we are all connected. They pass by and I am literally "moved."

This happens everywhere, every day. We need to recognize the power of even the smallest personal encounters, since every single transaction that we have in the grocery store, the drugstore, the bank, the dry cleaners affects us on some level. The energy you exchange in every single interaction is contagious. If your manner is curt and nasty, that venom spreads in a slow ripple effect. Likewise, if your manner is kind and friendly, that grace spreads in a slow ripple effect as well.

What Goes Around Comes Around

Recently I felt the ripple effect acutely when I was in a discount store with my children, in a hurry because we were late for an appointment, and I approached the check-out counter with one item at the exact same time that another woman approached the check-out counter with roughly ten items.

"Do you mind if we go first?" I asked. "We're in a big hurry."

"So am I," this woman snarled, though she clearly was not. And she sauntered in front of us, slowing putting each item onto the conveyer belt. My stomach began to knot. I felt annoyed, insulted. After we finally finished our own transaction, we began to run frantically to our car, and I saw that woman slowly meandering in the parking lot with a smirk on her face.

My chest felt tight for some time. I could feel the heaviness of my heart. True, I am responsible for my own responses. I couldn't cast the blame onto her for how I was reacting. So, I managed to do deep breaths in the car, a prayer or two, and then I called upon the centeredness of my inner grown-up to help me out.

But imagine the difference if this person had said, "Oh, yes, of course, please go ahead of me. That's no problem." I would have felt relieved, supported, and reassured about the generous spirit of humanity. I would have left the store grateful and pleased. Or even if the person had said, "No, I can't let you go first, but I'm awfully sorry. I'm in a terrible hurry as my sick mother-in-law is waiting for me to return and she's afraid to be alone. Otherwise I'd be happy to help you out." Well, of course I would have understood and would have sympathized with someone trying to fit too many activities into too little time, just like myself. But instead I encountered a patently nasty response for no apparent reason.

Every single time we are in a transaction, we have an opportunity to spread goodwill. Try complimenting the cashier the next time you check out at the drugstore—"What pretty earrings you have on," or "Thanks for your efficient service today, I really appreciate it." It takes no more effort to be nice than to be nasty. You will make someone's day and the karmic effect spreads tenfold. Energy is *contagious* whether it's positive or negative.

Random Gifts of Love

Spread a little love. It's so easy to do and makes everyone feel better. One way to do this is to implement a small, conscious routine into your life: give love gifts. You may have heard of "random acts of kindness"; well, consider these "random gifts of love." The intention is of love, of giving a gift. It need not be anything large or grand; perhaps it is as simple as pouring a cup of coffee for a colleague. Perhaps it is complimenting someone's new dress. The recipient need not even recognize that they have been given a gift, but that is irrelevant. *You* know that you have given something small, subtle, yet powerful. You are filled with the love that was the motivator behind the gift.

Whistle when you walk into a store. Comment positively on the weather. Say more than "fine" when a store worker routinely asks you how you are or if you found everything you needed. Take a chance. See what happens. You don't even have to say a word . . . choose to silently bless people, showering them with a wish for peace and prosperity. When you hear a siren, bless those in trouble.

If you implement this "gift"-giving practice into your daily living, you will be surprised by the results. Energy attracts like energy. When you pour love from yourself into the world, the world begins to pour love back in your direction. That which you release to the universe will come back to you.

The inner grown-up knows how to spread love.

God Is Love

I suppose no discussion on love is complete unless we mention God. I use the word God, coming from a Judeo-Christian tradition, but I could just as easily say Allah, Jehovah, Great Spirit, Higher Power, Goddess, Eternal One, or any other salutation to invoke the divine. My former minister used to often proclaim that God is not God's name, it is our name for that which is greater than all of us yet present in each.

As for love, when you choose to stay committed to love, when you choose to love the earth, your neighbors, your enemies, your family, and yourself, you choose to be an expression of God.

Try This . . .

For the next seven days, give one random gift of love each day. Consider including yourself, your partner, your parents, your children, a distant friend, and/or a stranger. The gift should be small but significant, intentional yet subtle. It could be a letter, phone call, unexpected visit, spontaneous purchase, pouring someone a cup of coffee, rubbing a friend's back, sending a condolence letter to a stranger . . . be creative. The recipient doesn't have to know you did it, but *you* know that it is a gift from love. Notice how you feel as you give these expressions of love. How does it impact your week?

Record your gift for each day.

Day	Recipient	Gift
Sunday		
Monday		
Tuesday		
Wednesday		
Thursday		
Friday		
Saturday		

Part of that love is also the truth, the absolute knowing that God loves *you*. There is a branch of counseling that draws on biblical theology and especially on God's love to aid in the therapeutic process. Christian counselors are convinced that relying on typical techniques of secular counseling, such as modes of "empowering the client" or looking within to love the self, ring hollow and fall short. Christian counselors, instead, rely on the power of God to convince their clients that they are indeed lovable and worthwhile. And sometimes, for those who feel unlovable, coming to know that God loves them is just what they needed.

Feeling loved by God is not the sole province of Christians, however. People of all religious traditions who are aware of the holy know deeply that God loves them and protects them. That means we are loved not only in times of joy and celebration, but also during times of fear, loss, terror, and misery.

Do *you* feel loved by God? What would it mean for you and for your life to feel loved by God? Our fourth and final pillar for examination is about spirituality. We will be analyzing the many complicated pathways for finding God, for establishing a life that is rooted in spirit and devoted to holiness.

The Love Pillar in Review

While inner child love is about having your own needs met, inner grown-up love is about meeting the needs of others. Both are essential for true love.

True love begins by loving the self. The inner grown-up loves and nurtures you, knowing that you are valuable, worthwhile, and lovable (no matter what messages you may have ever received to the contrary). Libby Roderick sings a song called "How Could Anyone," where the lyrics say, "How could anyone ever tell you you were anything less than beautiful? How could anyone ever tell you you were less than whole?"

Feeling loved from within, you are then free to pour love outward. Shower love on your partner. Shower love on your children and your parents. Shower love on your friends, neighbors, and colleagues. Shower love on your community, your country, your earth.

You will receive it back tenfold. And in so giving and receiving love, you will become an embodiment of divinity.

READING
"If Thou Must Love Me"
by Elizabeth Barrett Browning

If thou must love me, let it be for nought
Except for love's sake only. Do not say
"I love her for her smile . . . her look . . . her way
Of speaking gently, . . . for a trick of thought
That falls in well with mine, and certes brought
A sense of pleasant ease on such a day"—
For these things in themselves, Belovèd, may
Be changed, or change for thee,—and love, so wrought
May be unwrought so. Neither love me for
Thine own dear pity's wiping my cheeks dry,—
A creature might forget to weep, who bore
Thy comfort long, and lose thy love thereby!
But love me for love's sake, that evermore
Thou may'st love on, through love's eternity.

VISUALIZATION

Begin by getting your body prepared to relax. Stretch your arms high over your head. Then stretch them to your sides, reaching out. Drop your arms, and gently roll your head from side to side. Settle your body into a comfortable position and close your eyes.

Think about the words that you just heard from the reading. What do they make you think of? Did the reading evoke a feeling? Did the reading remind you of any experience from your own life? Take whatever message it is that you need from the reading.

Now bring your attention to your body and where you are in the room. Notice your breath, breathing in and breathing out. Notice the air around you and how it feels on your skin. Listen for any noises that may be near you. Notice any smells in the air. Become *mindful* of your environment and your place in it. Feel the weight of your clothes on your body. Feel the weight of your body on the floor or in your chair. Take three slow, deep breaths. Your consciousness is going on a journey.

Imagine yourself going down a flight of stairs. Down you go, and when you get to the bottom, there is a door. The door opens, and as you go through it, you find yourself by the ocean, on a beautiful beach. It is late in the afternoon and the sun is making its way down to the horizon. You smell the salty air and feel the spray of water on your cheek. You hear the sound of seagulls flying in the air. You feel the squish of sand beneath your feet. It is peaceful and quiet, with only the sound of the ocean waves as your music.

You begin to walk along the shore. It is not crowded and you feel at one with nature. Up ahead you notice a small circle of people holding hands. You feel compelled to approach them. As you get nearer to the cluster of people, you realize that you recognize each person in the circle. Each person in the circle is someone who has loved you in this lifetime.

You see people who are currently in your life, and you see people from your past who are no longer a part of your life. You see people who have died and people who are still alive. You see old teachers, perhaps your grandparents, old lovers, old friends, former colleagues—people who cared about you, who loved you, who shaped your life in some way. These people see you approach the circle, and as you do so, they break open the circle so that you might enter and stand in the center.

There you stand and look each person in the eyes. You move around the circle resting your eyes on each of the people there from your past and from your present. You feel their love cascading out to you, surrounding you with essential goodness. The love surrounds you, enfolds you, and you absorb the sense of compassion so that it emanates from you as well. You silently thank each of these people for the role they played in your life, however brief. You thank them for their love.

After a while the circle breaks open for you to exit. You leave this circle of loving people behind as you travel back along the beach to the place where you came from. You feel their love spilling out of your body, filling you with a sense of tenderness. In fact, you are so filled with love that you feel buoyant, almost as if you could skip or float back along the beach. You ease your way along the shore, back to where you first came, inhaling the salty breeze, feeling the mist, hearing the lap of the waves. You feel rested and at peace.

Now, when you are ready, your consciousness returns to your body on a wave of light. Start to sense your body in the room. Feel your mind and body getting grounded and integrated. Wiggle your fingers and toes. Take a deep breath. Start to move your arms and legs gently from side to side. Take another deep breath. Allow yourself to feel a vibrant energy coursing through your body, revitalizing you. I'm going to count from one to five, and when you are ready, after the count of five, you may open your eyes. One . . . two . . . three . . . four . . . five. You may open your eyes.

JOURNAL QUESTIONS

Core Question: Do you love yourself? Do you live with the knowledge that you are lovable? How do you know?

If you looked at your life: your diet, exercise, sleep habits, home, work, friends, and overall lifestyle, would you conclude that you love yourself, or not? If not, how can you change your life to reflect that you love yourself? Or what would your life need to look like for you to know that you loved yourself?

What frightens you the most about giving love?

What frightens you the most about receiving love?

What did you learn about love when you were a child?

Who is your teacher now about love ... what is he/she teaching you?

What do you teach others about love?

What commitments do you currently try to keep in your life? How do you feel about them?

What commitments have you broken in your life? How do you feel about them?

EXERCISES

DARE Thought System: Look for ways to apply this technique to the love pillar.

Notice this week and fill in:

SITUATION	DETACH	AWARE	REORIENT	ENACT
What happened	Pull back	How I was regressing (inner child)	Remember that things can be different now; I am a grown-up	How I did change or could've changed thoughts/ behaviors
				EVALUATE How did it work?

Lists: A. List ten things that you should be doing regularly to take care of yourself, but aren't. Think of things that would really *nourish* you (exercise, long walks, lunch with a friend, reading a travel magazine, massages, overnight trips, sporting events, meditation and prayer time, going to a movie alone, singing or dancing, playing cards, a long, hot bath, listening to music, looking at the mountains/ocean, for example). A friend of mine told me that in her "free time" she pays bills and responds to e-mails. Of course, these activities' need to and will get done somehow, but they're not exactly top of the list for refilling the well. Consider that the things for nurturing and replenishing you—whatever those are for you—are more than luxuries; they are necessities to keep you going in a multifaceted life.

Now pick two items from your list and make a commitment to yourself to implement them regularly this month. Really stick to it. How does it feel?

B. List ten qualities that your friends and family members admire about you.

C. List ten words to describe yourself. How many of these words are positive? How many of these words are negative? For each negative, analyze if it really is true (yes, I really do have a bad temper) or if it is a lie that you tell you about yourself (I'm stupid). If it's a lie, challenge it when it comes up. If it is the truth, ask yourself how that quality serves you in your life. Is it useful in some way? Is it destructive and rooted in problem child motivation? Stand back and take an honest inventory of yourself—what do you notice?

Spend Time with Elders: It is so important to spend time with people who are one or more generations older than us. Other cultures tend to revere the elderly. We are more apt to recoil from them. I encourage people to spend time with older people, whether it's their own family members or strangers in a nursing home facility. We need to strengthen intergenerational ties. Being around our society's senior citizens helps broaden our perspective on and love for life. Listen to an elder and see what there is to give and to receive.

Spend Time with Children: Likewise, it is vital to spend regular quality time with children. If you don't have your own young children or grandchildren, I recommend volunteering in a day care or preschool or elementary school. Consider coaching a local team sport or tutoring a young student. Perhaps you could even visit a classroom to talk about your profession or an unusual hobby. There is much to share with children, and being around them helps broaden our perspective on and love for life. Listen to a child and see what there is to give and to receive.

Positive Affirmations: Choose several affirmations that describe yourself that are loving and full of self-worth. Write each one on an index card as a positive statement in the present tense. You may not believe this statement at the moment, but state it in the present anyway. For example, "I am a beautiful person," or "I am a strong and resilient person." Design several positive statements that fit you or describe the you that you want to believe in.

Put the cards beside your bed and read them *out loud* every morning and every night, both when you wake up and right before you go to sleep. Stay committed to doing this for an entire week. See what comes up.

Love Letters: Write a letter to yourself from someone who loves you. In it, explain why he or she loves you.

Write a letter to your best friend about why you love them.

Write a letter to yourself on why you love you and what makes you special.

Write a letter to yourself as a newborn infant from the perspective of you being your own mother.

Write a letter to yourself from God on why God created you and why God loves you.

CHAPTER EIGHT

Pillar IV—Stairways to Heaven

People see God every day, they just don't recognize Him.

—Pearl Bailey

I once had a debate with a friend on the issue of whether you can be totally and completely fulfilled in life without having any sense of spirituality. She argued that, yes, you could be happy—she was perfectly happy—without any spiritual life, any sense of a God, any religious convictions. And although I could understand her point, in the end I had to disagree with her. I believe that so-called "happiness" without a spiritual foundation is ultimately hollow. Without a spiritual life as an anchor for the soul, something—whether you realize it or not—is missing.

I liken this phenomenon to the following story. When I was a girl growing up in Texas, my father used to take me to a hole-in-the-wall kind of place called Shanghai Jimmy's, which was famous for its chili and rice. I ate the chili and rice plain, with no beans or fixin's and I loved it. In fact, I didn't think chili could get any better. Now, many years later, I still love chili and rice, but I eat it with beans and shredded cheese and chopped celery and crushed corn chips and sometimes even hot sauce. And you know what, chili really did get better. I loved my plain chili then; I love my loaded chili now.

But when I compare the two chilis, I see without a doubt

that my current chili fare is richer and fuller and more multidi-
mensional. My appetite roots sink deeper and farther. I never
would have known what I was missing or what was to come.
So you see, you can genuinely be happy and satisfied, and yet
there's a whole different level of existence available to you that
will make you even more expanded and more satisfied.

It's like believing that there is only AM frequency on the radio. You enjoy listening to AM; you are perfectly happy listening to AM . . . but then one day you discover that there is FM,
and a whole new world opens up to you.

The Void

On the other hand, there are those who have no spiritual life
and feel a tremendous emptiness inside; they may have seemingly everything they desire, and yet they are keenly aware that
something vital is missing. They feel a longing, a yearning . . . and
they are searching for the answer to their pain. The thirteenth-
century poet Rumi, a Sufi mystic, captures the poignancy of such
a void:

> *"Anyone apart from someone he loves understands*
> *what I say.*
> *Anyone pulled from a source longs to go back. . . ."*
> —*Rumi*

Some people try to fill the void by compulsive shopping,
eating, drinking, gambling, sex, or working. I have learned firsthand that nothing will fill that bottomless pit except a connection with the divine spirit. Only God—and when I say God, I
do not mean a white man with a beard sitting on a cloud; I
mean anything and everything connected to the mystery of life:
earth and ocean waves and baby giggles and spring breezes
and autumn leaves and compassionate gestures and the profound creative energy that runs through the universe providing
order and rhythm to our days, all of this spirit and more,

known by many names and images—only this God can ultimately satisfy our soul's longings.

Charting the Course

But how do you come to know this God? Which path will
take you there most directly? Some people will plainly tell you
that there is only one route, the route they follow, of course. I
believe, however, that there isn't only one "correct" way to
reach God, not one sole (or soul) saving way. I personally
think that there are many paths, each equally valid, to making a
connection with the eternal force.

I'm reminded of an often told story of three blind men
touching an elephant. One says, "I am certain that this creature
is long and skinny with hair at the end." He was feeling the tail.
Another says, "No, I know the truth: this creature is tough and
thick and wide." He was feeling the body. The last said, "No,
no, I am enlightened—this creature is wide but thin and dry
and papery." He was touching the ear. Each felt something different, but each confidently concluded that he knew the truth.
Each was partially correct. The truth was, it was all the same
elephant. Likewise, with God, there are many ways to experience and describe and proclaim the truth . . . but it's all the
same elephant.

Before we continue our discussion on this pillar, however, I
think it's important to make a distinction between religion and
spirituality. I happen to think that both are vital to the life of
the inner grown-up, though they are, in fact, quite different.

Religion—as I refer to it—means that which men and women have created to get in touch with the spirit. It means the
churches and mosques and temples, the community of people,
the sets of beliefs and creeds, the sanctioned rituals. Being religious means committing to regular attendance in the organized
church, mosque, or temple of your choice. It means connecting
with and caring for a community of like-minded people who
share your belief system. It means supporting this institution

with your time, talents, and finances. It also might mean electing to wear certain clothing, eat certain foods, perform certain activities. And it could mean witnessing if not participating in the inevitable politics of such an organization. Religion has always been a social and historical force in our culture. All of this may or may not actually lead to a relationship with the spirit.

Spirituality, on the other hand—as I refer to it—is that private and personal relationship that one builds with the divine, just you and God together. It isn't necessary to have a "religion" in order to do this, though it may be helpful. Typically a spiritual practice facilitates your relationship with and connection to the Holy. This could mean private rituals of prayer and meditation, inspirational readings, listening to music, attending workshops and retreats, developing spiritual friendships, performing yoga and other forms of exercise, connecting with nature. One's personally tailored spiritual life can be filled with a variety of practices drawn from a variety of religious traditions.

Research shows that *both* religion and spirituality have a positive effect on your health, your well-being, even your longevity. This evidence demonstrates why this pillar is an important one. (Not to mention that it makes life more meaningful.) The problem is that both religion and spirituality are very complicated, sometimes accounting for much pain and misery in our world.

Some people tell me that they are spiritual but cannot tolerate the hypocrisy of organized religion. Others tell me that they belong to a church but they do it for social reasons and have no private relationship with (or even necessarily a belief in) God. Still others tell me that both religion and spirituality leave them cold and that they have no use for such nonsense in their lives. I think it's important to begin exploring what this pillar means in your life by going back to the beginning, that is, examining what sort of religious background you grew up with. Often, for better or for worse, as with most things in our lives, our childhood experience sets the stage for our grown-up realities.

> **Try This . . .**
> Chart the progression of your faith along a chronological line,
> beginning with your birth through the present year, connecting
> the highs and lows along a line, moving up and down like a
> mountain range (or think of it as a spiritual EKG if you're medi-
> cally minded). Note the peaks and valleys in your journey of
> faith. Do you have mostly peaks? Mostly valleys? Where do you
> place yourself currently?

The Power of the Past

One of the exercises I am fond of assigning in my groups
and workshops is asking people to draw three God pictures:
the God of their childhood, the God of their youth, and the
God of their present. With astonishing predictability, most people draw the God of their childhood as one of a stern, rather
fierce guy with a white beard peering from the clouds, often
with a lightning bolt in his hands ready to hurl at the sinners
below. This God was vengeful, rather ornery, and had a downright nasty disposition. No wonder adults who grew up with
this image of God later have issues with organized religion.

Unfortunately, many people, having had a negative experience with the rules, regulations, and perhaps even fear that religion offered them as children, close the door on the whole
issue. Rather than search for a new relationship with a religion
or with God, they let a negative association from the past get in
their way. In other words, their wounded inner child replays itself, convincing them that a church or synagogue is a bad
place, full of judgment and wrath, filled with fanatical people.

Similarly, if a person had a negative experience with his parent, say a mother who was emotionally distant, withholding,
even punitive, there is an unconscious projection that God, the
heavenly parent, operates in the same way. We learn from our
parents—or so we think we do—how the world, and perhaps
even heaven, operates.

Isn't it possible that just as inner child baggage like fear, pain, or anger may interfere with your psychological and emotional life, it could also be interfering with your spiritual/religious life? Perhaps a negative experience with religion, or with your parents, is getting in your way now of plunging deeply into a committed life of the spirit.

Or perhaps it wasn't an overtly negative relationship with religion so much as just a superficial experience, or a nonobservant one. Many people grow up practicing no organized religion. As humans, we seem predisposed to worship something beyond the limited scope of ourselves. Even our culture influences us to worship *something*, even if it's only money and power. Furthermore, while children especially seem to have an innate sense of the holy, if it is not nurtured, this sense becomes weaker and weaker over time.

So whether your past brings heavy negative baggage or lighter invisible baggage, it is still up to you to choose for things to be different now. It is your choice to develop your own spiritual relationship with all that is holy. It is your option to drop the baggage, let go of past assumptions, and commit yourself to a different kind of grown-up spirituality.

Try This . . .

Create your own God pictures:

Draw a picture of the God of your childhood.

Draw a picture of the God of your youth.

Draw a picture of the God of your present.

How do these images affect your current views on spirituality and religion? Are they holding you back or have you integrated them?

Refurbished Faith

What I have found in my specialty as a bereavement counselor is that many people develop a new, reconfigured spirituality after a major loss. Suddenly a world that seemed to make sense has been shattered, and often that includes a person's faith. At this point faith requires a major overhaul.

Jeremy was a thirty-nine-year-old sales manager with a wife and three children and a basically happy life. He and his family were driving home, ironically from a funeral, when Jeremy's wife, Marsha, slumped over in the car. Her head fell over onto him. Jeremy thought maybe she was emotionally fatigued from the funeral. He called to her, "Honey, what's wrong?" Silence. "What's wrong?" Marsha had had a heart attack. After a dramatic sequence of pulling off the road to get help, administering CPR, riding in an ambulance to an emergency room, Jeremy's wife died at the hospital. They had just celebrated their eighteenth wedding anniversary.

That was over ten years ago. Jeremy had quite a journey afterward. He learned how to grieve and he learned how to raise three children alone. He eventually went back to graduate school and became a grief counselor himself in order to help others. But it was his faith that most dramatically changed. In some ways it became less naive, less childlike. His theology became riddled with more questions and fewer answers. But he told me, "That's what good spirituality does; it's not having the answers but having better and better questions."

He also told me, "It changed my focus and my image of God to one who struggles with you, one who walks with you in your pain." And although there was now a crack in his cosmic egg, he told me that the crack serves to let in more light.

After a death, a divorce, or a job loss, this is often when faith is questioned, reworked, lost, and found. Our contextual frame is stretched. And for some the frame first collapses. It may have to be painstakingly rebuilt over time. But surely the process of doubt and struggle can ultimately end in renewed faith.

Fortunately, a major loss is not necessary for this kind of spiritual shift to occur. Our spiritual and religious lives can become deeper, stronger, more complicated, richer simply because we decide that this should be so. It doesn't happen haphazardly but is born of choice and determination. I do believe that those who earnestly seek shall find.

Remembering Religion

David came to me in a broken state. He was abusing alcohol and marijuana, was having trouble concentrating at work, and had just been dumped by his girlfriend. He spoke of an emptiness inside, a longing for something "more" in his life. In the course of our work together, I asked David if he would consider looking for a church. He was not raised in a particular faith, thus it had never even dawned on him to consider looking for a religious community. But fortunately for him, since he didn't have negative baggage about religion from the past, he agreed to go to a Sunday service and see what it was like.

Although he felt odd at first, David went to several church services, exploring and experimenting as he went. What he eventually found was a community where he felt welcomed; he was amazed by the dimension of connectedness that it added to his life. Simultaneously, he cut back on his drinking and gave up marijuana altogether. For him, he found a religion, but his spiritual life has been slower to develop. He says he feels awkward when praying. He doesn't automatically express gratitude to a deity for the blessings in his life. He's not sure what he thinks about God. But he is open to developing a spiritual life, just as he was open to finding a religion. And although he still has many questions and doubts, he is willing to put these aside to experience the warm, enveloping, peaceful feeling that he has when at church.

DARE to Believe

Sometimes, what we grew up with no longer fits. Like a snake that sheds its skin as it grows, we sometimes have to cast off ideas that no longer work or that get in our way and hold us back. That's when it becomes time to rethink religion.

Martha grew up in the Catholic tradition and recalls being terrified of the nuns who slapped her hands with a ruler when she misbehaved. She tried to make religion work for her as an adult, but she could never make the connection. She married. She raised her children with no religion. But as she grew older, she realized that something was missing in her life, and she began to reexamine her beliefs.

Using the DARE technique she *detached*, stepped back from the situation, and saw that there was a void. She became *aware* that her negative experiences with nuns when she was a child had virtually informed her entire religious life since. She saw that her baggage with the Catholic Church had caused her to reject all religion, even a religious upbringing for her children.

So, Martha *reoriented* to her inner grown-up by realizing that things were different now. She was no longer a frightened child subject to the dogma being taught. She was a grown woman who could make her own informed decisions. She could explore and pick and choose where she felt comfortable. She asked herself, "Isn't it possible that I could have a broader sense of God and religion now?"

Thus, she *enacted* by embarking on a spiritual pilgrimage. She explored Eastern religions and New Age philosophies as well as traditional Western religious concepts. She began to pray and was happily developing a rich spiritual life.

Still, she felt that something was missing, and for her that was a religious community to belong to. Having a private spiritual life was tremendous, but she felt she was falling prey to a brand of spiritual narcissism that can come from practicing all alone. She needed a group of like-minded individuals to share the journey.

After much searching, finally, at the age of sixty-five, she landed in the religiously liberal tradition of the Unitarian Universalist Church. Describing herself as a "recovering Catholic" (and not to bash Catholicism, because many people feel negatively about other traditions as well), she said she felt like she had come home at last when she found the Unitarian Church.

Here was a group of people who honored questions and doubts as much as the answers. Here were people who were open and inclusive.

And the final step of DARE for Martha, to *evaluate*, confirmed for her that as a result of her open search, she discovered a place and a practice that has brought depth and meaning to her life. It's never too late to embark on the journey to find the right religious community for you. The rewards are well worth the effort.

On the pilgrimage to seek community and seek divinity, it is useful to know that there are different ways to relate to one's faith. There are two distinct positions—inner child spirituality and inner grown-up spirituality—both of which are vital aspects to a relationship with the Holy.

Inner Child Spirituality

The inner child possesses an openness and experiences a sense of awe when contemplating the spirit. He isn't overly concerned with matters of proof, scientific evidence, logic, or rationalism. The life of the spirit operates on a certain amount of faith—a leap that perhaps defies logic and reason but is grounded in a deep "knowing." The inner child isn't afraid of such a leap because she is accustomed to operating from a gut level.

And coming from this level, a place of pure intuition, can be highly emotional. When you are touched by the spirit and filled with grace, and when you experience this miracle with inner child vulnerability, it can move you to tears and take your breath away.

Being like a child with God means that we turn to God for comfort, strength, guidance, and help. With our hands open in supplication, we cry to our God for support and we yearn for the love that only this heavenly parent can supply.

Deborah is a woman whose twelve-year-old nephew was recently diagnosed with lymphoma. She was initially overcome by her own grief, pain, and fear. Then she took on her sister's pain and fear. Finally she realized that she couldn't handle this situation by herself. Despite support from friends and family, she needed strength from a source beyond this world. Part of claiming her inner grown-up was knowing that she needed help, and in this case divine help. She began going to church daily and also intensifying her prayer practice. The result, she said, was amazing. She felt that she was turning the burden over to God, knowing that she could not control the outcome. It was both liberating and calming for her to have a set of divine "shoulders" to lean on.

While inner child spirituality—being able to depend completely on God—is healing at times, it should not be confused with what I call Santa Claus theology. You cannot pray to God for whatever you wish and hope to have every prayer answered: such as, "Dear God, please let me win the lottery." God is not a genie. And just because you pray for God to save your mother during her battle with cancer and then she dies anyway, doesn't mean that God has disappeared or spurned your prayers.

God is with us even when it seems that he is not. Perhaps everything is part of God's plan, perhaps not. In the end, we don't really know why things happen the way they do. I certainly don't have the answers, but I have learned to tolerate and even revere mystery. I do know that God is present no matter what, as a support and comfort, answering our prayers for strength and guidance, loving us and caring for us, in both the good times and the bad.

Inner Grown-up Spirituality

If you leave your spiritual life at the level of only the inner child, then you will be missing an entire dimension of what it means to live a life centered in spirituality. To expand your spiritual experience, to activate your inner grown-up, requires becoming God's partner, a co-creator on this planet.

I wouldn't go so far as to say that we become "peers"

with God exactly; I would say that the mature shift in perspective is to see yourself as "like" God, an imitator of God—a creator and compassionate presence. William Ellery Channing, a great American nineteenth-century philosopher and theologian, preached a sermon in 1828 entitled "Likeness to God." He said,

> It is plain, too, that likeness to God is the true and only preparation for the enjoyment of the universe. In proportion as we approach and resemble the mind of God, we are brought into harmony with the creation; for, in that proportion, we possess the principles from which the universe sprung; we carry within ourselves the perfections, of which its beauty, magnificence, order, benevolent adaptations, and boundless purposes, are the results and manifestations. God unfolds himself in his works to a kindred mind.

Imagine thinking of ourselves as a kindred mind with the ultimate power in the universe. Then we may become an extension of God, a channel for God's work, collaborators in bringing about peace, love, justice, truth, and healing. We become kindred spirits with God and have a common mission.

I heard someone share the following reading at my church, and it beautifully points out the potential of being a messenger for God's word on this earth. The source is unknown but the wisdom profound:

> At the last session on the last morning of a two-week seminar on Greek culture, led by intellectuals and experts in their fields, Alexander Papaderos rose from his chair at the back of the room and walked to the front. . . . He turned and made the ritual gesture, "Are there any questions?" Quiet quilted the room. These two weeks had generated enough questions for a lifetime, but for now there was only silence.
>
> "No questions?"
>
> Papaderos swept the room with his eyes. So I asked, "Dr. Papaderos, what is the meaning of life?" The usual laughter followed, and people stirred to go. Papaderos held up his hand

and stilled the room and looked at me for a long time, asking with his eyes if I was serious, and seeing from my eyes that I was.

"I will answer your question." Taking his wallet out of his hip pocket, he fished into his leather billfold and brought out a very small round mirror, about the size of a quarter. And what he said went like this:

"When I was a small child, during the war, we were very poor and we lived in a remote village. One day, on the road, I found the broken pieces of a mirror. A German motorcycle had been wrecked in that place. I tried to find all the pieces and put them together, but it was not possible, so I kept only the largest piece. This one. And by scratching it on a stone, I made it round. I began to play with it as a toy and became fascinated by the fact that I could reflect light into dark places where the sun would never shine—in deep holes and crevices and dark closets. It became a game for me to get light into the most inaccessible places I could find. I kept the little mirror, and as I went about my growing up, I would take it out in idle moments and continue the challenge of the game. As I became a man, I grew to understand that this was not just a child's game, but a metaphor for what I might do with my life. I came to understand that I am not the light or the source of the light. But light—truth, understanding, knowledge—is there, and it will only shine in many dark places if I reflect it.

"I am a fragment of a mirror whose whole design and shape I do not know. Nevertheless, with what I have, I can reflect light into the dark places of this world—into the black places in the hearts of men—and change some things in some people. Perhaps others may see and do likewise. This is what I am about. This is the meaning of my life."

If you are an ambassador of God, a goodwill agent, it means your mission is to reflect light into dark places. But God is more than just a force outside of the self, a bigger something that you become the spokesperson for. Inner grown-up spirituality is coming to know that God dwells within you as well, that you are connected to God from the inside out.

Divinity Within

With the other three pillars, we started within and worked
our way out. With the responsibility pillar, you learned to own
your core and be responsible to yourself before you could look
outward and become a forum for an interconnected web of being responsible to others. With the maturity pillar, you learned
to forgive and accept yourself, even with all of your imperfections, before you could forgive others and transcend emotion.
And with the love pillar, you learned to love yourself first before you could spill that love out to others. This inward first
orientation is a sound principle. Even the airlines recommend
that, in the event of an emergency, you fit your own oxygen
mask on first before you attempt to assist others.

With the spirituality pillar, however, we start by becoming
aware of something larger than ourselves first. It is by initially
looking outside of the self, beyond the self, that we make a
connection to the spirit that can later lead us back inside, to the
spark of divinity that glows within. Each week the benediction
from All Souls Church in New York City reminds us of this: "For
the light of God shines upon us and out from within us."

It is the inner grown-up who recognizes the paradox that
this source of life transcends the self yet is within the self, that
the kingdom of God is beyond you yet within you. But this is
not the same as the New Age notion that you *are* God. I ask,
"Did you create the trees, the seasons, the stars, the universe?"
No, but some energy force did. And you are a part of that.

One woman who wrote me with her thoughts on spirituality
shared the following:

Even though I sometimes need to see God as an all-loving
Father/Mother figure, I also cherish the concept of possessing
the divine within me. I had never quite thought about it this
way until one of my teachers challenged me by saying, "What
would it take for you to believe that you are divine?" At the
time I told her I had enough trouble dealing with the human
part! But over time, I came to realize that the same truth had

been taught to me in grammar school, that we "are temples of the Holy Spirit."

Now I know that each of us possess God within, we too are touched by the divine, "built in the image and likeness." I now really believe that each of us, no matter how bad or wicked we appear to be, possess within us, God. It is our choice to hide that presence or not acknowledge or recognize it.

I see God as all the goodness in the world, all the love that each of us can possibly possess and then magnified into infinity. I see and know God as the source of love, inspiration, and creativity. I see God as the Connector, the invisible thread. So, my growing up has allowed me to see God far beyond anything any church or religious organization could teach me. I see a God without limit, and that presence is inside of me!

Being aware of that presence within brings enormous power and strength into your life. I was once watching an old rerun of *Gunsmoke* (believe it or not) and in this episode, the hero, marshal Matt Dillon, had been shot in the back. They were transporting him by train to Denver for surgery when the train was hijacked by robbers. The "doc" refused to operate on Matt because he said he was too old, didn't have the proper instruments, and so forth . . . but time was running out and they still weren't on their way to Denver. Then a priest on board told the doctor something to the effect of, "Of course you cannot perform the operation, not on your own. But if you let God help you and let Him work through you, then you'll be able to do the surgery." P.S. Doc did the operation and Matt came through with flying colors, just in time to shoot the bad guy and save the train. The point, of course, is that when you connect to God within you, you access a power that enables you to scale mountains that would otherwise be too treacherous.

But how do you connect to that awesome power within? How do you get to know God? How do you experience the presence of the Holy? How do you open yourself to a spiritual life?

Building a Relationship

I once belonged to a prayer group that met monthly. Each time we gathered we began with an opening focus question: "How is your relationship with God now?" Every month each of us answered this question differently. Having a relationship with God means first becoming aware of God's presence . . . seeing God's handiwork in the smiling face of a child, hearing God's voice in the wind that dances through the treetops, tasting God's grace in a lusciously ripe summer peach.

I have a friend who says that she cannot be aware of or talk to God because she has neither the time nor the energy. She has the labor-intensive job of caring for a two- and a four-year-old. She thinks she needs a quiet sanctuary, a retreat to invoke the Holy. I tell her that God isn't only in heaven. He doesn't require a specific devout manner of address. God is present when your two-year-old smooshes a peanut butter sandwich on the table. Talk to God then. God is present when your four-year-old refuses to put on her shoes and socks before preschool. Talk to God then.

God is present with the inmate on death row who may or may not have committed the crime. God is there in chaos and in order. God is there in the darkness and in the light. Don't wait for your world to become divinely quiet and ordered before you seek the eternal ground of all being. You can notice God in grocery lines. You can talk to God while at a stoplight. You can pray while brushing your teeth, while taking a shower. There's no reason to wait.

But what eventually happens is that once you begin to notice God's presence everywhere, once you become more cognizant of and appreciative of the sunlight and the fresh breezes and the spring flowers, once you feel God guiding you and sustaining you, then fast-food prayers squeezed into your life don't seem to be enough. You realize that you need "quality time" with God. You need to make a commitment to making that relationship in your life a priority.

Spiritual Practice

I was in a women's discussion group once and we were talking about the "commitments" in our lives, our covenants, the promises we keep (or don't keep). Most people were talking about commitments to their children, their husbands, their work. Then one woman quietly admitted that one of her most important commitments was her commitment to God.

I remember being very struck by her comment. In our predominantly secular society, we often overlook our covenant to God, while other cultures, particularly those in the Middle East, build spiritual practices into their daily routines. This woman in the group went on to say that for her, commitment to God meant being a loving and kind and honest person. And it also meant committing herself to a spiritual practice, a special time to talk to God every day (prayer) and a time to listen to God every day (meditation).

Part of inner grown-up spirituality means making a deep spiritual commitment—commitment to a life of holiness, to a religious institution, and to a regular discipline of connecting with the sacred.

One aspect of a spiritual practice is prayer. But what is prayer exactly? I once talked with a young man susceptible to anxiety and depression, and I commented that he didn't seem to feel anchored in his soul to any presence outside of himself. He readily agreed. He told me, "But I don't have any idea how to pray. I never learned any prayers."

Now reciting the Psalms or the Lord's Prayer is lovely indeed, but is it the only way to pray? Is that the only way God hears? Personally I don't think so. I told this young man to just have a conversation with God. "Talk to him the way you might to your wife or to a friend. Just say, 'Hey, God, how's it going today?' "

Prayer as a spiritual practice is a time to momentarily stop the craziness of the world and to get centered in the depths of your soul. It's a time to quietly connect with what matters in this world. It offers an opportunity to get centered and focused. You can offer prayers of thanksgiving and gratitude. You can pray for others who are in need. You can pray for strength and guidance and direction. In the end, prayer isn't so much about what you *get*, but about what you *become* as a result of it. But for this to occur, you need to make time regularly for this pause in the rhythm of your life.

Try ten minutes after you wake up or ten minutes before you go to bed. You'll find that this becomes holy time, a prized reflective period that becomes necessary for your restoration and replenishment. At some point you may want more—twenty minutes daily for meditation. An hour. Certainly, it takes commitment and discipline to make this happen, just as it takes the same to implement an exercise regime. But think of this time as healthy exercise for the soul.

Other methods of spiritual practice include fasting, observing holy days, doing acts of service, and volunteering. Whatever rituals you can develop that stretch your soul and connect you to a holy spirit are suitable for your spiritual practice.

But you have to work on your relationship with God just as you would work on your relationship with any other loved one. And as with any relationship, that work requires time, attention, focus, and prioritization. I'm not saying that this is necessarily easy to do given our busy, overscheduled lives. And certainly you might encounter internal resistance if you happen to remember all the jarring and unpleasant memories that religion and God language used to evoke. That's when you need to dust off the DARE four steps to pull you out of the past and to mindfully bring you back to the present and the possibility that things can be different now.

The payoff, I believe, is a depth of peace and connectedness that gives life transcendent, luminous moments. Having a personal relationship with God, the great spirit of life, and having a commitment to a religious community can lift us beyond our daily lives of potential drudgery and minutiae. For me, tending my own religious and spiritual gardens makes me aware of the grace in my life and helps me know that I am not alone. Of course, there are always a few weeds that crop up, or sometimes I'm just too tired to tend the garden. But the potential harvest for each of us when we cultivate our inner grown-up qualities, such as discipline and an open-mindedness that honors the past but is freed from its constraints, is a bounty that helps anchor our being.

Spiritually Centered

In his book *Who Needs God*, Harold Kushner writes that Freud was once asked to summarize psychoanalysis in one sentence and he said, "Where id is, let ego be." I thought this was a very inner grown-up position, since he is advocating choice over impulse. Kushner wrote that if he had to summarize the Bible in one sentence, it would be "Don't do what you feel like doing; do what God wants you to do." Also a very inner grown-up perspective, I might add.

How do you know what God wants you to do? Well, you can assume that generically God wants you to be loving and forgiving and honest and helpful. Moreover, you can assume that there's something specific that God wants you, and only you, to do. When you spend quality time with God, when you work on the relationship, when you spend time listening, you eventually get a sense of being guided and directed. You come to feel or "hear" your calling.

A "calling" is not just reserved for the ministry, as is so often assumed. There can be a calling to medicine, to helping people, to being an artist, a writer, a parent, a scientist, a social activist . . . really the possibilities are endless. Few people have mystical callings from burning bushes or from visions in the night sky. Most of us perceive our callings by listening to that quiet voice within, the voice of intuition, the voice of God that persistently nudges and directs us. You know it's a calling when a certain feeling takes hold in your mind, heart, and soul and just won't let go. Try though you might to silence it, it continues.

Of course you can resist a call, as many people do. You might think, "Oh, no, I couldn't possibly do *that*; it's too risky/stupid/scary/dangerous/impossible. Many people spend their lives not fulfilling their spiritual potentials because they do not answer their callings. Free will gives us the opportunity to choose whether or not to do what is being asked of us.

Your calling may or may not result in an actual career—it could be a serious hobby or a serious volunteer commitment. And callings change through the years as you continue to change and grow. There isn't necessarily one big Calling (with a capital *C*); there might be many smaller callings (with a lower-case *c*).

Are you using your God-given talents for good? Are you answering your callings? Are you fulfilling your spiritual potential?

Peaks and Valleys

As with any relationship, there will be times when your spiritual practice is flowing smoothly and you will feel spiritually centered and on track in your life. And then there will be other times when you feel estranged, distant, removed from God. When you listen for guidance, you will hear only the silence. This is okay. Don't be afraid to allow natural rhythms to emerge . . . natural highs and lows.

It's important to remember that religion and spirituality *change* over time. P. D. James writes, "It is a condition of faith that it gets lost from time to time, or at least mislaid." Religion and spirituality are fluid. By this I mean that at some points in your life you might be active in a religious institution, serving on the board, chairing committees, then at other times, you don't even manage to attend weekly services. Similarly, at times you might, for example, feel very close to God. You might rely on a consistent prayer life, meditation, walks in the woods. But at other times, you might feel distant, even estranged from God, and find yourself unable to pray.

I heard a minister once tell her congregation, "If your spiritual life is the same five years from now as it is on this very day, then something is wrong." Your insights shift and deepen as life continues to unfold, as you continue to be shaped by your experiences, and as your perspective continues to shift as you age.

The Sustaining Spirit

Having a faith-filled life, even with its inevitable ups and downs, enables us to go on and live deeply in spite of the fact that life will end. Death is not an option, no matter what we pretend to tell ourselves. The Reverend Forrest Church, minister and author, says, "Religion is our human response to the dual reality of being alive and having to die."

Many religions focus on what may happen after this life, be it eternal life in heaven, eternal damnation, or the wheel of reincarnation. For many, some other celestial world brings hope and consolation to this world. Of course, none of us *really* knows what will happen after we die (despite near-death experience accounts). But having faith, trusting in God, carries you through the uncertainty and assures a sense that, somehow, all will be well. This is a comforting, supportive thought for both your inner child and your inner grown-up.

If you're still having trouble imagining a spiritual life for yourself, think of God as your pilot light. Your stove burner may not be on, but the pilot light is still glowing within, keeping the possibility of heat alive. All you have to do is turn on the burner and the pilot light will ignite a flame. Even when you see no evidence of fire, the pilot light burns persistently inside.

To put it another way, it's important to search and find your road. There are many pathways to truth, many windows facing toward the light. The spiritual journey—in whatever forms it may take and wherever it may ultimately lead you—is in the end, I believe, an essential journey for growing up and for making this life adventure worthwhile and meaningful.

The Spirituality Pillar in Review

The void—existential angst, the dark night of the soul that we all eventually face—becomes tolerable with the help of a divine presence. Connecting with this powerful peace, coming to know a sacred spirit that is both within and beyond us, of which we are a part, brings a rest to the soul. This holiness is found in private spiritual realms and in public religious communities.

It is time to release any former negativity that has trapped you in a secular prison. It is time to look for a new way, a way that embraces mystery and possibility.

The inner child is comforted by God. The inner child finds awe and majesty in God's universe. The inner grown-up becomes God's partner, creating and serving and shining light in dark places.

Work on your relationship with God—work on it despite its inevitable ups and downs. Make your faith a priority and embrace the call to follow a spiritual path. You will never regret it.

READING
"On Prayer"
by Gordon B. McKeeman

How Does One Address a Mystery?

Cautiously—
> *let us go cautiously, then,*
> *to the end of our certainty,*
> *to the boundary of all we know,*
> *to the rim of uncertainty,*
> *to the perimeter of the unknown*
> > *which surrounds us.*

Reverently—
> *let us go with a sense of awe and wonder,*
> *a feeling of approaching a powerful holy*
> *whose lightning slashes the sky,*
> *whose persistence splits concrete with green sprouts,*
> *whose miracles are present in every place and moment.*

Hopefully—
> *out of the need for wholeness in our lives,*
> *the reconciliation of mind and heart,*
> *the intersection of the timeless with time.*

Quietly—
> *for no words can explain the inarticulate*
> *or summon the Presence*
>> *That is always present even in our absence.*

But what shall I say?

Anything—
> *any anger, any hope, any fear, any joy, any request,*
> *any word that comes from the depth of being*
> *or perhaps,*
>> *nothing—no complaint, no request, no entreaty,*
>> *no thanksgiving, no praise, no blame,*
>> *no pretense of knowing or not knowing.*

Simply be in the presence of Mystery,
> *unashamed—unadorned—unafraid.*

And, at the end, say—Amen

VISUALIZATION

Begin by getting your body prepared to relax. Stretch your arms high over your head. Then stretch them to your sides, reaching out. Drop your arms, and gently roll your head from side to side. Settle your body into a comfortable position, and close your eyes.

Think about the words that you just heard from the reading. What do they make you think of? Did the reading evoke a feeling? Did the reading remind you of any experience from your own life? Take whatever message it is that you need from the reading.

Now bring your attention to your body and where you are in the room. Notice your breath, breathing in and breathing out. Notice the air around you and how it feels on your skin. Listen for any noises that may be near you. Notice any smells in the air. Become *mindful* of your environment and your place in it. Feel the weight of your clothes on your body.

Feel the weight of your body on the floor or in your chair. Take three slow, deep breaths. Your consciousness is going on a journey.

Imagine yourself deflated, emptied, like a flattened balloon. Then imagine a cord from your back that dangles behind you. You notice a wall outlet near you that is radiating light. Reach the cord to the wall and "plug in" to this divine outlet. See your body filling with light, a buoyant luminosity that floods throughout your limbs. Feel your body being filled with holy air and energy, filling up the deflated balloon. Absorb God's strength, peace, love, and power that is charging through you. Bask in this divine energy letting it saturate your body. Then unplug from the outlet, retaining the energy within and knowing that you can plug in again whenever you need to be recharged.

Now, when you are ready, your consciousness returns to your body on a wave of light. Start to sense your body in the room. Feel your mind and body getting grounded and integrated. Wiggle your fingers and toes. Take a deep breath. Start to move your arms and legs gently from side to side. Take another deep breath. Allow yourself to feel a vibrant energy coursing through your body, revitalizing you. I'm going to count from one to five, and when you are ready, after the count of five, you may open your eyes. One . . . two . . . three . . . four . . . five. You may open your eyes.

JOURNAL QUESTIONS

Core Question: Do you believe in a spiritual presence in this world that loves and sustains you?

Have you ever taken a "leap" of faith? When and how?

How does your faith translate into concrete action?

Do you allow yourself to be angry at God?

What gets in your way of developing a relationship with a higher power?

How is your life different because of your faith? How could it be different?

What is your spiritual practice? How can you deepen it?

What are your gifts/talents to share? Are you sharing them?

What is your ministry in this life?

What are you called to do? How do you know? Are you doing it?

How does your spirit become restored? Are you doing this regularly?

EXERCISES

DARE to Change: Look for ways to apply this technique to the spirituality pillar.

Notice this week and fill in:

SITUATION	DETACH	AWARE	REORIENT	ENACT
What happened	Pull back	How I was regressing (inner child)	Remember that things can be different now; I am a grown-up	How I did change or could've changed thoughts/ behaviors
				EVALUATE How did it go?

Visit a Cemetery: (I'm not kidding . . . especially a historic one, if possible.) Walk among the tombstones. Read the names of those who have lived and died before you. This isn't a morbid activity; it is a way to put your own life in perspective, to trivialize the trivial. Know that you will end up in a cemetery yourself one day (or somewhere comparable). Do not be afraid to face your mortality. Knowing that you will die can infuse your life with purpose rather than aimlessness.

What do you plan to do with this one precious wild ride of your life before it's over? What does God want you to do with it?

Attend Religious Services: Over the course of the next six months, attend six different religious services from a variety of denominations and faiths. Think of yourself as a reporter, someone observing from a distance. What do you notice that feels right? What feels awkward or uncomfortable? What are the people like who attend these services? What is this experience like for you?

Prayer: Pray and pray and then pray again. Don't pray to God as the big Santa Claus in the sky who may grant your wish on Christmas morning. Talk to God and ask for guidance, peace, strength, understanding. This may be incredibly difficult. If so, "act as if." In other words, pray even if you don't believe in it or understand it. Pretend. Ask others about how and whether they pray. Talk to people. Explore. Read books about prayer. Question and struggle. But pray. Every day. Build it into your daily routine. See what miracles happen.

List: Make a list of fifty blessings in your life for which you are grateful. Think of these as graces, unearned gifts, in your life for which you should give thanks. Think broadly. As you reflect on this list, what does it say about you? Is it difficult to list blessings in your life? Is it difficult to thank a holy power for these gifts?

Card for God: Make a thank-you card for God, a valentine card of sorts. Feel free to use a variety of materials to make this card/collage of gratitude, thanking the holy one for the graces in your life. As the author Sam Keen wisely notes, "The more you become a connoisseur of gratitude, the less you are the victim of resentment, depression, and despair."

PART

III

The Best of Both

CHAPTER NINE

Integrating Your Inner Child and Your Inner Grown-up

Believe that life is worth living, and your belief will help create the fact.

—William James

He was sitting at my kitchen table. This was a man I had known since I was a child. He had always been so serious, so formal. He had built his life on being a prominent doctor, as well as chief of staff of a prestigious hospital. When I heard that he was retiring early at the age of fifty-seven, I, like everyone else, thought he would be lost without his work. He would probably become depressed, idle, rootless.

But instead, he surprised us all. He was having the time of his life. He told me, "I realized I'd never had any fun in my life. Now I'm making up for lost time." He spends his days down on the floor playing with his grandchildren. He goes golfing, reads novels, meets friends for lunch, travels. At the age of fifty-seven, he has finally integrated the best aspects of his inner child with the best aspects of his inner grown-up.

The Wonder Child

The inner grown-up without a doubt *needs* the inner child, especially the wonder child. Remember, that is the part of the self that nurtures fun, awe, enthusiasm, creativity, joy. All of these aspects are vital for good mental health. Without them, we run the risk of frowning too much, feeling the weight of the world on our shoulders, or, worst of all, falling prey to the perspective of the cynical chic. The cynical chic take pride in their high-brow negativity.

Did you ever see the classic movie *Miracle on 34th Street*? The young Natalie Wood plays a little girl who is so practical that she doesn't believe in Santa Claus. Her mother has raised her with a "realistic" perspective on life. Here is an example of a child who, ironically, has more inner grown-up than inner child in her system. By the end of the movie, however, she does claim that wonder child within her.

The wonder child cleanses skepticism from our systems, offering us innocence again. She restores an elusive quality of mystery to our days. She makes us more productive, more curious, and more alive. She keeps us dreaming. Remember, the wonder child is an idealized version of childhood. Many of us may have never actually lived a childhood so magical, but the idealized essence is still available to us.

Happily, it's never too late to claim the wonder child. I was having lunch with a friend, and she was describing to me the unbridled joy that she used to experience when she was a child and she sang in church. "I have images of myself as a little girl singing in choir where there's this joyous contemplation of singing to God . . . but I lost that through the years. I lost that image of myself. I'm starting to recapture it now that I've gotten sober and pulled my life together. I'm finding my way back to feeling that way, that flash of the little girl—she's still there inside of me—who was so joyful in her praising God. It's coming back to me."

My friend realized the irony that by "growing up" she could reconnect with her child self. Often it is in going forward and growing up that we are then free to reach backward, retaining the best from an idyllic, romanticized past. The inner child (the wonder child) brings a refreshing perspective to each of the four pillars: to responsibility he brings a lightness and freedom, lest we get overwhelmed by obligations; to maturity he brings surprise and adventure, lest we get stifled by seriousness; to love he brings a passion and playfulness, lest we get mired in the heaviness of commitments; and to spirituality he brings an awe and reverence, lest we get dulled by religious routine.

Try This . . .

When you are feeling overly stressed, take some time off and let your inner child take over. Go out and *play*. When was the last time you . . . swung on a swing? went to a funny movie (try renting a Marx Brothers film)? played dress-up or cops and robbers? painted with finger paints? made a mud pie? jumped in a pile of autumn leaves? Think of your favorite game when you were a child and go play it. Get creative. Get silly. Give yourself a break.

The Problem Child

Remember, as we discussed in chapters 1 and 2, the inner child is more than the wonder child. The inner child is also, at times, a problem child—the child who was hurt and abused and neglected, whose pain continues to contaminate the present. It's this child who is selfish and angry and fearful and impetuous. Consider this: Just as the wonder child sometimes needs to come out and loosen things up, occasionally the problem child needs to come out and throw a tantrum (as long as the inner grown-up is nearby to set limits and make sure things don't get out of control).

Just as the inner grown-up and the wonder child make a fabulous team, so do the inner grown-up and the problem child. To begin with, the inner grown-up is a wonderful influence on the problem child. The inner grown-up gently reminds this unruly toddler/adolescent that perhaps it's time to let go of the self-absorption, to be a little patient, to bravely act in spite of the fears. The inner grown-up comforts, instructs, and challenges the inner child. You just need to get them talking to each other.

Try This . . .

The next time you feel really scared or sad or disappointed or wronged, give yourself a time-out. Parents use a variation of this technique when their children are throwing tantrums. Allow yourself a short period of time and give your problem child free rein. Go in your room and cry, scream, throw pillows, and host a big-old pity party for yourself. Whine like a baby. Howl over your hurts. Throw a nice tantrum and let it all go. Afterward, reassert the inner grown-up's authority and use the DARE thought system to deal effectively with the problem. Remember to set limits!

Developing the Dialogue

One woman shared with me that she often has a conscious conversation between her inner adult and her inner child. It comes up the most, she said, around exercise. She said, "My inner child will whine, 'But I don't want to go for a run. I'm tired.' And my inner grown-up will tell her, 'That's too bad, but you're putting on your sneakers and we're going to go out for a run.' I just listen while they have a conversation about it and then I assert, 'It's okay if you don't want to, but we're going on a run anyway.' That's maturity for me."

Of course I myself was thirty years old before I really understood this lesson . . . when I was, in fact, giving birth to my first child. I had been in labor for over twenty hours and was feeling frightened. Because of my preexisting squeamishness and aversion to all things medical, I was a mess. A sweating, shaking mass of nerves and fear. I wanted the whole thing to be over (so much for the spiritual epiphany of childbirth for me).

Along the way, I developed a fever and the doctors became concerned that the baby needed to come out quickly as her heart rate was being elevated by my fever. But first they wanted to rule out whether I had strep throat—you know how they do that: that horrible swab they stick down your throat that makes you gag? The doctor came at me with the swab as I clamped my hand over my mouth and whined, "No, I can't." She tried again and I refused to comply. She tried a third time and I just shook my head and whimpered. Then she boomed, "Good God, woman, you are about to become a *mother.*"

As my husband recalls the incident, I reacted as if I had been slapped across the face. I thought to myself, "She's right." (My inner grown-up said to my inner child, "Get a grip.") I opened my mouth, accepted the swab, gagged accordingly, and got on about the business of giving birth to my daughter. My husband had never seen me so instantly changed.

Of course the trick is learning to activate your inner grown-up on your own. For me, at that time, I needed my ob-gyn to open my eyes. I'm learning to motivate myself, however, more and more often with the DARE technique. Similarly, I once was working with a couple on marital problems. The husband was being verbally abusive to his wife; essentially he was reacting from a frightened problem child position. I told him that his words were belittling and inappropriate. He thought about that for a minute and replied, "You're right. I guess I just needed someone to tell me to stop." I told him, "No, you don't need me to tell you that. *You* know when you've crossed the line. *You* know deep down when you should stop." We shouldn't need outside limits enforced upon us—children need that. The inner grown-up knows how to set the limits on his own.

Basically your inner grown-up needs to dialogue with your inner child, saying things like "Let's calm down and do what we need to do. Let go of that victim talk. Time to move on. Patience. Don't act out. Stop pouting." Your inner child needs to dialogue with your inner grown-up as well, saying things like "You need to relax. Let's take the day off or plan a vacation. You need to chill out and have some fun." Really, they can be the best of friends if you just get them talking!

Reframing the Picture

In chapter 6 on maturity, we talked about how the inner grown-up can actually look at the past in a new light, seeing it for more than we originally envisioned. This concept is worth revisiting since it is also the embodiment of how the inner grown-up can work with the inner child in a positive and helpful way, a way that allows us to reinterpret past events.

It's like taking the pieces from the past and rearranging them into a new puzzle. As Virginia Woolf said, "Arrange whatever pieces come your way"—the point is that you can choose how to arrange them. The inner grown-up takes the inner child by the hand and says, "Let's order these pieces differently. Let's see what other picture we can create." The inner grown-up, you might say, knows about "spin."

A forty-nine-year-old gay man, Charles, came to see me because he still was having trouble coping with the painful memories of his father abandoning him when he was nine years old. Charles's father apparently fell in love with another woman, left his wife and two sons, and never looked back. Charles has never heard from him to this day, some forty years later. In fact, he's not even sure whether his father is dead or alive. He told me that he felt like a "burn victim," so burned by the circumstances of his life that he couldn't seem to move past them.

His fears of abandonment were causing him severe distress and anxiety. He asked me, "How can my painful memories become just memories of pain?" In other words, how could he learn to detach from the emotional content of his past? How could his memories be without their customary potency?

In my work with Charles, he worked with the DARE technique. He got in touch with his inner grown-up. He tried other exercises from the Four-Pillar Program. We talked about his past. We reached out to his wounded child. All of this helped to a certain degree, but it wasn't until I asked him about the *benefits* of his difficult childhood that he really began to make progress.

I asked Charles what aspects of himself, what pieces of who he is now—especially the good qualities—are a direct result of his father's abandonment. He was stunned at first and couldn't grasp my meaning. But then, the light began to dawn. "I see what you mean," he gasped. "I am a more sensitive, compassionate man *because* I was burned. And I help others; I am a 'bridge over troubled water' to others in need *because* of what I experienced." Charles was very active in a Big Brothers program as well as a volunteer in his local homeless shelter. If his childhood hadn't happened the way it had, he might have grown up to be a very different kind of man, maybe one not quite so generous of heart.

He mused, "I never considered that the aspects of me that I consider treasures, my golden nuggets, could be traced directly to my pain and directly to my past."

In fact, when I asked him a fantasy question, he surprised himself by the response. I asked, "If I had a magic wand and I could change the past, but doing so would change the you who you are now, and that means all aspects of you, would you want me to change your childhood?"

Incredulously, after he thought about it for a few minutes, he answered, "No." When he reframed his past and saw it as the link to his current self (a bit anxious but loving and self-less), he no longer needed to bemoan it. When he rearranged the pieces of the past into a new puzzle, he liked the image he saw. Consider that it is an *irritant* (a grain of sand) that is eventually, over time, transformed into a pearl. Try to see your irritants as pearls in the making.

Let your inner grown-up initiate this internal shift so that instead of focusing on "Oh, this sad and terrible thing happened to me—woe is me," you begin to connect with "Yes, this sad thing happened, but look at how it changed the direction of my life and look at how it formed me into who I've become." Come to see pain as a pathway for your evolutionary growth, and you will attain a fresh vision.

Try This . . .
   Write a letter from your inner grown-up to your inner child.
Your inner grown-up has a perspective that your inner child never
had, that is, the future, or how things have turned out. Tell your
inner child what happened after you grew up. Tell your wounded
self from the past how you developed and how you grew because of what he experienced. Discuss all aspects of your development that resulted from that wounded child, even the good
ones (especially the good ones) and look for how they link back
to the past.

The Integration Advantage

In the end, in order to achieve a well-balanced sense of
peace and wholeness, we must incorporate the best of *all* inner
worlds. The inner child without the inner grown-up could
result in an existence devoid of purpose, and the inner grown-
up without the inner child could result in an existence devoid
of joy.

Think of it this way: the wonder inner child is basically like
a dessert. But if you only ate sweets all the time, you wouldn't
get the nourishment you need to grow. The wounded inner
child is like your vegetables. Some of them may not be as tasty
as a dessert, but they do provide vitamins and minerals for
growth. The inner grown-up is the substantial meat and pota-
toes meal. Of course, if you had that all the time, with no
dessert ever, after a time your diet would grow bland and un-
appealing. You need all of it: you need balance; you need
wholeness.

When the inner child and the inner grown-up are integrated, it's a source of regeneration and new vitality, a source
of completeness.

The integration image I use to represent this blending of the
inner grown-up and the inner child is a tree. The roots of the
tree are *spirituality*, anchoring the tree to the earth, keeping it

strong and grounded. The trunk of the tree is *love*, the solid center of one's life. The branches of the tree are both *responsibility* and *maturity*, weaving a wide network of support and strength. The wonder inner child is symbolized by the leaves— lots of waving, dancing, beautiful leaves that are at times fresh and green and other times a blazing colorful display. The wounded inner child is symbolized by the barren tree. Yet, while the leaves may fall and scatter, they do come back in the spring, renewed, in fresh form.

An important note: While the tree's weight is found in its trunk and branches, the tree is ultimately sustained by the leaves, which feed its internal system. Thus a tree that has no regenerating leaves will die. The tree is a complex plant that needs each of its parts in order to be whole and alive. Likewise, if *you* are missing any of the components to the self, for example, the wonder child, the wounded child, the pillars of the inner grown-up: responsibility, maturity, love, and spirituality—if you are missing any of these, then your being is less than whole. Your tree won't make it. Similarly, each piece is vital to the puzzle of your life. Each strand is an integral aspect to what makes up the unique tapestry of *you*.

The inner grown-up balanced with the inner child is intent on relishing all the gifts that life has to offer—connect to this energy source. Let your inner grown-up and the inner child together show you how to delight in your life.

Using Your Time Wisely

One way to value and love your life is to not waste it. How many of us just "kill" time, loads of time, useless time? I have a friend who felt like his life wasn't full enough. He assessed how he was spending his time, and he realized that he was spending hours and hours every week watching television. So, as an experiment, he gave up television for a month. The difference was amazing, he said. He honestly hadn't realized how much of a drain TV was having on his brain, on his life in general. I don't mean to be a television basher (all things in moderation), but a disproportionate amount of television viewing is a waste of valuable time. My friend found that he had loads of free time once he gave up the tube, so what was he going to do with it?

He decided to do something he had always wanted to do, even as a child. He took up the recorder, an early form of a flute. He took lessons. He practiced for hours. He joined ensembles. He began to perform locally. In fact, he started enjoying this newfound passion so much that he never went back to the television! He now spends his free time playing music and traveling to national music conferences to meet other musicians. His life is fuller. Note that he only developed this interest when he took the leap to love life and give up his drug of choice—that which deadened him, zoned him out—for him, the television.

A few summers ago, I read Stephen Covey's *First Things First*. As the title implies, it's about making your priorities in life and sticking to them. In this book, he makes a wonderful suggestion of writing a personal mission statement. You may have heard about mission statements for businesses and corporations. Often they are framed and prominently displayed or proclaimed on brochures. Usually the group devises one succinct sentence that summarizes their overall goals. For example, the national organization of Mothers Against Drunk Driving's (MADD) mission statement is "Our mission is to stop drunk driving, support the victims of this violent crime and prevent underage drinking." Or the Mount Washington Hotel in Bretton Woods, New Hampshire, states "Our commitment as staff and management is to provide each guest with a truly memorable experience, one which exceeds their expectations and entices them to visit us time and time again."

Or perhaps it could be several statements, even a paragraph, that summarizes a group's mission. I read in a local public school's newsletter: "Our Mission: Learning is a voyage. We are dedicated to awakening curiosity and creating an acceptance and respect for each individual. We will provide meaningful academic experiences through the ebb and flow of the ever-changing world."

So how about creating a mission statement for your life?

Writing a life mission statement means taking the time to reflect, prioritize, and pointedly capture in a sentence or two what is the purpose and meaning and mission of your life. Is it to sleepwalk through the journey? Certainly not. Awaken. Be present. Seize and savor. Maybe a mission statement will help you focus on what it is you need to be doing.

Try This . . .
Write a personal mission statement. Write one or several sentences that sum up what your life is about and what direction you should be moving in. Let this reflect, and perhaps become, the guiding vision for your life.

For the Love of Life

Occasionally someone is amazed and perhaps even horrified that I am a bereavement counselor. "Isn't it terribly depressing?" they ask. And they look at me as if I have been brushed by the cobwebs of the grim reaper.

It is at times heartbreaking to hear stories of trauma and sudden loss and tragic deaths. I am affected deeply by each person whom I work with. But what makes it meaningful and sustainable work is that I also find it incredibly inspiring. I see people broken by life . . . and then transformed. I see people walk through the valley of the shadow of death and not only emerge, but emerge with new strengths and new perspectives.

Also, I find that death blows the dust off my own life. It keeps me from taking a single thing for granted. Believe me, when you sit with a bereaved parent whose heart has been shattered, and then you come home to your own children, you want to hold them and never let go. It doesn't matter that the house is a mess, that they didn't do their homework, and that their shoes and socks are in the middle of the living room . . . at least they are alive.

Having chosen a profession that forces me to face death regularly reinforces for me how precious life is. Most people seem to be unaware of the awesome gift that life really is. They numb themselves with alcohol and drugs and overeating. They anesthetize themselves to any and all deep feelings. They rush through life in a whirlwind of busyness hardly stopping to notice what a gift it is to be them.

Are you strung out on substances, on work, deadened to the reality of this one precious lifetime? Do you seize and savor each day as if it were your last? When I was in high school, I played the part of Mrs. Webb in our drama department's production of Thornton Wilder's classic play *Our Town*. As Mrs. Webb, I was mother to the character Emily, who ends up dying in childbirth. In the third act of the play, Emily has the opportunity to relive a day. However, not only does she get to relive the day of her choice, she has to *watch* herself live it.

Emily chooses a happy day, her twelfth birthday, but she doesn't realize given her current perspective how painful this will be. Upon going back, she sees how blind living people are to their gifts. She implores her mother, "Oh, Mama, just look at me one minute as though you really saw me." She is overcome by their seeming indifference to the significance of life events and thus begs to be taken back to her new life with the dead. She says:

> It goes so fast. We don't have time to look at one another. I didn't *realize*. So *all* that was going on and we never noticed! Take me back—up the hill—to my grave. But first: Wait! One more look! Goodbye! Goodbye, world! Goodbye, Grover's Corners—Mama and Papa—Goodbye to clocks ticking—and my butternut tree! And Mama's sunflowers—and food and coffee—and new ironed dresses and hot baths—and sleeping and waking up!—Oh, earth, you're too wonderful for anyone to realize you! Do any human beings ever realize life while they live it—every, every minute?

No, most of us don't, can't . . . unless something strips clear our vision. I recently spoke at an annual Cancer Survivors' Day event in my town that was filled with men and women who were fighting for their lives. Some of them were in remission. Others may not live to see next year's celebration. Not a single person there takes their life for granted anymore. They savor time, knowing it is as ephemeral as a child's bubble blown through a pink plastic ring. Their view of life has been stripped down, cracked wide open to expose the most essential meanings. Most of us value something only after we have lost it, or are about to lose it.

When you are fully integrated as a person (with both your inner child and inner grown-up), complete and whole, you are free to love life with abandon, reverence, and gratitude. The integrated self urges you to relish this life—it's the only one you have.

A Package Deal

Loving life means, of course, savoring every step in the developmental journey, absorbing the smallest of details as a holy experience. But it also means accepting (if not loving) the darker sides of life. It means knowing that suffering and loss and death are inevitable. It means that unfairness and injustice occur daily and that free will accounts for atrocities even as it leads to acts of tender mercy. The joys are supreme but the costs are dear, and all of this is *life*. The darkness doesn't make life any less good any more than the goodness eliminates the shadows (though it takes only one candle to dispel the darkness).

Joy and sorrow, inextricably linked, forever entwined. Life—full of mysteries and enigmas that we may never understand. Life—full of questions that we will never have the answers to. But it's all part of the package deal. And even given these conditions, wouldn't you still choose life in spite of all the risks and ultimate pains? Wouldn't you still consider it a bargain to be allowed to live in this precious and wondrous world?

A Place of Peace

Calling forth your inner grown-up and letting him coexist with your inner child will bring more peace and security than you ever thought possible. You will love living in your own skin. You will take joy in the pleasures of your inner child, and you will take pride in honoring your inner grown-up. You will feel the lightness of your inner child tethered to the weight of your inner grown-up. And with that, you will sleep with a clear conscience and rise to greet each new day full of promise and opportunity.

Integration in Review

Your inner child and your inner grown-up *need* each other. They each are a positive influence on the other. So, keep them dialoguing—let them regularly communicate.

A critical element of integration is to see how the wounded inner child has developed into the current you. Your inner grown-up can spotlight the wonderful, loving, lovable, divine aspects of you that exist precisely because of your past. Remember that all of *that* has created all of *you*. Embrace the entire process and be grateful.

When your inner child and your inner grown-up are fully integrated, you become whole in a way that leads to balance and peace. This is when your vision comes into sharp focus for appreciating all that life has to offer, and the rewards are many.

READING
From *The Prophet*
by Kahlil Gibran

Your joy is your sorrow unmasked.
And the selfsame well from which your laughter rises was oftentimes filled with your tears.
And how else can it be?

The deeper that sorrow carves into your being, the more joy you can contain.

Is not the cup that holds your wine the very cup that was burned in the potter's oven?

And is not the lute that soothes your spirit, the very wood that was hollowed with knives?

When you are joyous, look deep into your heart and you shall find it is only that which has given you sorrow that is giving you joy.

When you are sorrowful look again in your heart, and you shall see that in truth you are weeping for that which has been your delight.

Some of you say, "Joy is greater than sorrow," and others say, "Nay, sorrow is the greater."

But I say unto you, they are inseparable.

Together they come, and when one sits alone with you at your board, remember that the other is asleep upon your bed.

VISUALIZATION

Begin by getting your body prepared to relax. Stretch your arms high over your head. Then stretch them to your sides, reaching out. Drop your arms, and gently roll your head from side to side. Settle your body into a comfortable position, and close your eyes.

Think about the words that you just heard from the reading. What do they make you think of? Did the reading evoke a feeling? Did the reading remind you of any experience from your own life? Take whatever message it is that you need from the reading.

Now bring your attention to your body and where you are in the room. Notice your breath, breathing in and breathing out. Notice the air around you and how it feels on your skin. Listen for any noises that may be near you. Notice any smells in the air. Become *mindful* of your environment and your place in it. Feel the weight of your clothes on your body. Feel the weight of your body on the floor or in your chair. Take three slow, deep breaths. Your consciousness is going on a journey.

Imagine yourself going down a flight of stairs. Down you go, and when you get to the bottom, there is a door. The door opens, and as you go through it, you find yourself at the edge of a lake. It is a beautiful and sunny day. You feel the warmth of the sun on your face. You feel a soft breeze blow on your body. You feel safe and relaxed. You breathe in deliciously pure air, deeply into your lungs. You notice that someone is rowing a boat toward the edge of the lake in front of you. You look to see who is in the boat and then you realize that it is you, as a child. Your inner child. You see that she is quite capable of rowing herself to the shore. As you watch, you see that someone else comes to greet your inner child as she makes her landing. It is your inner grown-up, the you that you met in the castle. You are surprised to see her here. She offers a hand to your inner child and helps her out of the rowboat. They walk together to the edge of the trees and then they beckon you to follow.

Your inner child and your inner grown-up are holding hands and you join them. You make a circle together and look into one another's eyes. You smile, seeing yourself like this. You begin to draw closer together, huddling close, when suddenly you all three merge into one being, and as you do so, feeling yourself whole, you amazingly begin to transform into a tree. You are not afraid.

At first you feel your body becoming a trunk. This is the solid center of love. Next you feel roots shooting out from your legs, anchoring you into the ground. This is your foundation of spirituality. You cast your arms up into the air as they become branches reaching toward the sky. These arc to become an umbrella of responsibility and maturity. And then, finally, your branches sprout leaves. Beautiful, tender green leaves that dance in the wind. These are your inner children.

You stand amazed at yourself, fully integrated and fully transformed into a tree, a symbol of strength and towering majesty. The tree becomes stronger and more beautiful with age. As do you. You feel fully integrated and whole. Take a moment to bask in this wondrous state. Then, gradually, you transform back into your own body.

Now, when you are ready, your consciousness returns to your body on a wave of light. Start to sense your body in the room. Feel your mind and body getting grounded and integrated. Wiggle your fingers and toes. Take a deep breath. Start to move your arms and legs gently from side to side. Take another deep breath. Allow yourself to feel a vibrant energy coursing through your body, revitalizing you. I'm going to count from one to five, and when you are ready, after the count of five, you may open your eyes. One ... two ... three ... four ... five. You may open your eyes.

JOURNAL QUESTIONS

On a scale of 1 to 10, how much *fun* do you have in your life? How can you include more fun on a weekly basis?

Did you have any specific hobbies, talents, interests, activities that you pursued as a child/teenager? Are these interests still a part of your life?

What do you do that's creative in your life? Are you creating something out of nothing on a regular basis? When you do create something, how do you feel? When you're not creating anything, what do you think is the cost to your soul?

If you were a scale, would you say that you are balanced (emotionally, physically, spiritually)? Where do you need to focus more attention? What's stopping you?

Are you the kind of grown-up now that you imagined you'd be when you were a child?

What is the meaning of your life?

EXERCISES

Create Something: Think about something that you can create. Envision a project. You may decide to visit a craft store for
ideas and materials. Perhaps you'll gather materials from nature
and create something new. Arrange a rock garden. Plant a window box. Create something new that didn't exist before. Write a
poem. Paint an abstract painting full of bright colors. Let go of
all the old baggage, the negative tapes, that tell you you're a
terrible artist or an inept craftsman. Take the time to learn a
new skill that could assist you in your mission to create. Think
broadly. Cast a wide net. Create.

***List Your Areas of Vulnerability (retriggered wounded
child):*** These may continue to crop up from time to time. List
ten ways your inner grown-up can nurture and comfort that
sensitivity in your inner child. A Chinese proverb says, "Whatever is flexible and flowing will tend to grow. Whatever is
blocked and rigid will tend to die." Let your inner grown-up
unblock the past and honor it for all that it was. Become like
the bending willow in the winds of life.

Turn Off TV Week: My children's school recently had a turn
off TV week (that means no videos, either). At first I was ap-
prehensive. I rely on the electronic baby-sitter as much as anyone, so I know how hard it is to give up that crutch. I figured it
would be harder on me than on them. But then we made the
commitment and we did it. What happened? My children read.
They drew. They played together outside. They played with the
dog. They made up imaginary games. I was amazed. It wasn't
that hard after all. We've dramatically reduced our viewing time
since. Try it. See for yourself. There's a lot more of your own
life available to you when you stop sitting around watching
other people's lives.

Go on a News Fast: Dr. Andrew Weil recommends a "news
fast" in his book *8 Weeks to Optimum Health.* He claims that
most news is inconsequential and that furthermore much of it
negatively impacts one's mental health (repeated exposure to

violence, trauma). So, no newspapers, no news magazines, and no TV news (of course, if you're doing the previous exercise, you're not watching TV this week anyway!). Think of this as a means for connecting with your inner child. Kids generally don't watch or read the news. Stay in the moment. Connect to your life. See what it's like. Does it feel uncomfortable?

Take Yourself Out to Lunch: Go out to lunch with yourself as you would with a friend. Don't just put your nose in a book while you're eating, either. Actually look up and observe people. Actually taste and savor the food. Think about yourself, your childhood, perhaps. Reminisce with yourself. Think about the happiest times in your life. Plan for the future. Develop a wild fantasy. Tell yourself a joke! Enjoy your own company. Be happy to be with *you.*

Write a Haiku: The haiku is a formal Japanese poem with the following very disciplined form: a total of 17 syllables; line 1 has five syllables, line 2 has seven syllables, and line 3 has five syllables. No exceptions. Write a haiku about your life.

Line 1: _____

Line 2: _____

Line 3: _____

Have a Cocktail Party Shake-up: The next time you attend a party, try shaking up the usual small talk and chitchat. Try asking people, "What is the meaning of your life?" You can tell them you're working on a project, or writing an article, or taking a survey. See how people respond, whether they laugh it off or answer seriously. It could be the best party you ever attended!

Imagine a Projected Life Review: Part A. Imagine that you are eighty-eight years old, on your deathbed. Imagine how you might look, dress, sound, and feel. Look back over your life. What was meaningful in your life? Who did you love? What kind of life did you live? What were some of your accomplishments? Are there things that you wish you had done? What were the major turning points in your life, and where did these lead you? Are you pleased with the life that you led? What are your regrets? Do you believe that you fulfilled your promise? Did you live the life that you were meant to live? How are you to be remembered? What legacy did you leave?

Now write your own eulogy.

Part B. Now imagine that you are in the present, today, on your deathbed. Ask yourself the same questions as above. Do you answer the same now as you would then? What work needs to be done between dying now and dying when you are eighty-eight so that you have a life that you are proud of? Are you fulfilling your potential? What are you waiting for?

Write your eulogy based on your life if you were to die today. What was this exercise like for you?

Afterword

And the day came when the risk to remain tight
in a bud was more painful than the risk
it took to blossom.

—Anaïs Nin

I said to my daughter, who was six years old at the time, as I was brushing her hair, "Did you know that you have a grown-up inside of you?"

She glanced down at her tummy and first shook her head no. Then she thought about it some more and commented, "Ooooh, gross."

"What I mean is, inside of you, you have all the tools you need to be strong, brave, and smart. It's there inside of you and you just have to connect to it." (Who knows? If you believe in reincarnation, as more than half the planet does, she may actually have *been* a grown-up before.)

But she rolled her eyes at me, much as she might when she asks, "Where is God?" and I say, "Everywhere." The abstraction of each concept is cognitively too much for her at this stage in her development. I can't prove to her that she has an inner grown-up any more than I can prove that God exists—though watching a morning glory open on a sunny summer day is proof enough for me! Some things must be accepted on faith and faith alone.

I do pray that as she grows, she will unite with that internal resource—I know it will not fail her.

And I know that when you unite with your own inner

grown-up—your highest and best self—it will not fail you, either.

Working the Program

The inner child concept has had a huge impact on our nation's overall mental health. It has taught us to nurture our wounds from the past and helped us retain the excitement and curiosity of four-year-olds. But in the real world, you cannot and should not always maintain the stance of a four-year-old. Four-year-olds are self-absorbed, entitled, and impulsive. Thus, the inner child concept ultimately falls short, leaving us developmentally stuck, curiously incomplete.

Claiming your inner grown-up is the missing companion piece. By doing so, we can move forward emotionally and discover richer, more mature possibilities for living.

If you work the Four-Pillar Program, you will attain psychological and spiritual growth. And when you employ the four steps of DARE, you will free yourself from old habits and blind spots to develop the full range of your powers. By asserting your adult authority over yourself and your behaviors, you will be an authentic adult. Growth will not always be smooth and may come in bursts and spurts. And sometimes it will feel as if you are shrinking instead of growing. When this happens, do not be discouraged. Think of it as the movement of a bow and arrow. The bow must be pulled backward before the arrow is launched forward, springing into the future.

Don't just read this book; put it into practice. There is a big difference between reading about swimming versus actually diving into the water. Take the plunge. I urge you to go back through the book and try the exercises, if you haven't already. Really write the journal entries; stop and do the visualizations. Of course, some of them will resonate with you more than others, but give them all a try. You may not notice immediate results, but stick with it.

The program will work, if you work the program. It offers ideas beyond clicking your ruby red shoes together and chanting, "There's no place like home," to realize that what you seek is available inside of you and has been all along.

- Analyze the Four Pillars and reflect on them in your life: Responsibility, Maturity, Love, and Spirituality
- Use the four essential steps of DARE (Detach, Aware, Reorient, and Enact/Evaluate)
- Use the "act as if" exercise
- State inner grown-up affirmations
- Write the journal entries
- Try the suggested exercises in each chapter
- Use the visualizations, especially the one from chapter 4 when you meet your inner grown-up
- Develop a spiritual practice

In the end, the Four-Pillar Program is about creating a life that has meaning and purpose. This cannot happen if you are self-absorbed. It happens through self-transcendence. I've heard it said that when you're all wrapped up in yourself, you make a pretty small package. Each of the pillars encourages you to first focus within, but then to rise above your own concerns, to expand your wrapping. Each of the pillars guides you to connections outside of yourself that will help build a supportive, interdependent web. When you do this, you gain perspective on your life in particular, and on life in general. Move from a house of mirrors (where you can see only your own reflection) to a house with windows (where you can view the world around you).

Rewriting Your Story

The litmus test of claiming your inner grown-up is answering this question affirmatively, "Can you be grateful for your childhood, however painful it was, and all that has happened to you, because it was integral in making you the *you* that you are?" In other words, if you are truly happy to be you and feel positively about where you stand in terms of all four pillars—

your maturity and responsibility levels, your ability to love, and your spirituality—you must know that you are the unique and special you *only because of the experiences that you have had.* If you had had a different childhood, you would not be the you who you are now.

And if you cannot yet answer that litmus test question affirmatively, then I ask you to be open to getting there eventually. Consistent open-mindedness and persistent attempts to grow and gain a broader perspective will eventually take you there.

In the *Family Therapy Networker* magazine, Frank Pittman reviews the movie *Shakespeare in Love*, observing, "Shakespeare gave us characters who could listen in on their own conversations or soliloquies, observe themselves, gain awareness of who they were and what they were doing and consciously choose to change. Shakespeare's characters are . . . not at the mercy of their past, their hormones or their gods, but are capable of 'reconceiving' themselves." So are we! *Claim Your Inner Grown-up* offers a road map to do just this.

Don't be afraid to expand your story. Let your story be more than just the bad things that have happened to you. Let your story be about redemption and triumph. Let your story be about growth and transformation. Let your story be multichaptered, ever unfolding. Don't be afraid to change the paradigm of your life, to develop a new vocabulary. Even Scrooge changed in the final hour. Do you need three ghosts to visit you to open your eyes?

There is a saying from the Talmud: "We do not see things as they are. We see them as *we* are." In other words, perception is reality. Everything you see in life is being filtered through the lens of who you are, what your past was, what your beliefs are. The Four-Pillar Program helps cleanse your eyes. It helps to give you a fresher vision.

When You DARE to Change

One concern that may crop up is that after completing this program, your experience could be summed up: "Great, I'm growing, but what about everybody else?" As a person begins to claim her inner grown-up, she may notice more clearly those people around her who have not. This could cause some tension, to say the least.

One of two possible outcomes is likely: influence them or distance yourself from them. For example, after Mary Beth began working the Four-Pillar Program, she shared the information with her friends and family. She talked about what she had learned; she convinced her sister to sign up for a workshop. She became a teacher herself of that which she had just discovered. And her loved ones were receptive. But remember, you can only *introduce* them to ideas that helped you. After that, you must let go. You cannot change them. Really, don't waste your time trying. Let me repeat: *You cannot change them*. You can only change yourself.

Judy discovered firsthand the cliché that "you can lead a horse to water, but you can't make him drink." Her family just wasn't interested in what she had to share. She could not change them, nor did she try, and they did not want to change on their own. Thus, she found that she had to distance herself from certain people in her life. As painful as it was, she realized that she didn't have time anymore to hang around people who were either attached to their victim status or too immature, irresponsible, insecure, or otherwise "toxic" to her. She calls it "negatronics." If anyone is too negative, she knows that it drains her of her own power. It's as if their emotional poison leaks out to contaminate her own emotional world. So she has had to limit her time with people, and consequently has lost some friends and become distant from some family members.

The antidote to this dilemma is that Judy has drawn new people into her life. She attracts like-minded people who place a high premium on personal growth and development. These friends support her on her journey and add to her overall quality of life.

Who knows? Maybe your example of growth will eventually inspire others in ways that you cannot begin to imagine. Nelson Mandela writes about inspiration:

Our deepest fear is not that we are inadequate. Our deepest fear is that we are powerful beyond measure. It is our light, not our darkness, that most frightens us. We ask ourselves, "Who am I to be brilliant, gorgeous, talented, and fabulous?" Actually, who are you not to be? . . . Your playing small doesn't serve the world. There's nothing enlightened about shrinking so that other people won't feel insecure around you. We were born to make manifest the glory that is within us. It's not just in some of us; it's in everyone. And as we let our own light shine, we unconsciously give other people permission to do the same. As we are liberated from our own fear, our presence automatically liberates others.

Dare to dream big and to become *awakened* to life. So many of us go through life in a trance, sleepwalking through all the significant and insignificant moments of our lives. Or as one woman said to me, "I think I've been in a virtual coma for most of my life. Until now." At the age of fifty-seven, she's claiming her inner grown-up, learning to love herself, and awaking to life. It's never too late. As the sun comes up, dawning each new day, there is always hope for the future.

Empower Yourself

So ask yourself, "What am I *doing* here?" "What am I *doing* with my brief time here on this planet?" And if you don't have an answer that pleases you, then go on the quest to figure it out. The time is now. Do not wait. S t r e t c h your frame of possibility. As William Congreve said, "Defer not till tomorrow to be wise, Tomorrow's sun to thee may never rise."

Each of our lives is so precious and potentially powerful. In the Disney movie *Mulan*, the emperor points out, "A single grain of rice can tip the scale. One man (or woman) may make the difference between victory and defeat." And so it was, for Mulan herself saved China.

So may it be with you. Save yourself and then reach out to touch the world. You matter. You make a difference. Claim your inner grown-up. She's right there inside waiting to join forces with you.

You *can* claim the transcendent self that shines light into dark and shadowy inner places of the mind and spirit. You *can* tame your problem children so that they behave themselves. All children deep down long for consistent discipline, after all, which is an expression of ultimate love. You have the pillars inside of you, though they may be lying dormant. Together we can awaken the sleeping giants.

I hope this book has been a starting point to launch you on your exciting journey of self-discovery. I hope it has been your wake-up call to grow while there's still time. Have patience. But dare to reach for the brass ring. The results will bring you the life that you've always wanted and so richly deserve.

Take the magic, mystery, awe, creativity, and sensitivity of your inner child and balance that with the wisdom, the courage, the discipline, and the strength of your inner grown-up. And plunge them both deeply into the river of life.

I wish you many blessings along your journey.

SOURCES AND RESOURCES

Introduction

Prend, Ashley Davis. *Transcending Loss: Understanding the Life-long Impact of Grief and How to Make It Meaningful.* New York: Berkley, 1997.

Chapter 1

Bradshaw, John. *Homecoming: Reclaiming and Championing Your Inner Child.* New York: Bantam, 1990.

Taylor, Cathryn L. *The Inner Child Workbook: What to Do with Your Past When It Just Won't Go Away.* New York: Jeremy P. Tarcher, 1991.

Whitfield, Charles. *Healing the Child Within.* Deerfield Beach, FL: Health Communications, 1987.

Chapter 2

Albom, Mitch. *Tuesdays with Morrie.* New York: Doubleday, 1997.

Epstein, Mark. *Thoughts without a Thinker.* New York: Basic Books, 1995.

Myss, Caroline. *Anatomy of the Spirit: The Seven Stages of Power and Healing.* New York: Three Rivers, 1996.

Peck, M. Scott. *Further Along the Road Less Traveled: The Unending Journey Toward Spiritual Growth.* New York: Touchstone, 1998.

Chapter 3

Coles, Robert. *The Story of Ruby Bridges*. New York: Scholastic, 1995.

Graber, Ann V., and Mark Madsen. *Images of Transformation: A Unique Blend of Psychotherapy and Music* (audio cassettes, 1994). Fountain Publishing, P.O. Box 80011, Rochester, MI 48308-0011; (248) 651-1153; www.fountainpublishing.com.

Kottler, Jeffrey. *Travel That Can Change Your Life*. Jossey-Bass, San Francisco: 1997.

Linnea, Ann. *Deep Water Passage: A Spiritual Journey at Midlife*. New York: Pocket Books, 1997.

Pittman, Frank. *Grow Up! How Taking Responsibility Can Make You a Happy Adult*. New York: Golden Books, 1998.

Surya Das, Lama. *Awakening the Buddha Within: Tibetan Wisdom for the Western World*. New York: Broadway, 1997.

Chapter 4

Graber, Ann V. and Mark Madsen. *Images of Transformation: A Unique Blend of Psychotherapy and Music* (audio cassettes, 1994). Fountain Publishing, P.O. Box 80011, Rochester, MI 48308-0011; (248) 651-1153; www.fountainpublishing.com.

His Holiness the Dalai Lama and Howard Cutler. *The Art of Happiness: A Handbook for Living*. New York: Riverhead, 1998.

Oriah Mountain Dreamer. *The Invitation*. HarperSanFrancisco, 1999.

Chapter 5

Crum, Thomas. *The Magic of Conflict*. New York: Touchstone,1987.

Nouwen, Henri. *Reaching Out*. New York: Doubleday, 1986.

Quindlen, Anna. *One True Thing*. New York: Delta, 1994.

Chapter 6

Casarjian, Robin. *Forgiveness: A Bold Choice for a Peaceful Heart*. New York: Bantam, 1992.

Chodron, Pemo. *Awakening Loving-Kindness*. Boston: Shambhala, 1996.

Holabird, Katharine. *Alexander and the Dragon*. New York: Clarkson N. Potter, 1988.

Houston, Jean. *A Passion for the Possible: A Guide to Realizing Your True Potential*. New York: HarperSanFrancisco, 1998.

Simon, Richard. "Awakening Our Wisdom." *Family Therapy Networker* (November/December 1999).

Whiteman, Thomas. *Innocent Victims: How to Help Your Children Overcome the Trauma of Divorce*. Nelson, 1992.

Chapter 7

Carter-Scott, Cherie. *If Love Is a Game, These Are the Rules*. New York: Broadway, 1999.

Chapman, Gary. *The Five Love Languages*. Chicago: Northfield, 1992.

Gibran, Kahlil. *The Prophet*. New York: Knopf, 1993.

Silverstein, Shel. *The Giving Tree*. New York: HarperCollins, 1986.

Chapter 8

Church, Forrest. *Lifecraft*. Boston: Beacon, 2000.

Coles, Robert. *The Spiritual Life of Children*. Boston: Houghton Mifflin, 1990.

Kushner, Harold. *Who Needs God*. New York: Summit, 1989.

McLennan, Scotty. *Finding Your Religion: When the Faith You Grew Up with Has Lost Its Meaning*. San Francisco: HarperSanFrancisco, 2000.

Moody, Harry, and David Carroll. *The Five Stages of the Soul*. New York: Anchor, 1997.

Robinson, David, ed. *William Ellery Channing: Selected Writings*. New York: Paulist Press, 1985.

Salkin, Jeffrey. *Being God's Partner: How to Find the Hidden Link between Spirituality and Your Work*. Woodstock, VT: Jewish Lights, 1994.

Weems, Renita J. *Listening for God: A Minister's Journey through Silence and Doubt*. New York: Simon & Schuster, 1999.

Chapter 9

Ackerman, Diane. *Deep Play*. New York: Random House, 1999.

Bloomfield, Harold. *Making Peace with Your Past: The Six Essential Steps to Enjoying a Great Future*. New York: HarperCollins, 2000.

Covey, Stephen. *First Things First*. New York: Fireside, 1996.

Weil, Andrew. *8 Weeks to Optimum Health: A Proven Program for Taking Full Advantage of Your Body's Natural Healing Power*. New York: Knopf, 1997.

INDEX

of life story, 226–27; search for, 59–60, 86, 107
Media, 3, 43–45
Meditation, 82; *tonglen,* 158
Meir, Golda, 88
Miracle on 34th Street (movie), 244
Missildine, Dr. W. Hugh, 18
Mission statement, 252–53
Mitzvahs, 142
Money, 127
Mulan (movie), 268
Myss, Caroline, 40–41

Narcissism, 5, 45–46
Neighbors, 144–45, 202–3
Nelson, Portia, 149–50
Never Ending Story, The (movie), 188
New York Times, 4–5, 143
Niccolini, Julian, 30
Nin, Anaïs, 263

Objects: inner child, 29; inner grown-up, 111–12; your core, 140
Oklahoma City bombing, 51
Orphan archetype, 92
Our Town (Wilder), 254

Parent, 91; becoming, 79–81; –child love, 198–201; forgiving, 164–67
Past, 9, 36–42; finding meaning in, 174–77; and image of God, 219–20
Peace, 256
Pearson, Carol S., 92
Peck, M. Scott, 58
Peter Pan, 3
Pinocchio, 126
Pittman, Frank, 85, 266
Power: of others, 135–37; of you, 137–40
Preschool self, 21–22
Priorities, 252
Problem child: dark side of, 42–56; integrating, 245–46; mastering, and maturity, 155; shadow side of, 56–61
Prophet, The (Gibran), 201, 256–57
Proust, Marcel, 1
Punctuality, 127

Rage, 50–51
Readings, 9, 10, 30; "Autobiography in Five Short Chapters" (Nelson), 149–50; *Awakening Loving-Kindness* (Chodron), 179; *Book of Qualities* (Gendler), 62; *Grow Up!* (Pittman), 85; Hindu master, 117; "If Thou Must Love Me" (Browning), 209; "On Prayer" (McKeeman), 236–37; *Prophet* (Gibran), 256–57; *Where the Wild Things Are* (Sendak), 30–31
Realm of the Hungry Ghosts, 42
Reason, 161–62
Red Hat society, 173
Reinvestment, 6, 98
Religion, 217–18
Reorient step, 7, 102
Reparenting (self-parenting), 24–26, 38–39, 190
Resolution stage, 157
Responsibility, 7, 73, 125–53; and codependence, 147; defined, 93; exercises, 152–53; and getting beyond self, 141–42; to improve the world, 146–47; integration, 251; reading, 149–50; as self-blame, 148
Retriggered Wounded Child Log, 39, 48
Rewriting your story, 265–66
Ripple effect, 203–5
Roderick, Libby, 208
Rodgers and Hammerstein, 156, 191
Roosevelt, Eleanor, 88
Rumi, 216

Schlessinger, Dr. Laura, 2
School-age self, 22
Schweitzer, Albert, 143
Seinfeld (TV series), 3
Self: covenant to, 194–95; facing true, 188–89; getting beyond, 99–100, 141–43
Self-blame, 148
Self-love, 188–89, 195, 212–13
Self-obsession, 4
Sendak, Maurice, 30–31
Seven Habits of Highly Effective People, The (Covey), 47
Sexual abuse, 18, 166

Index